THE ROCKETMAKERS

THE ROCKETMAKERS

BY HARRY WULFORST

ORION BOOKS / NEW YORK

Published by Orion Books, a division of Crown Publishers, Inc., 201 East 50th Street, New York, New York 10022

ORION and colophon are trademarks of Crown Publishers, Inc.

Manufactured in the United States of America

Library of Congress Cataloging-in-Publication Data

Wulforst, Harry.
   The rocketmakers / by Harry Wulforst.—1st ed.
      p.   cm.
   1. Rocketry—United States—History.   I. Title.
TL781.8.U5W84   1990
621.43'56'0973—dc20   90–32532
ISBN 0-517-56586-2

10 9 8 7 6 5 4 3 2 1

Design by Lauren Dong

First Edition

To Nicholas
and all members of his generation
who will share knowledge and opportunities
originated by the rocketmakers

Contents

PART ONE

The Dreamers

1

Lost in a World of Make-Believe

Winter 1928–1929
Berlin, Germany

FRITZ LANG PATIENTLY watched scores of extras take their places in a cavernous studio of the Ufa Film Company. Satisfied, he nodded, then glanced over his shoulder. The cameramen were ready. Turning back to the scene before him, he gave a signal. At the far end of the set, a huge rocket, its bullet-shaped nose aimed menacingly skyward, was wheeled slowly out of a hangar. In the foreground, actors impersonating news reporters and photographers milled about, angling for a better view. Beyond them, police lines held a crowd in check while searchlight beams flashed over the rocket's surface. The filming of *Frau im Monde* had begun.

A science-fiction potboiler about four men, a woman, and a boy who rocket to the moon, *Frau im Monde* would be billed as another exciting Fritz Lang epic. Lang, then one of Germany's most successful silent-film producers, directed the production and also co-authored the script. His wife and collaborator, Thea von Harbou, credited her inspiration for the story to the published works of Willy Ley and Hermann Oberth.

Ley, a journalist who specialized in science reporting, and Oberth, a professor of physics and mathematics, had little in common apart from their shared interest in rocketry. Ley, a native Berliner, steeped in the ways of the big city, was a brash young man of twenty-two, precociously assertive and cocksure of himself. By Ley's standards, Oberth was a country bumpkin, having lived a sheltered life in Schässburg and other small villages in Transylvania. The fact that Oberth was twelve years older than Ley, and endowed with impressive academic credentials, should have evened the score. But unhappily, Oberth was a follower, not a leader, in his present situation.

In 1923, Oberth had created a stir with the publication of his doctoral thesis *Die Rakete zu den Planetenraumen* (By Rocket to Interplanetary Space), which demonstrated, through elaborate mathematical proofs, that rockets could be built to transport man beyond the reach of Earth's gravitational pull. Three years later, Ley published a popularized version of this astounding thesis in his *Trip into Space*.

During preproduction planning in the fall of 1928, Fritz Lang lured Oberth to Berlin to serve, in association with Willy Ley, as a member of the film's technical advisory committee. Oberth was to be the rocket expert; Ley, the idea man. Bringing Oberth and Ley aboard was a shrewd business move. Oberth's high academic standing would lend an aura of legitimacy to an implausible story line. And Ley, through his own writing and influence on fellow journalists, would stimulate coverage of the film in the press.

Ley loved the glamorous and exciting business of moviemaking. Oberth hated it. His decision to accept Lang's invitation and take a leave of absence from his teaching duties in Transylvania was triggered by the hope that, in Berlin, he would find financial backing for his future research in rocketry. Regrettably, Oberth was poorly equipped to exploit this opportunity. He was a scientist, not a salesman. While his association with Lang brought him into contact with many influential businessmen, Oberth was so intimidated by their aggressive style that he shrank into the background.

Now, standing on Lang's set as floodlight beams flicked across the ersatz rocket he had designed, Oberth yearned fervently to be somewhere else. This world of tinsel was not to his liking. Nor were the people in it. Fast talking, frequently lapsing into French, English, or Russian (none of which Oberth understood), his present companions were an alien breed, vastly different from those with whom he shared an easygoing, well-ordered life back home. Further aggravating his discomfort was his failure to prevent himself from being maneuvered into an impossible situation by Willy Ley.

The previous evening Lang jubilantly revealed that Willy Ley had come up with a blockbuster idea. Warming quickly to Ley's suggestion that a real high-flying rocket be launched on the day *Frau im Monde* premiered in Berlin, Lang ordered Oberth to bring it off. Until that moment, the film's resident technical expert was merely an adviser. Now, at the wave of Lang's hand, he was project manager, responsible for designing and building a rocket from scratch. Fuels must be tested. Materials secured. A suitable launch site found. How was all this to be accomplished? Oberth barely knew his way to the railroad station and now he was expected to scour Berlin, and its suburbs if necessary, to gather all the needed components and enlist the craftsmen to fashion them into a rocket.

Lang, by nature a visionary, was nevertheless enough of a realist to see that Oberth could not handle the assignment unaided. He therefore empowered Oberth to hire two assistants. Ley then stepped forward and volunteered to find the right people. But Oberth, asserting himself, said no. True, Ley had gotten him into this mess. Yet Oberth was determined to extricate himself without any meddling by Ley.

Oberth, however, probably should have welcomed rather than rebuffed aid. Once, looking back years later, Ley offered some thoughts about the kind of help Oberth should have looked for: Oberth "needed an assistant who was a professional engineer, preferably with some specialization, preferably, too, a native [of Berlin], who did not need the telephone directory to find a place which could do a good job on aluminum welding but would know the phone number by heart and be on a first-name basis with the foreman."

To find such expertise, Oberth could have retained an employment agency, staffed with trained interviewers to screen the candidates. But he chose not to engage one, possibly because Ley had suggested that he do so. Instead, Oberth wrote a brief "Help Wanted" advertisement, which he placed in the classified columns of several Berlin newspapers. Jobs were scarce at the time and he was swamped with responses, some from well-qualified applicants. Oberth, however, was not up to separating the wheat from the chaff. Although a learned professor and a renowned rocket expert, he was a neophyte when it came to that most delicate of management skills, picking the right man for the job.

For his deputy, a man Friday to open doors and get things done, Oberth chose a heel-clicking former German flying ace with eleven Allied planes to his credit. Rudolf Nebel was a graduate engineer "with diploma" but without experience applying those skills in industry. Unable to find a job in engineering in the years after World War I, Nebel had supported himself mostly by selling mechanical kitchen gadgets. While displaying a laudable zeal for work, he was nonetheless ill-prepared to relieve Oberth of any major responsibilities on the rocket project.

For his second assistant, Oberth might have picked one of many other applicants who responded to the newspaper advertisement. But he passed over this pool of talent to seek out one Aleksander Borissovitch Shershevsky, a destitute Russian student of aviation who had come to Germany to study glider design. Having overstayed his visa, and afraid to return to Russia to face punishment, Shershevsky lived in a Berlin garret, eking out a living by writing articles for various German aviation magazines. Oberth, who had read these pieces and was favorably impressed by them, contacted one of the magazine editors and got Shershevsky's address. Then Oberth arranged a meeting and hired him.

Oberth now had his assistants, but Nebel and Shershevsky could do little until Oberth disposed of a charge that challenged his competence. A prominent chemist, apparently with enough technical clout to be taken seriously by the Ufa Film Company, predicted that Oberth's rocket would never get off the ground. Oberth's plan for launching a vehicle into space was based on the premise that power for such a feat would be provided by liquid propellants. The dissenting expert, who claimed years of experience using liquefied gases, maintained that liquid oxygen and volatile fuels could not be combined to sustain a controlled thrust. His prediction: Oberth's rocket would blow up the instant oxygen and fuel ignited.

Responding to pleas from Ufa Film publicists, who were grinding out press releases touting the rocket launch plan, Oberth agreed to an experiment to prove he was right and his critic wrong. When all was in readiness, Oberth squirted a fine stream of gasoline into a bowl of liquid air. For a moment, nothing happened. Then, an explosion. The device igniting the mixture fired later than it should have. Other than wounding Oberth's pride, the damage was minor. Some papers were blown from tables and shelves, and a windowpane was pushed out.

Undaunted, Oberth repeated the experiment several more times. Much to everyone's relief, all were successful. He not only achieved a controlled burn with each ignition but also demonstrated that in a given time frame larger quantities of fuel could be injected into a confined space (producing more thrust) than his earlier estimates.

Hurrying back to their typewriters, the Ufa publicity team churned out more press releases trumpeting these findings. But that wasn't all they were saying. Every scrap of information was grist for their mill.

Newspaper editors were swamped with stories about the rocket's design (a torpedo-shaped cylinder about six feet long), projected maximum altitude (about forty miles), and hundreds of other details, including the choice of Greifswalder Oie as the launch site.

Naming Greifswalder Oie, a small island in the Baltic Sea, was saying too much too soon. Getting the news out while it's hot may be shrewd public relations, but not waiting to be sure that all bases are covered is a stupid blunder. Bristling and indignant because they were not consulted about the plan to launch Oberth's rocket from Greifswalder Oie before reading about it in the newspapers, government authorities flatly refused to sanction the event.

The lighthouse there, the official line went, would be endangered. Falling from a great height, the spent rocket might seriously damage this vital maritime beacon. Not so, argued the Ufa Film spokesmen. The rocket shell, void of fuel, weighing less than thirty pounds, and slowed by a parachute, could not threaten a structure built to withstand the buffeting winds and waves of the Baltic. The bureaucrats, however, would not budge, and a search was organized for a new site. Eventually permission was grudgingly granted for them to fire the rocket from the seashore resort of Horst. But now the publicists were bound by a gag order because Greifswalder Oie was well within the radius of descent of any rocket launched from Horst.

Meanwhile, the pressure increased. Nebel, after much searching, found a machine shop equipped to build a rocket casing within the specifications drawn up by Oberth. But work had not yet started on the parachute release mechanism. While doubts about liquid propellants had been dispelled, the question of fuel was still up in the air. Although Oberth always stressed the superiority of gasoline, he was now leaning toward the use of methane. Finding a supplier of a pure form of this gas was consuming a great deal of Nebel and Shershevsky's time.

Unnerved by Fritz Lang's prodding, Oberth resorted to short cuts. One day, in his haste, critical precautions were bypassed during a fuel experiment and the resulting explosion nearly blinded him in one eye and forced his confinement to bed for several days. Upon his return to work, he suddenly changed the plan. Assuring Lang that a less ambitious altitude goal would be no less spectacular, Oberth started anew. His modified design was a narrow aluminum cylinder, about forty feet long, to be packed with a substance rich in carbon. A space surrounding the core was to be filled with liquid oxygen. When ignited, exiting gases generated by the burning carbon and oxygen would propel the cylinder upward. A much simpler technique, but it failed. After hundreds of experiments, the precise mix of carbon and inert materials needed for an even burn remained a mystery.

On the verge of panic and unhinged by overwork, Oberth disappeared. Perplexed and not knowing what to do, Shershevsky telephoned Willy Ley. "He ran away," the distraught assistant wailed. Oberth, however, returned three days later to tell Lang that he had given up. After hurried consultations with Ufa Film management, Lang abruptly announced the cancellation of the rocket launch. No reason was given other than some vague allusion to unpredictable weather conditions on the Baltic during the winter.

If Oberth's rocket was a failure, the film it was meant to promote did not fare much better. At the time Lang was filming his outer-space epic, the advent of motion pictures with sound was taking Germany, and the world, by storm. In every town large enough to support three or more cinemas, at least one was equipped to show the new "talkies." Because new sound films garnered more box-office revenues than silents, Ufa Film management pressed Lang to revise the script and produce a talking picture. Lang refused, saying that he did not want to lengthen the shooting schedule, increase the budget, postpone the premiere, and delay any return on money he had invested in the project.

When shown in movie houses during the spring of 1929, *Frau im Monde* drew a lukewarm response from critics and ticket buyers. Shrugging off this artistic and financial disappointment, Lang moved on to other film ventures. Oberth was not as resilient. Abandoning his rocket paraphernalia to gather dust in a Berlin warehouse, he returned, chastened and despondent, to his home in Transylvania.

2

Goddard's Lament

Summer 1929
Worcester, Massachusetts

IT MIGHT HAVE been the classic chase scene in a Mack Sennett comedy. Over the crest of a hill bounced a dozen automobiles, moving as fast as the bumpy ground would permit. Clouds of dust obscured all but the lead vehicles and policemen, perched on the running boards of ambulances at the head of the caravan, waving their arms excitedly while directing the drivers toward the base of the slope.

Minutes earlier the switchboard in the Worcester police headquarters had been buzzing. Dozens of callers had reported that an airplane had caught fire and then crashed beyond a hill just outside of town. The first policeman to reach the scene was told that no one was hurt, nor in danger, and therefore the incident merited no further interest. But keeping things quiet was now impossible. Drivers and passengers clambered out of cars, and reporters for Worcester's evening newspapers led the crowd racing down the hill.

For Professor Robert H. Goddard, a senior member of the faculty at nearby Clark University, this was an awkward situation. There had been no plane crash, he said. It was just a routine experiment with a new propellant. The reporters, who could smell a good story, would not be put off. Bombarded with questions, Goddard argued that there was little to be excited about. There was only the twisted remains of a small rocket that had been launched from a tower barely two hundred feet away. Curious onlookers milled about the spot where the rocket had crashed. Others gathered around the tower. Much of the vegetation around it had been burned off by earlier, less spectacular tests, and rocks were black, some even disintegrating, from long exposure to high heat.

Seeing that no more answers could be wrung out of Goddard, the reporters snapped some pictures and left as quickly as they had come. Then Goddard and his assistants packed instruments and equipment while the crowd dispersed. Back in Worcester two hours later, Goddard phoned the editors of the two evening newspapers. Growing anxious about a potentially hostile reaction to his experiments, he tried to persuade them to play down the incident. But that tactic backfired. Headlines in the *Evening Gazette* blared: "GOD-DARD EXPERIMENTAL ROCKET EXPLODES IN AIR . . . BLAST HEARD FOR MILES . . . FALLING EMBERS LED TO BELIEF THAT MAJOR AIR CATASTROPHE HAD TAKEN PLACE." The *Evening Post* was more imaginative: "TERRIFIC EXPLOSION AS PROF. GODDARD OF CLARK SHOOTS MOON ROCKET." The next day, July 18, the *Boston Globe* reinforced the canard: "MOON ROCKET MAN'S TEST ALARMS WHOLE COUNTRY-SIDE."

Goddard, appalled, at first decided to say nothing. But linking his name with a "moon rocket" was holding him up to public ridicule. Sensing that he was the subject of furtive snickering and finger pointing all over town, he hastily issued a statement to the press: "The test . . . was one of a long series of experiments with rockets using liquid propellants. There was no attempt to reach the moon or anything of such a spectacular nature. . . . The test was thoroughly satisfactory; nothing exploded in the air, and there was no damage incident to landing." Goddard's explanation changed few minds. The press depicted him as an eccentric academic. And that was the way many would remember him.

Perhaps this viewpoint was widely held at the time because Goddard had been viciously lampooned by journalists in the past. In December 1919, the Smithsonian Institution Press published a Goddard monograph entitled "A Method for Reaching Extreme Altitudes." Less than two thousand copies of the sixty-nine-page document were printed because the potential number of readers was small. It was heavy stuff—page after page of mathematical formulae relieved, occasionally, by photographs and drawings of rocket-engine experiments, then pages of tables listing in tedious detail the relative efficiencies of various combinations of powder and wadding ignited in a small combustion chamber. But a minor digression, inserted only to illustrate how a rocket, once launched, could be seen at the peak of its trajectory, stirred up a national controversy. Proving that a rocket had pierced the upper atmosphere when not visible to the naked eye would be difficult, Goddard wrote, for "even if a mass of flash powder [were loaded in a rocket and] arranged to be ignited after a long interval of time . . . the light would at best be very faint, and it would be difficult to foretell, even approximately, the direction in which it would be most likely to appear." When a publicity writer at the Smithsonian read Goddard's next sentence, he knew he had struck gold. "The only reliable procedure," Goddard concluded, "would be to send the smallest mass of flash powder possible to the dark surface of the moon [at the time of a new moon] . . . in such a way that it would be ignited on impact. The light would then be visible in a powerful telescope."

A rocket to the moon! This was utter nonsense to many who viewed flying the mail between New York and Washington, D.C., as a death-defying adventure. But since this bizarre idea was offered in a news release bearing the imprimatur of the prestigious Smithsonian Institution, news editors from Maine to Florida took notice. Their handling of this little gem was typified by the *Boston Herald*. On January 12, 1920, it blared: "NEW ROCKET DEVISED BY PROF. GOD-DARD MAY HIT THE SURFACE OF THE MOON—Clark College Professor Has Perfected Invention for Exploring Space—Smithsonian Society Backs It." An editorial in the *New York Times* echoed the thoughts of many. Professor Goddard should forget this foolishness, said the *Times*, and undertake projects more in keeping with the dignity of his profession.

Sitting in his study nine years later, Goddard brooded that again the newspapers had made him a laughingstock. In the public's eye, he was just a crazy professor who shoots rockets. When will it end?

3

Dead Ends in High Places

November 1929
Sands Point, New York

Embers glowed on the hearth beneath a massive stone mantelpiece as Caroline Morton Guggenheim leafed through a magazine. Lounging on a sofa near the fireplace, she read while half listening to her husband, Harry, converse with their visitor, a young aviator from Minnesota.

Harry Guggenheim, then a vigorous thirty-seven, was the grandson of a Swiss immigrant who, a half century after landing in Philadelphia, had climbed from penniless obscurity to head one of the wealthiest families in America. Harry's father, Daniel, one of seven sons of Meyer Guggenheim, was then chief operating partner of Guggenheim Brothers and nominal head of the family. From his baronial mansion, Hempstead House, perched on a promontory overlooking the sound at Sands Point, Long Island, Daniel ruled like the proverbial lord of the manor. On the three hundred acres of rolling hills surrounding the main house were a nine-hole golf course, a swimming pool, tennis courts, a dairy, a hennery, pheasant and peacock houses, and Tally-Ho, Daniel's on-site amusement center. Not far from Hempstead House, on another bluff overlooking Long Island Sound, stood Falaise, the mansion Daniel had built for his son Harry. There, on this chilly autumn afternoon, Harry sat in its great hall, too engrossed by the problem presented by his visitor to notice his wife suddenly sit upright on the sofa.

Only thirty years had elapsed since the Wright Brothers' historic flight at Kitty Hawk, North Carolina. Yet it now seemed that the propeller-driven aircraft was nearing the peak of its potential. Significantly faster flying speeds could not be achieved solely by propellers biting through air. Guggenheim's guest thought that rocket power might be the answer. A move to develop a solution along these lines at E. I. Du Pont de Nemours in Wilmington, Delaware, had ended almost as soon as started. Engineers there had concluded that to generate the needed forces, the interior of the rocket engine required a coating of firebrick, adding far more weight than the resulting thrust could lift. A net loss.

Caroline Guggenheim jumped up excitedly, holding a copy of *Popular Science* in front of her. "Hey, you two. Listen to this: 'Aims Rocket at Roof of Sky. Goddard tests new missile to explore the upper air for science.' " Harry's wife then continued reading aloud the account of Goodard's experiment in the meadow near Worcester, Massachusetts, four months earlier. When she had finished, Guggenheim turned to their guest and said, "Maybe this man Goddard can help. It's worth a try." Colonel Charles A. Lindbergh thought so, too. Perhaps it was worth a try.

Lucky Lindy, the Lone Eagle, the first to fly alone across the awesome reaches of the North Atlantic, had been introduced to Guggenheim on May 19, 1927. They had met only hours before Lindbergh's *Spirit of St. Louis* lumbered off into the darkness and then, barely clearing treetops, headed east into the unknown. Guggenheim, who had gone to inspect Lindbergh's monoplane as president of the Guggenheim Fund (a foundation established by his father, Daniel, for the advancement of aeronautics), invited Lindbergh to visit Falaise when he returned from France. Lindbergh eventually accepted Guggenheim's hospitality, a welcome respite from the galas and receptions he had been obliged to attend ever since the wheels of his *Spirit of St. Louis* had touched the surface of Le Bourget outside Paris. At Falaise, sealed off from the outside world, Lindbergh wrote *We*, the hour-by-hour account of his epic flight. And it was there that he and Harry Guggenheim planned the three-month flying tour, financed by the Guggenheim Fund, that took Lindbergh and the *Spirit of St. Louis* to scores of public celebrations in more than sixty cities across the length and breadth of America.

A few days after hearing Caroline Guggenheim read the account of Goddard's rocket experiment, Lindbergh went to Cambridge for a meeting at the Massachusetts Institute of Technology. While there, he approached C. F. Taylor, a professor in MIT's department of aeronautical engineering, and spoke about his interest in Goddard's work. Taylor, who knew Goddard, agreed to act as go-between. But

Taylor procrastinated. A week went by before Taylor sat down on November 22, 1929, and wrote to Goddard explaining that Lindbergh "asked me if there was a possibility that he could get in touch with you and arrange a visit to your laboratory at Worcester."

Growing impatient because he had received no word, Lindbergh bypassed Taylor and telephoned Worcester direct. The unexpected call startled Goddard, and for a minute he was not sure whether he was talking to the famous aviator or to a practical joker. Finally persuaded that it was Lindbergh on the line, Goddard agreed to a meeting in Worcester the following day. As soon as Lindbergh arrived, he went straight to the point. Are rockets sufficiently powerful to accelerate aircraft for brief intervals, say ten seconds or so, on short takeoffs or landings? After asking about the amount of thrust needed for such short bursts, Goddard said yes, either powder or liquid propellants would do nicely.

Exhilarated by the positive response, Lindbergh intimated that his high-placed contacts in the corporate world would guarantee generous funding if Goddard agreed to build rockets for him. Goddard, forced to scrimp continuously and limited to a modest annual grant from the Smithsonian Institution, was understandably entranced by the prospect of coming into some real money now that names like Du Pont and Guggenheim were being bandied about. He quickly assured Lindbergh that he would seriously consider any proposal put forth in good faith.

Four days later, Goddard was at work, of all places, on a road gang at Fort Devens. The avalanche of publicity after the July 17 incident had drawn an intolerable number of kibitzers, hangers-on, and gawkers to the test site outside Worcester, making it impossible to continue there. Through friends at the Smithsonian, Goddard wangled permission from the War Department to transfer his experiments to an undeveloped sector of the nearby army post. With winter beginning, he wanted to ensure ready access to the test site. Filling in potholes before the prolonged subfreezing temperatures was a prudent precaution.

While Goddard was wielding a shovel, Lindbergh called and left an urgent message. The Du Pont people wanted Goddard to come down to Delaware for a meeting the next day. Following a sleepless night on the train from Boston, he arrived in Wilmington at 11:00 A.M. and was quickly ushered into the office of Henry Du Pont himself. After a hurried handshake, Du Pont escorted Goddard to a waiting limousine and they were driven to Du Pont's home, where Lindbergh and three men from the company's research laboratories were waiting for them.

When introduced, one of the trio informed Goddard that they had considered, but later terminated, research on a rocket to deliver added thrust to an aircraft on takeoff. They had asked Goddard to come down, they explained, because they were interested in his thoughts about such a project. As they settled into chairs and a large sofa in Du Pont's library, the questioning began. One of the three took notes while the other two queried Goddard. Du Pont and Lindbergh sat quietly, saying nothing. Goddard, who assumed that this quiz was the prelude to a discussion of funding for his own research, grew restive as the session wore on. In a letter a few days later to C. G. Abbot of the Smithsonian Institution, Goddard described his uneasiness: "I realized soon that the object of this questioning was not so much to determine what could be done on airplanes as to find every last detail of the rocket I have developed during the last nine years, and after I saw this, I evaded [answering] further questions [about] constructional details as much as possible."

With Goddard clamming up, the meeting rapidly wound down. Finally, Lindbergh and the others adjourned to a corner of the room out of Goddard's earshot. While most of their whispering was unintelligible to him, Goddard overheard one of the research men admit that what they had learned from the conversation with Goddard would "save us a lot of grief" in future development work. Lindbergh then rejoined Goddard, who was sitting alone by the fireplace, and invited him to fly back to New York instead of waiting for the next train out of Wilmington. Goddard readily accepted. Knowing that the unheated cabin in Lindbergh's plane would be unbearable without a flying suit, Henry Du Pont, who had walked over and heard this exchange, sent a servant to find one for Goddard.

Annoyed because he suspected he had been summoned to Wilmington under false pretenses, Goddard was in no mood for conversation during the flight to Newark, New Jersey. After landing, Lindbergh went to great lengths to make his personal position clear. First, he emphasized that he disagreed with the posture adopted by others at the meeting. In fact, said Lindbergh, the Du Pont people "did not have the right attitude," being more interested in reaping immediate benefits than in investing in research that offered much future potential but no near-term profit. Lindbergh further volunteered the opinion that he and Goddard should now seek support from someone "interested in the scientific side of things" rather than an immediate practical application.

Later that evening, when boarding the train in New York for the remainder of the trip back to Boston, Goddard concluded that nothing had changed. He was still grubbing fruitlessly for funds to expand the scope of his rocket research. And in doing so, he remained continuously vulnerable to ruthless exploitation by others intent upon stealing his ideas. As the train steamed north into the darkness, he worried about the future. For Goddard, it would be a long, hard winter.

4

Raketenflugplatz

THE DIRECTOR OF *Chemische-Technische-Reichsanstalt*, a government-sponsored research center in Berlin, sat in his office listening sympathetically to his two visitors.

For several days, Hermann Oberth and Rudolph Nebel had been making the rounds of Berlin's numerous scientific foundations seeking financial support to carry on the experiments that had been terminated at the Ufa Film Studios the previous year. Whenever he had been in the company of Fritz Lang's coterie of wealthy businessmen—those with the means to finance the advanced rocket research he hoped to undertake—Oberth never had mustered the courage to speak up. But on this day, talking to one of his peers, he was more at ease. After all, the director of the *Reichsanstalt*, the learned Dr. Alexander Ritter, was an academic, too.

Oberth's money-raising presentation covered two points. First, he cited the superiority of liquid-fuel motors over all other rocket propellants. Liquid fuel alone, he emphasized, could deliver measuring instruments to the unexplored reaches of the upper atmosphere. Second, with all the restraint he could summon, Oberth tried to neutralize any adverse talk about his competence that Ritter might have heard from Fritz Lang or others at the Ufa Film Company. If given sufficient time and resources, Oberth assured the patiently attentive director, he would build a rocket powerful enough to guarantee collection of valuable scientific data from high altitudes.

When Oberth finished, Dr. Ritter leaned forward and said that he regretted that the *Reichsanstalt* had no funds for rocket development. Oberth, however, might be interested in a proposition. It concerned the several prototypes of a liquid-fuel motor that Oberth claimed he had completed for the Ufa Film project. Get one in shape for a demonstration, Dr. Ritter suggested. If successful, he would give Oberth an affidavit certifying the length of the burn and the amount of thrust generated.

Seeing that an endorsement by Ritter would enhance his credibility when seeking support elsewhere, Oberth accepted. Oberth's reputation had elevated him to a position of leadership in the eyes of many whose interest in rocketry transcended the froth dished out in cheap science fiction. In June 1927, a dedicated cadre of rocket enthusiasts had met in the back room of a Breslau restaurant to found the *Verein für Raumschiffahrt*, the Society for Space Travel. In the three years since that meeting, the VfR had grown to more than eight hundred members including Oberth, who, shortly after joining, was elected president. For Oberth, the VfR was a godsend. As defined by Willy Ley, the VfR's main purpose was "to interest as many people as possible [in rocketry], collect membership dues, solicit extra contributions and maintain a fund for experimental work."

With more than half of the VfR membership living in or near Berlin, there was no shortage of volunteers to help Oberth prepare for the demonstration. Nor did Oberth suffer from a lack of financial support. The society's board of directors also approved payment of a long-overdue bill from a machine shop that had fabricated some parts for Oberth. The shop then released a *Kegelduse*, one of the cone-shaped firing chambers originally designed for the initial Ufa Film rocket.

A month after his meeting with Dr. Ritter, Oberth was ready. A time was set for the demonstration, and on the appointed day, Oberth, Ritter, Nebel, Ley, a contingent of VfR members, and a few newspaper photographers gathered at the edge of a small clearing in a pine grove on the outskirts of Berlin. Conditions were far from ideal. It had rained steadily for forty-eight hours. The ground was soggy, a heavy mist hung over the treetops, and dampness permeated the only shelter, a crude shack adjacent to the clearing. Oberth's *Kegelduse* was mounted on a stand equipped with a registering scale, which was then placed in a slit trench.

Klaus Riedel, a graduate engineer and a new member of the VfR, was deputized by Oberth to handle the loading of liquid oxygen and monitor the related equipment. As he poured the fluid from one container to another, much of it vaporized and, drawing moisture from the humid air, quickly formed a layer of ice around pipes and valves. Riedel, while scraping ice from control switches, continued to load the liquid oxygen with the aid of another VfR recruit, a tall blond youth with an engaging smile. The youthful Wernher von Braun, a recent high-school graduate, was demonstrating a skill beyond his years in deftly responding to Riedel's instructions.

Watching from the sidelines, Oberth tried to ignore Nebel's whining about not being a part of the show. Distressed because his own rocket motor was not yet ready to demonstrate and seeing this golden opportunity slip by, Nebel jealously bemoaned the fact that his brainchild was not the focus of all this flattering attention. Riedel eventually had everything in order. Oberth stepped forward and threw a switch while, from a safe distance, photographers snapped pictures of this odd contraption spewing flame and smoke. At the end of the burn, everyone shook hands, and Dr. Ritter returned to his office, where he certified in writing that Oberth's rocket motor "had performed without mishap on 23 July, 1930, for 90 seconds, consuming six kilograms of liquid oxygen and one kilogram of gasoline, and delivering a constant thrust of about seven kilograms."

The demonstration of the *Kegelduse* marked the end, for the time being at least, of Oberth's rocket work in Berlin. Now he had to face up to the necessity of making a living. And so, shortly after accepting the certificate from Dr. Ritter, Oberth departed for Mediash, the town in Romania where he lived and taught at a technical institute. Nebel had his own plans. He talked of little else than his precious *Mirak* and how it would win him a place of honor in the ranks of the VfR. While Dr. Ritter's presence endowed Oberth's demonstration with immunity from official censure, Nebel knew that the growing public demand for a ban on all rocket experiments, following the recent tragic death of Max Valier, might halt his work on *Mirak*.

Valier, a member in good standing of the VfR, had not seen eye to eye with Oberth. For many years, Valier had been an outspoken advocate of powder-burning rockets. Oberth, Ley, and many others viewed Valier's commitment to solid fuels as leading to a dead end, which, when reached, would bar further performance improvements. This was bad enough, but the high profile that publicity about Valier was giving to powder propellants was creating a bad image for rocketry in general. Another concern was that Valier's experiments, while amusing to watch, added nothing significant to the body of scientific knowledge.

Instead of aiming at the heavens, like any other self-respecting member of the Society for Space Travel, Valier mounted his rockets on automobiles. For more than two years preceding his untimely

death, his rocket-powered cars had burned up the tracks at various
fairs and exhibitions around Germany. But six months before he died,
finally recognizing the limits of solid fuels, he switched his allegiance
to liquid propellants. Only days before he was to drive in a widely
publicized extravaganza, Valier was working alone late one night in
May 1930. While he was observing, apparently at close range, the
operation of the gasoline and liquid-oxygen motor, it exploded. A
fragment pierced Valier's aorta and he bled to death.

The public outcry following Valier's fatal accident made it impossible for Nebel to test his rocket in Berlin. With no place to experiment
without risking arrest by the police, Nebel decided to get out of town
until things cooled off. He discreetly passed the word to a few trusted
VfR members that he needed a remote hideaway for his work on
Mirak. Eager to curry favor with anyone building a rocket, Klaus
Riedel, the young engineer who had loaded fuel for Oberth's recent
demonstration, brashly offered his grandparents' farm near Bernstadt
in Saxony. When a letter from Riedel advised the elderly couple that
he was bringing a friend for a prolonged summer visit, whatever
doubts they may have harbored were dispelled by their grandson's
assurances that Nebel was indeed a fine fellow. As his grandparents
prepared to welcome Nebel into their home, Riedel and other VfR
members helped Nebel organize his gear for the drive south. On the
morning of their departure, they hurriedly jammed parts of a test
stand, sundry pipes and canisters, and the *Mirak* itself into the back-
seat of a touring car that Nebel had acquired. With everything
stowed, there was handshaking all around and Nebel climbed into the
driver's seat. Before clambering aboard beside him, Riedel turned to
Willy Ley and, with a sheepish grin, confided that they were
transferring operations to Saxony "to keep further casualties secret."

With Oberth in Mediash and Nebel down on the farm, Ley was left
to mind the store in Berlin. Throughout the summer of 1930, Ley, as
secretary of the VfR, dutifully issued mimeographed bulletins on the
latest developments in rocketry. These missives, circulated regularly
to the VfR membership, achieved two important objectives. Though
geographically isolated from each other, rocket buffs throughout Germany, Austria, and Romania now enjoyed a common communications link. And funds to support promising rocket experiments could
be solicited from a large and sympathetic contributor base.

Ley, continually scratching for news to publish in his bulletins,
impatiently awaited a progress report from Saxony. One arrived,

penned on a postcard, not long after Nebel and Riedel erected the test stand in a secluded gully. The message was brief and not encouraging: "The *Mirak* burns, but the recoil is too small to be measured with our homemade thrust meter . . . probably a pound or so." A couple of weeks later: "The *Mirak* now produces a recoil of three to four pounds." And then: "The recoil now exceeds *Mirak's* own weight . . . it would rise if we released it." Ley, who featured these pithy reports in his bulletins, editorialized that far greater gains would come when readers loosened their purse strings.

At first, the response to Ley's appeals for funds was barely enough to pay for mimeograph supplies and postage. But late in August, an engineer whom Ley remembered as Herr Dilthey, told Ley that he intended to contribute 3,800 marks (about $1,000) to support VfR's research. Dilthey, who later paid this sum in two cash installments, was not sufficiently troubled by news from Nebel in September to withdraw his pledge. Ley somehow managed to put the last postcard message in the best possible light. Nebel's final report from the farm in Saxony, while disconcerting, paradoxically exuded optimism: "The *Mirak* has exploded, no harm done; we'll return and build a new one."

With the VfR now comfortably solvent through Dilthey's largess, Ley was further buoyed by a commitment by Hugo A. Hückel, a well-to-do businessman, who agreed to contribute about $150 a month. Prospects were indeed brighter, and Nebel, having returned to Berlin, set out to find a permanent proving ground for the society's rocket experiments. Because the furor over Valier's death had subsided, Nebel drove around inspecting potential sites with cocky bravado. His objective: an isolated retreat, out of the way and off the beaten path. Several tracts met that requirement but none better than one in the district of Reinickendorf on the northern edge of Berlin.

Abandoned soon after the armistice ending World War I, the two square miles of hilly woodland never had been improved for commercial purposes because of a dual jurisdiction. The land was owned by the city of Berlin, but during the war the site had been an army ammunition depot upon which the German War Ministry built eight huge concrete bunkers. Each was surrounded by an earthen wall forty feet high and sixty feet thick at the base. Whenever the city tried to lease the property, the deals were quashed by the War Ministry, which refused to permit even minor modifications to the bunkers.

The War Ministry's intransigence reduced the commercial value of the tract to virtually zero. As a result, when Nebel visited the city official responsible for administering public property, the bunkers and adjoining acreage had been unused for over ten years. Nebel said that he and his associates wanted the property for research purposes but refrained from mentioning the VfR or the firing of rockets. The official was pleased to learn that Nebel wanted to lease the bunkers as they were, promising not to make any structural changes within them.

There were other conditions. Only two of the eight bunkers could be occupied, and Nebel and his friends must enter and leave through one of two gates in the high wire fence that surrounded the property. Finally, no machinery was to be brought in that could not be removed on forty-eight hours' notice.

Nebel agreed to observe the restrictions, signed a lease, and handed over the nominal sum of fifteen marks (about four dollars) for twelve months' rent. A few days later, on September 27, 1930, he moved in. Proudly proclaiming to his confederates that the site was the first *Raketenflugplatz* (rocket airdrome), Nebel set up housekeeping in a guardhouse near the main gate.

5

The Masterful Touch of Ivy Lee

July 1930
New York City

HIGH ABOVE THE bustling clamor of Manhattan's financial district, Ivy Ledbetter Lee presided over a tranquil domain. Visitors entering his handsome suite of offices on the thirty-first floor of the Equitable Trust Company building were subtly mesmerized by an aura of dignity and decorum: walls adorned with fine etchings of great European cathedrals, rich oriental carpets, huge glass cabinets containing expensive objets d'art. But it was the courtly southern charm of Ivy Lee himself that ultimately captured their confidence. He exuded assurance in the face of uncertainty, wisdom in a world of fools, direction in the midst of chaos.

Ivy Lee & Associates was an anomaly on Wall Street. Engaging the services of the many other firms occupying the skyscrapers south of City Hall brought advice about a bewildering array of investment opportunities. Lee, however, offered different counsel. While the money men responded only to hard facts on a balance sheet, Lee dealt in the abstract. He was less concerned with how much a company earned than with the respect it commanded from the public. His phenomenal success in the esoteric art of influencing people was corroborated by the long list of corporate executives flocking to him for advice. They represented every facet of American business, from breakfast cereals to steel making, tobacco, petroleum, motor cars, and motion pictures. He also counseled political candidates on projecting an image that attracts votes and showed philanthropists how to give away their money gracefully.

Lee was a masterful salesman of ideas and a skilled promoter of his own abilities. With his carefully indexed file of the world's most important people, he had a rich potential client base at his fingertips. But many were not merely names on cards. He personally cultivated the great and near great, adroitly using each contact to gain entry to another. He was granted audiences with prime ministers, cabinet officers, and important industrialists, and he exploited his membership in numerous private clubs to proselytize otherwise inaccessible prospects.

Nor was he inclined to soft-pedal his hobnobbing with the high and the mighty. Crowding the walls of his reception room were dozens of personally inscribed photographs including those of the John D. Rockefellers, King Boris III of Bulgaria, songwriters Jerome Kern and Irving Berlin, German financier Hjalmar Schacht, steel titan Charles M. Schwab, and the international literary and political celebrity, the Right Honorable Winston S. Churchill. Churchill's portrait was a prized possession, which, Lee assured the future prime minister of Britain, occupied "a place of honor among my gallery of notables."

Lee had the advantage of neither a powerful family nor an old-boy network to smooth his way into the big time. His parents were of modest means and the properties of both his maternal and paternal grandparents had been left in ruins by Sherman's earth-scorching march through Georgia in 1864. A little more than a decade later, Lee was born near Atlanta on July 17, 1877, one month before his mother's fourteenth birthday. His father, twenty-seven at the time, was an itinerant preacher serving a small circuit of Methodist churches. Frugality and hard work enabled young Ivy Lee to go north in 1896 and enroll at Princeton University. His degree from that hallowed institution might have ensured, with the help of influential alumni, a promising future in banking, finance, or the law. Lee's prizewinning debating skills prompted aspirations for a career in the courtroom, but limited resources forced him to leave Harvard Law School after his first semester. He then turned to his other strength—writing. As campus correspondent for some New York newspapers, he had covered lectures, concerts, and sports while a student at Princeton. Charles Edward Russell, who was editor of the *New York Journal* and had used many of Lee's dispatches, promptly hired him when he came seeking a job.

Lee, however, did not fit the mold of the freewheeling, hard-drinking New York reporter of the turn of the century. In the words of a colleague, John C. Mumford: "He did what most newspapermen don't . . . [he] made a business of his business." Mumford meant that, unlike most journeymen reporters of his day, Lee never coasted. An interview with a prominent person was invariably preceded by hours of research in a library. When helping out at the drama desk, his off hours were crammed with intensive studies of the art of criticism, during which he compiled a bulging notebook of commentaries on the work of the great playwrights. While a reporter's customary equipment was limited to a notebook and pencils in a coat breastpocket, Lee augmented these bare essentials with an armful of books carried from one assignment to another.

From the *Journal*, Lee eventually gravitated to the *New York Times* and then to Joseph Pulitzer's *New York World*. Spare time was work time. Searching for ways to supplement his income (for he now was married and a father), he turned to free-lance writing. One of his early pieces, "Savings Banks," argued that these much maligned institutions generated sociological benefits for the common man as well as profits for their owners. Lee wrote: "the savings of the poor should be invested for them . . . sound finance demands that the savings of the people should be made available for the productive needs of the community." He went on to laud the public schools and the few companies that encouraged thrift. Singling out the board and management of the Baltimore and Ohio Railroad, who had set up a savings plan for their employees, Lee concluded: "these public-spirited men . . . have made themselves creditors of civilization."

Lee's arguments drew high praise from the banking community, and shortly thereafter a consortium of New York bankers, unable to convince property owners to sell a right of way for a new railroad they were backing, went to Lee for help. Lee sought out and talked to the men of influence in every town affected by the proposed train route and finally convinced them that their communities had much to gain by granting the right of way.

In bailing out the New York bankers, Lee had made the first move in a redirection of his career. Writing, until then his full-time occupation, was gradually subordinated to another pursuit: helping businessmen achieve their goals without arousing the wrath of the populace. By 1916, after he had served as a consultant to the Rockefeller family and a corporate policymaker for the Pennsylvania Railroad, Lee's reputation as an independent adviser to business was well established. By 1925, many of the most powerful men in the country called on Lee when they needed a troubleshooter.

One of these was Daniel Guggenheim. After engaging Lee to look into some problems relating to the family's extensive copper-mining interests, Guggenheim sought Lee's advice about the disposition of funds he had set aside for philanthropic purposes. At the time, Lee had a close working relationship with Daniel's son, Harry, a navy flier during World War I and still an ardent aviation enthusiast. Sharing the younger Guggenheim's belief that aviation in the United States was on the verge of spawning a great new industry, Lee joined him in persuading his father to endow a school of aeronautics at New York University. Lee then campaigned to carry this initiative one step further. Education is important, he argued, but so is research. Lee then proposed setting up a dedicated capital resource for experimentation and development. Responding to the enthusiastic endorsement of Harry, the father acquiesced and the Daniel Guggenheim Fund for the Promotion of Aviation was formed.

Throughout the 1920s, the firm of Ivy Lee & Associates handled many tasks for the Guggenheims. In addition to overseeing labor and government relations in the family's businesses, other special services were performed. When Lindbergh returned to America after his historic transatlantic flight in 1927, it was the Lee organization that coordinated the three-month triumphant nationwide tour by the Lone Eagle. In 1929, when Harry Guggenheim was appointed United States ambassador to Cuba, Burnham Carter, an associate in Lee's firm, was assigned to go along as his secretary.

Now, on this warm morning early in July 1930, Ivy Lee was spearheading another project for the Guggenheims. Looking around the conference table during a meeting with key members of his staff, Lee turned to Harcourt Parrish. Parrish, like most of those present, had served his apprenticeship as a newspaper reporter, first for the *Louisville Courier-Journal* and then for the Associated Press in New York. He was a seasoned member of Ivy Lee's team, having successfully managed several projects for foreign clients and the Rockefeller family.

Lee wanted to know the status of a news release that Parrish was drafting. A few days earlier, on July 3, C. G. Abbot, the dispenser of the modest annual grants that the Smithsonian Institution doled out to Professor Robert Goddard, received a telegram from Ivy Lee: "We are preparing for the newspapers a statement relative to Dr. Goddard's experiments. Would appreciate by special delivery three hundred to five hundred word explanation from you on the value of this work to aviation, possibly in making high elevation weather maps." Abbot's reply was received in Lee's New York office after the Fourth of July hiatus and immediately turned over to Parrish.

Parrish retrieved a copy of his draft from the stack of papers in front of him and passed it to Lee. Reading the first paragraph, Lee noted approvingly that although "Mr. Daniel Guggenheim has made a grant [to Robert H. Goddard] for the continuation of the [rocket] work which has been in progress for fifteen years," no amount was mentioned. As former newspapermen, Lee and Parrish knew that the size of the grant was an essential part of the story. But they were newspapermen no longer. Now they cautioned their client to downplay the money angle. For to most suffering souls in a depression-ravaged world where millions went to bed hungry every night, spending many thousands of dollars on rockets was an obscene extravagance.

Daniel Guggenheim had disclosed the generous terms of the grant a month earlier in a confidential letter to Wallace W. Atwood, the president of Clark University: "I take pleasure in offering Twenty-Five Thousand Dollars a year for two years of work [by Dr. Goddard]. I understand that Clark University [will organize] an advisory committee. . . . If at the end of two years this advisory committee considers that the results attained warrant further expenditure, I should be glad to give Twenty-Five Thousand Dollars per year for two years more."

After conferring with Clark University's Board of Trustees, Atwood quickly accepted Guggenheim's offer. In his reply, he assured Guggenheim that "the University will make these funds available to Dr. Goddard upon his requisition and will aid him in the prosecution of his work." Less than a week went by before Atwood finished recruiting a distinguished roster of advisory board members. For chairman, he tapped the learned Dr. John C. Merriam, president of the Carnegie Institution of Washington. C. G. Abbot, Goddard's longtime mentor, was also invited to serve, as was Daniel Guggenheim's technical adviser, Charles A. Lindbergh, and the Guggenheim family attorney, Henry Breckinridge. Rounding out the rest of the committee were: Walter S. Adams, director of the Mount Wilson Observatory; John A. Fleming of the Carnegie Institution; C. F. Marvin, chief of the United States Weather Bureau; Robert A. Millikan, director of the physics laboratories, California Institute of Technology; and Atwood himself.

For Goddard, the Guggenheim grant was truly a bonanza. Everything, it seemed, had changed for the better. No more cutting corners to stretch skimpy resources. Gone, too, was the frustration of working in a hostile environment. He was now free to get away. Far away. Writing to advisory committee chairman Merriam, Goddard complained that the experiments at Camp Devens had "proved too difficult to be effective. The camp is used [for training many recruits] in the summer and the soldiers have even stolen apparatus which I thought well hidden." During an earlier meeting with Lindbergh in New York, Goddard was urged to find a test site in the southern part of the Midwest region's Great Plains. When he returned to Worcester, Goddard went to see Charles Brooks, a Clark professor of meteorology. After studying climatic and topographical maps, Brooks suggested the southwestern portion of the Great Plains around Roswell, New Mexico, because it was least subject to wind and dust storms.

While Harcourt Parrish rechecked the facts in his news release, Goddard, at home in Worcester, prepared for the move west. He and his wife, Esther, planned to leave first. His work crew—Charles Mansur, Henry Sachs, and Al Kisk—and the wives of Sachs and Kisk were to start later. The three assistants, all experienced craftsmen who fabricated components for many of Goddard's earlier experiments, would remain behind until tools, materials, and shop equipment were crated and loaded aboard a boxcar in the Worcester railroad depot.

Though exhilarated by the prospect of a new start in the west, Goddard was ambivalent about the proposed news announcement sent by Ivy Lee. True, there was no speculative nonsense about rocketing to the moon. Nor were there any brash predictions of a technological breakthrough. Harcourt Parrish had skillfully downgraded the objective as stated by Abbot: while "barometers, electrical measuring apparatus, and air traps to collect samples of air may be sent to extreme altitudes . . . it is admittedly a matter of years" before any of Goddard's rockets will return to earth with information of value to "meteorology, astronomy, radio broadcasting, aviation and science in general."

Goddard knew from bitter experience that some newspapermen were prone to amplify the less relevant in order to produce a sensational impact. Although Abbot's statement, as a whole, was a restrained assessment of the potential value of Goddard's rockets, some sentences, if taken out of context, were not. The reference to improving high-altitude weather prediction, for example: "With the parachute rocket . . . automatic instruments will be sent to any desired height and will bring back their records safely within a few minutes. Thus by means of a network of stations, the Weather Bureau will be in a position to map the weather of the air as successfully as it now maps the weather of the earth's surface."

Goddard may have feared that Abbot's attempt to create a practical objective was promising too much too soon, but he said nothing. He returned the draft to Lee without comment and hoped for the best. Lee then distributed the announcement to the press on Wednesday, July 9. When the New York papers were delivered to Lee's suite of offices the following morning, Harcourt Parrish breathed a sigh of relief. All adhered meticulously to the facts stated in the announcement.

Parrish was less sanguine, however, about the telephone call later that morning from David Lasser, a free-lance science writer. Lasser, who had been commissioned to write a follow-up story for the Sunday edition of the *New York Herald-Tribune*, wanted more information. Parrish was troubled by his line of questioning. The queries relating to the possible use of rockets on aircraft were worrisome enough, but Lasser also asked for Goddard's views on rocketing to the moon and planets. In a quick note to Goddard, Parrish tried to absolve himself from blame for any irresponsible speculation in Lasser's story: "I am quite sure that in [Lasser's] article we will have wild dreams about interplanetary communication, although I called his attention especially to the fact that no mention of such possibilities was made in the news article sent out by this office." In his reply a few days later, Goddard reassured Parrish: "You have done very well in keeping the press notices to the purely scientific side. The problem is especially difficult to handle because the interplanetary application is really physically possible." Happily, Goddard had no complaints about Lasser's report in the *Herald-Tribune*, for he later wrote from New Mexico that he appreciated "your well written article."

As he and his wife motored west, Goddard felt free at last. Free of the curious, the kibitzers, the pilfering soldiers. Free, too, of harassment by such nervous nellies as the spinster in Fitchburg who wrote warning that the Camp Devens experiments "are dangerous to the cities and small towns in the vicinity." That missive, addressed to the War Department in Washington, D.C., wound up on the desk of Major General C. H. Bridges, who, with considerable relief, informed the lady that the army was not responsible. Told to contact the Smithsonian Institution, she sent a letter to C. G. Abbot voicing her conviction that she suffered personal injury: "Think I was struck by the radio experiment near the apex of the heart one day last year." Abbot, controlling his annoyance, replied that "no actual rocket flights were made at Camp Devens during the year 1929–1930. The apparatus has now been entirely removed therefrom, and there is no intention of making further rocket experiments in the neighborhood."

Ten days after they waved farewells to friends and neighbors, the Goddards reached Roswell in southeastern New Mexico. After seeking directions to the U.S. Weather Bureau office, where, by pre-arrangement, their mail had been forwarded, they checked into the Hotel Nickson, rested, and prepared to start scouting the area the following day. Within a week, they narrowed their search to a small ranch about three miles northeast of town. On August 2, they signed a two-year lease, agreeing to a $115 monthly rental for the sprawling single-level house that had enough living space to accommodate comfortably both Goddards, the three worker assistants, and the two wives.

The ranch, however, lacked an outbuilding large enough for a workshop. To remedy this deficiency, Goddard, in five busy days, drew plans for a single-story structure thirty feet wide and fifty-five feet long, ordered blueprints, secured estimates, and signed a contract with a carpenter. Also, during the same week, he purchased a used truck, ordered steel plates and framing for a metal launching tower, gave a talk at a luncheon meeting of the Roswell Rotary Club, and supervised the unloading of the boxcar that had just completed the long journey from Worcester. Construction of the workshop began two days after the contract was signed. While the carpenter and his helpers hammered frames for the cement foundation piers, Goddard turned to the one remaining order of business. By this time, his three assistants had arrived and settled in. Their first assignment was the assembly and erection of the launching tower. On the morning of August 22, Goddard, accompanied by Mansur, Sachs, and Kisk, trucked the sheet iron and pipes for the tower to a remote site on the prairie ten miles northwest of town.

While Goddard and his crew labored in the sweltering New Mexico sun, Ivy Lee savored the light breeze wafting through his New York office windows. Sitting at his desk and leafing through several hundred newspaper clippings announcing the Guggenheim grant, Lee concluded that Harcourt Parrish's assessment was right. The news

coverage was overwhelmingly positive. There were no brash speculations about rocketing to the moon and, more importantly, scant
criticism of the Guggenheim support for Goddard's experiments—
just well-reasoned presentations of the facts Lee had judged suitable
for public disclosure. An editorial in the July 14 edition of the *New
York Herald-Tribune* echoed best the high hopes Lee had wanted to
convey: "The financial aid by Mr. Daniel Guggenheim may mark
an important step in exploration of the upper air. . . . It is a reward,
too, for perseverance and moderation. For nearly twenty years, Professor Goddard has maintained the possibility of rocket motors for
flight. . . . During this time, he has refrained from the wild statements
characteristic of [some] European advocates of this variety of motive
power. Well balanced enthusiasm is none too common, even among
scientific men. It is good to see it rewarded." Ivy Lee nodded his
agreement as he closed the file on another Guggenheim project.

6

Nebel Takes Charge

March 1931
Berlin, Germany

Bʏ ᴍᴀsᴛᴇʀᴍɪɴᴅɪɴɢ ᴛʜᴇ acquisition of the test site near Reinickendorf, Rudolf Nebel became the overlord of all VfR rocket experiments. It was not that he had abruptly toppled Hermann Oberth from his pedestal. Clearly outclassed by the academic achievements of the brooding professor from Mediash, Nebel was poorly equipped to engineer such a coup. Oberth's stature was also buttressed by the fact that he was the duly elected president of the VfR, which, during his tenure, had grown from a small cadre of rocket buffs into a government-chartered society with a thousand dues-paying members. Yet, for those flocking regularly to the *Raketenflugplatz*, Oberth was a leader in hiding.

Still smarting from the humiliation he had endured following the promotional fiasco for Fritz Lang's film, Oberth remained holed up in Mediash, stubbornly refusing to admit that returning to Berlin was better than working in self-imposed isolation. Nebel, a skilled opportunist, moved adroitly into the void created by Oberth's absence and exploited his seniority, the one strength no one could challenge. Though only thirty-one at the time, and five years younger than Oberth, Nebel successfully used his age to command the allegiance of others in the inner circle of the VfR.

Willy Ley, at twenty-four, was one of the oldest in this select group. Unlike most VfR members, who opted to watch from the sidelines, Ley and his companions were not afraid to get their hands dirty. But Ley's brashness, a personal trait that enabled him to outmaneuver Oberth when the two had been advisers to Fritz Lang, was less effective in dealing with Nebel. Ley was also burdened by other handicaps.

For one thing, Nebel occupied the territory. Little was done at the *Raketenflugplatz* without his knowledge and consent. Just a few steps from Nebel's bachelor quarters in the old guardhouse were all of the material assets of the VfR. Machinery, rocket parts, and other equipment acquired for Oberth's experiments at the Ufa Film Company were now secure in his protective custody. Even the gleaming shell of Oberth's unfinished rocket had been appropriated by Nebel as a symbol of his own expertise.

Nebel also dedicated much more time to the operations of the "rocket airdrome" than Ley's circumstances permitted. Somehow, he could afford to. Although lacking any visible source of income, Nebel mysteriously managed to conjure up the funds necessary to support a comfortable life-style. Ley was less fortunate. While captivating him since his teens, rocketry offered neither the substance nor the stability necessary for a livelihood. But some years earlier, Ley had stumbled upon a new way to make money. After detecting a serious error in a report of a recent scientific discovery published in a Berlin newspaper, Ley promptly dispatched a rebuttal. A few days later, he was delighted to see his argument in print and, soon thereafter, absolutely astounded to receive a small check from the editor.

Having discovered that publishers paid money for well-expressed viewpoints, Ley composed commentaries on every scientific happening that piqued his interest. As these essays appeared in more newspapers and magazines, Ley bolstered his reputation by turning out, with incredible speed, several book-length manuscripts. The first, *Trip into Space*, was published in 1926. In 1928, he wrote a sequel: *By Rocket to the Moon*. Broadening the scope of his research and drawing upon earlier university studies in zoology, Ley then produced a book about dragons and a biography of Konrad Gestner, the distinguished biologist.

While his prolific writing output limited Ley's participation in the daily activities at the *Raketenflugplatz*, others were not bound by comparable constraints. Klaus Riedel, for example, was, like Nebel, virtually a permanent resident. Possibly to return the hospitality Riedel had arranged the previous summer in Saxony, Nebel invited his young protégé to move into one of the vacant rooms in the old guardhouse by the gate. Curiously, Nebel did not consider Riedel a threat to his leadership even though Nebel's limited engineering skills were no match for Riedel's technical ingenuity. Riedel, who was aware that Nebel's ego would never tolerate a rival, prudently kept his ideas to himself.

Riedel's resourcefulness, nonetheless, was a major factor in solving the overheating problems that plagued Oberth's original *Kegelduse* and later Nebel's *Mirak*. Sustained burning of the liquid-oxygen mixtures used in these motors soon elevated the temperatures inside the cone-shaped firing chambers beyond the melting points of the inner walls. All sorts of remedies were proposed, including lining the interior surfaces with fire-resistant ceramics. Though deemed the most promising solution, the ceramics idea was subsequently abandoned. Disenchantment with these hardy yet brittle materials came when a small piece of interior lining cracked and broke off during a test. Instead of blowing harmlessly away, it lodged in the exhaust nozzle, causing the entire engine to explode.

Finally someone suggested attacking the problem from another direction. If we cannot formulate a reliable heat-resistant material, let's prevent the destructive high internal temperatures by cooling the walls themselves. Much discussion ensued on this point, culminating in the design (masterminded by Riedel) of a water jacket surrounding the firing chamber. Riedel's technical savvy was rivaled only by the expertise of a nineteen-year-old engineering student who, while not attending a *Technische Hochschule* in Zurich, dedicated much of his holiday and vacation time to the pursuit of his "scientific hobby." Ever since reading a story about an imaginary trip to the moon, Wernher von Braun had been obsessed with the notion that one day he would "soar through the heavens and explore the mysterious universe." Such thoughts naturally moved him into the orbit of the VfR and, after joining, his talent and enthusiasm soon propelled him into its inner circle, where his imaginative solutions to technical problems were hailed with admiration by Riedel and accepted in sullen silence by Nebel.

The second of three sons of a wealthy gentleman farmer, Wernher von Braun enjoyed the many privileges of a landed aristocracy. His father, Baron Magnus von Braun, a high government official in the pre-Hitler Weimar Republic, was sufficiently affluent to support his family in a manner well beyond the reach of most Germans. Wernher attended the best schools, traveled widely throughout Europe, and through his father's political and professional contacts enjoyed easy access to the intelligentsia and social elite of the time.

Von Braun learned early in life that his family's wide circle of influential friends could be used for personal advantage. Consequently, he was not above occasional name-dropping to establish credibility or make a point. One such instance occurred in Switzerland in March 1931. Von Braun was telling an acquaintance that one day huge rockets would carry men into space. To Constantine D. J. Generales, a medical student at the University of Zurich, the prospect was ridiculous and laughable. And he said so. Von Braun, his face reddening, withdrew an envelope from his pocket and, thrusting it at Generales, said, "Read this." The envelope was addressed to von Braun and bore a Berlin postmark. When he opened it, Generales found a letter filled with nearly indecipherable mathematical equations concerning problems and proposed solutions in rocket design and propulsion. Scanning the last page, Generales saw the signature of the internationally renowned Professor Albert Einstein.

While Generales gained new respect for the fixation of von Braun's "one track mind" on rocketry, the twenty-three-year-old medical student might never have listened to this outer-space nonsense if he himself had had nothing to gain. A week before seeing the Einstein letter, Generales had stood in the serving line of a cafeteria frequented by students of the university and the nearby *Technische Hochschule*. It was his first visit there since returning to Zurich from a vacation at his home near Athens. He tried to ignore the conversation around him, which was in German, French, and a local dialect known as *Schweizer Deutsch*, when, unexpectedly in the hubbub, he overheard a brief exchange in English.

Curious and eager to practice his rusty English, Generales turned and saw a "tall blond chap" to whom he introduced himself. Von Braun smiled, shook his hand, and cheerfully agreed to join him for lunch and some conversation. Generales would have welcomed chitchat on almost any subject except the one chosen by von Braun. Throughout their meal, and another the following week, von Braun spoke of nothing but rocketry. Finally, in desperation, Generales scornfully had belittled such talk, prompting von Braun to produce the Einstein letter.

After admitting that there might be some validity in von Braun's rocket theories, Generales offered this advice: "If you really want to reach the moon someday, you had better try with mice first." His point was that before subjecting anyone to the rigors of space flight much should be learned through experiments with animals. Because von Braun was worried about coping with the tremendous accelerative forces he anticipated during a rocket launch, Generales suggested some simple tests that might throw some light on any potentially harmful effects.

While von Braun was concerned about the inertial pull on tissues and organs as a rocket sped upward along a straight flight path, Generales thought that comparable forces could be simulated by centrifugal pressures generated by a rapidly spinning device. At first, an instrument almost as prevalent in biology research laboratories as the microscope seemed the best choice. But after testing the peripheral velocity limits of the standard centrifuge, Generales concluded that its radius was too short.

Then a brainstorm. Why not a bicycle wheel? The distance from hub to rim was much longer than the radius of any centrifuge around. And, unlike a centrifuge, Generales already had two of them. After smuggling the dismantled front wheel of his bicycle into von Braun's room, they set to work. They mounted the wheel on a horizontal wooden frame and attached a pedal to its hub. Using the pedal as a crank, they could rotate the wheel on its axis and calculate the velocity of fixed points on the rim with a tachometer and stopwatch.

Now they were ready for the next step: live subjects. Exploiting a friendship with an animal caretaker in the university's biology department, Generales acquired a dozen white mice. These were surreptitiously delivered to von Braun's room, where, for several days, they were given progressively faster rides on the Generales merry-go-round. After each, the mice were removed from four hammocklike sacks suspended at ninety-degree intervals around the rim of the wheel. Bug-eyed and staggering, some slowly regained equilibrium. Others succumbed. Generales performed autopsies on the dead and noted in his journal that "all of the organs in the chest and abdominal cavities, as well as the brain, were displaced and torn in varying degrees from the surrounding tissue. [Obviously] the force we had achieved was far greater than the mice could tolerate."

The inconclusive findings posed many more questions. As Generales and von Braun pressed on, an unfortunate accident brought their experiments to a halt. One day as the wheel spun at high speed, a mouse slipped from its cradle and was catapulted against the bedroom wall, leaving bloody stains that neither von Braun nor Generales could scrub clean. When the landlady discovered them the next morning, she issued an ultimatum: Get rid of the mice and that infernal contraption or move out!

Although forced to terminate the rooming-house experiments in Zurich, von Braun was cheered by news from his VfR friends in Berlin that things were heating up at the *Raketenflugplatz*. A crew of unemployed mechanics and metalworkers (recruited by Nebel to volunteer their skills in exchange for food and lodging) was turning out a sufficient number of motors to justify static test firings several times a week. Nebel presided over these demonstrations like a ringmaster in a circus. Barking orders and bustling about, he was too busy to notice that Riedel and his companions already knew what to do and, by ignoring Nebel's instructions, were actually running the show themselves.

Nebel reveled in the role he had created for himself. Playing to the audience of curious onlookers usually in attendance, he hinted broadly that they had been invited to the *Raketenflugplatz* to view the fruits of his own genius. Riedel and the others shrugged off this outrageous distortion, quietly accepting Nebel's bid for acclaim as well as his penchant for getting his fingers into everything. Even the audience was a product of Nebel's finagling. Always on the prowl for new ways to make money, Nebel concocted a scheme to make the more elaborate tests pay for themselves and perhaps even turn a profit. Because he could not risk arrest by openly advertising and charging admission, he arranged private demonstrations for a flat fee. The local chapter of an engineering society, for example, would be offered an opportunity to secretly witness a rocket motor firing for the payment of a few hundred marks (fifty dollars or so). Nebel solicited gifts of tools and materials from various businessmen in exchange for an invitation to the donor and his party to come and see the show.

Word of Nebel's theatrics even spanned the Atlantic. Thanks to Willy Ley's prolific correspondence with the co-founders of the newly formed American Interplanetary Society, David Lasser and G. Edward Pendray were well briefed on the demonstrations in Reinickendorf. Lasser, a science writer and editor of a popular radio-electronics magazine, and Pendray, a news reporter for the *New York Herald-Tribune*, had joined forces to organize a society that would "offer real inducements to American scientists comparable to those offered to scientists in Germany, Austria and France in the development of rockets and other proposed methods of travelling in space." In a letter written March 5, 1931, Pendray told Ley that he was planning a

vacation trip to France and Germany. Two weeks later, Ley, in
halting English, dispatched an answer to Marseilles in anticipation of
Pendray's arrival on the S.S. *France:* "I invite you to visit me in Berlin
and I shall show you our rocket field. I have told the chief manager of
the field, Dipl. Ing. Nebel, that you will visit us. He answered me
that he will show you an experiment with the Mirak, if possible."

On a Saturday early in April, Willy Ley drove into the *Raketenflugplatz* with a visitor from America. Pendray did not speak German.
Nor did Nebel, Riedel, and the others speak English. Ley, therefore,
became the medium through whom they conversed. After in-
troductions and a tour of the demonstration area and workshop,
Pendray asked Nebel what the American society should do first to
advance the cause of rocketry. Two things, said Nebel. First, start
experimenting: "There is no end to the things we must know before
we have solved the rocket problem." Second, cooperate by freely
exchanging information. Pendray replied that cooperation would be
easy, experimentation more difficult: "Materials, labor and land cost a
great deal in America and our society at present unfortunately has no
backer." Nebel, sensing a way to turn this lack of support to his own
advantage, bored in: "If you cannot make a beginning immediately in
America, you [could] send a little money to us for our experiments.
We already have a plant. Materials and labor are cheaper in Germany.
A hundred dollars will not buy much in America, but here it will pay
for a large part of a rocket . . . or make possible a series of experiments
on combustion chambers, landing apparatus and stabilizers."

Pendray, realizing that Nebel was maneuvering him into a corner,
backpedaled quickly. He was not authorized, declared Pendray, to
make any financial commitments on behalf of his colleagues back in
America. But this was only half the truth. Pendray knew that rocket
development must be encouraged at home. Goddard, with Guggenheim support, had made a start. Progress, even small steps forward, would eventually inspire others to provide more financial help.
But depleting American resources to benefit German research was
sheer madness. Nebel, accepting the rebuff, dropped the subject and
launched into his usual self-serving speech about the great gains
achieved under his leadership. The show was about to begin again.

By May 1931, however, Nebel's static motor demonstrations no
longer drew the crowds they once had. His reaction to the suddenly
shrinking audiences was an abrupt declaration that it was time for a
vacation. He announced that he planned to visit the seaport city of

Kiel, hastily adding that his trip would be more work than play. Because a huge aviation show was in Kiel at the time, he hinted that more financial backers for rocket experiments might be found there.

Knowing that glibness alone would not induce some fat cats to part with their cash, Nebel looked for an eye-catching prop. His ego prompted him to consider his Mirak or even one of the later standard motors. Yet these would not do. Unless fired, which was out of the question, they would be lost in a show dominated by the latest aviation technology. He eventually selected the gleaming shell of Oberth's first Ufa Film rocket. Though all sizzle and no substance, the shiny casing should capture the attention of passersby long enough for Nebel to start his pitch. With that settled, he loaded the rocket shell and his luggage into his touring car, waved a farewell, and drove off.

7

The Army Makes a Move

July 1932
Kummersdorf, Germany

STANDING ON A roadside deep in a pine forest near Berlin, Captain Walter Dornberger squinted at his watch. It was 5:00 A.M. and the first light of a summer sunrise silhouetted the treetops. Hearing the sound of approaching motor cars, he stepped quickly onto the crown of the road and waited. As the headlights of the first vehicle came into view, he signaled the driver to stop.

Among other things, Dornberger hoped that this early-morning rendezvous might hasten his promotion to higher rank. At thirty-seven years of age, he was beyond the point of no return, wholly committed to a military career. As a boy, he had yearned to be an architect, but as the second son in an upper-middle-class family, custom decreed that he become a soldier. His enlistment in the army just preceded the outbreak of World War I in August 1914, and by year's end, he was serving at the front as a second lieutenant of artillery. Lucky to survive four years of combat before capture in October 1918, he remained a prisoner in France for two years. Upon returning home, his outstanding war record qualified him for a commission in Germany's small postwar army.

Advancement was slow. After a leave of absence to earn a postgraduate degree in mechanical engineering to better his chances for promotion, Dornberger was assigned to the army weapons ballistics branch. Soon after, bountiful good fortune propelled this aging but ambitious captain into rocket research. Unlike his brother officers, he was not fettered by the constraints placed on German arms development by the Treaty of Versailles. The absence of any restrictions on rockets in that historic document provided a handy loophole for legitimately enhancing the fighting power of his vanquished country's scaled-down army. Assuming that Dornberger remained diligent and was graced with a little luck, prospects for a brilliant career were bright. He had moved onto the fast track.

Or had he? Colleagues working in other branches of weapons research were supported by a large reservoir of civilian talent. Huge engineering staffs in heavy industry and the prestigious faculties of numerous technical institutes were at their beck and call. Support for Dornberger's projects, however, was meager. Because most reputable scientists shunned any association with rocketry, he was reduced to dealing with amateurs, charlatans, and eccentrics. Adding to his frustration was the maddening irony that the army bureaucracy banned access to the one man who could help. Even if he succeeded in luring Hermann Oberth from seclusion, the high command decreed that Dornberger must turn him away. Oberth was a citizen of Romania, said Dornberger's superiors, and German arms research was too sensitive to be entrusted to foreigners.

As the approaching headlights grew brighter, Dornberger could rightly claim that he, not the army brass, had the last word on Oberth. True, he did not defy orders by surreptitiously consulting the learned professor from Mediash. But he was about to accomplish the next best thing: secure the services of Oberth's close associates, Rudolf Nebel, Klaus Riedel, and that remarkable young man, Werner von Braun. Many years later, Dornberger would recall his first impressions of von Braun at the *Raketenflugplatz:* "I [was] struck by the energy and shrewdness with which this tall, young student went to work and by his astonishing theoretical knowledge."

Brakes squeaked and an open touring car rolled to a stop beside Dornberger. Nebel, in the driver's seat, smiled and waved a greeting. A metal launching rack extended from the empty passenger seat beside him, across the rear seats, and protruded several feet beyond the back of the car. Then a second vehicle, occupied by Riedel and von Braun, pulled up behind Nebel. Packed in tightly around them were all the paraphernalia needed for a rocket launch, including liquid oxygen, petrol, rubber hoses, and an ample supply of tools.

Dornberger climbed on the touring sedan's running board and guided Nebel down a lane through the thick pine forest. Riedel and von Braun followed slowly. They soon came to a clearing where, von Braun recalled, "a formidable array of phototheodolites, ballistics cameras and chronographs . . . were set up." Never before had he seen such fine instruments. Although unable to secure hard data on VfR experiments during previous visits to the *Raketenflugplatz*, Dornberger had finally neutralized Nebel's hoopla. No longer able to sidestep requests for proof supporting his claims, Nebel now had to put up or shut up. Today, at last, Dornberger would get some reliable measurements and Nebel some money—maybe.

The conditions determining whether or not Nebel would end the day in a happy frame of mind were spelled out in a contract drawn up several weeks earlier. For successfully launching a rocket, he and his associates were to be paid one thousand marks, a handsome sum at a time a skilled worker fortunate enough to be employed earned less than fifty marks a week. Money would change hands only if all conditions were met, and Dornberger, not Nebel, would be the judge of that. Dornberger also insisted that the launching be in his own bailiwick, this isolated site between two artillery firing ranges at Kummersdorf.

With the dark blue sky yielding to the dawn's golden glow, everyone set to work. Riedel and von Braun began unloading equipment. Army technicians there to operate the measuring instruments checked their calibrations while Dornberger led Nebel to a stake marking the spot where he wanted the launch rack erected. Three hours later, much still remained undone. Nebel tried to justify the delay by reminding Dornberger that preparation at Reinickendorf was always quicker and easier. What must be assembled from the ground up here in Kummersdorf was already in place there. At 2:00 P.M., more than eight hours after he and his companions drove into the clearing, Nebel announced that he was ready.

Dornberger alerted the technicians and all eyes turned to the silver-domed rocket perched atop the launch rack. Then a shout: "Ready! . . . Fire!" White flames spurting from the nozzle diminished quickly with a roar as the rocket separated from the rack and accelerated upward. So far, so good. Nebel craned his neck waiting for the ejection of a red flare at the peak of its trajectory, a requirement specified in the contract. But at two hundred feet, far short of the intended altitude, the rocket turned on a course parallel to the ground and disappeared from sight, crashing into distant treetops.

Even the most liberal reading of the contract could not justify payment for that performance. Yet Nebel, the consummate salesman, argued otherwise. During subsequent visits to army headquarters in Berlin, he lobbied vigorously for some compensation as well as a new contract authorizing more tests. But the experts refused to yield. Nebel's rocket was unpredictable. No money was to be advanced nor resources committed for another launch attempt. Later, pacing back and forth in the old guardhouse in Reinickendorf, Nebel complained bitterly that he was forced to deal always with people who had no vision.

With Nebel stymied, von Braun decided to take matters into his own hands and see the authorities himself. Possibly because the army's background checks revealed that von Braun was everything that Nebel wasn't, an interview was granted with Colonel Karl Becker, the chief of ballistics and ammunition. Von Braun later recalled that Becker was not "such an ogre as had been represented by Nebel." Despite having the rigid authoritarian mien of a German officer in uniform, Becker appeared to be "broadminded, warmhearted, and a scientist through and through." At the outset, Becker hastened to dispel any suspicion that his refusal to accept Nebel's proposals sprang from a lack of interest in rocket development. "We are [very] interested in rocketry," Becker assured von Braun. Then, frowning slightly, Becker added that he did not like the way Nebel and his associates conducted their experiments: "There is too much showmanship. You [should] concentrate on scientific data [rather] than fire toy rockets." Von Braun countered that compiling data required money for parts, supplies, and measuring instruments, and the only way for them to generate needed funds was through showmanship. Becker shrugged his shoulders and said that secrecy, not showmanship, was the army's policy on rocket research.

Becker, however, did not agree to see von Braun merely to convey his scorn for Nebel's methods. Leaning forward, he narrowed his eyes as he studied his young visitor. "If we give you the support you want," Becker proposed, "will you and your friends work on our terms?" "That depends on the terms," von Braun replied. Becker was brief: all rocket development must be conducted within army jurisdiction and no funds would be disbursed to support testing at Reinickendorf or any other place not under military control. Von Braun asked for time to talk to Nebel. Becker sighed, nodded, and rose to his feet, indicating that the interview was over.

Von Braun was unprepared for Nebel's explosive reaction to Becker's conditions. Unwilling to subject himself to the whims of "ignorant" army bureaucrats, Nebel flatly rejected the offer. Riedel, too, refused to go along. Though never exposed to the frustrations of military discipline, he was strongly influenced by Nebel's feeling on the matter. An idealist, he naively believed that private enterprise, not government, would eventually provide the money to achieve such a worthy goal as space travel.

Von Braun, however, was the pragmatist. He knew that profit-oriented businessmen would not pour millions into research without a guarantee, much less a promise, of success. He was troubled, too, by the complex technical challenges. Actuators. Cutoff switches. Feed pumps. Gyroscopic controls. Electromagnetic valves. Jet vanes. How were these to be developed with the primitive resources at Reinickendorf? Convinced that Becker offered the only viable option, von Braun told his colleagues that he was going to work for the army. Nebel was furious.

8

Experiment at Great Kills

May 14, 1933
Great Kills Marine Park
Staten Island, New York

TINY BEADS OF perspiration glistened in his palms as Alfred Best crouched in a shallow dugout. Listening intently to the elapsed time called at thirty-second intervals, he glanced at the gasoline-soaked torch and the box of matches in the sand beside him. Rubbing his hands dry, he peered over the rim of the dugout and studied his objective twenty-five feet away. There, suspended between two pine poles, hung the American Interplanetary Society's Rocket Number Two.

Best drew some comfort from the fact that Rocket Number Two was not an unknown entity. Fuel tanks, motor, and most other parts now wedded into a working system on this beach overlooking the Atlantic Ocean had been scavenged from Rocket Number One. Though never launched, Number One had been successfully static tested six months earlier in an isolated field near Stockton, New Jersey.

That first rocket, like this one, was a simple device. The power source comprised two aluminum tanks, both five feet long and one and a half inches in diameter. Each tank was positioned parallel to the other, eight inches apart, and secured by clamps at the forward end. When activated, one tank containing liquid oxygen and another containing pressurized gasoline sprayed fuel and oxydizer into a combustion chamber mounted above the clamps. As the mixture burned, exhaust flame spewed from a nozzle between the tanks, providing the required thrust. Stability in flight was to be achieved by four guiding fins.

Weight was and continued to be a paramount concern. The guiding fins on Rocket Number One had been fashioned of thin metal, so thin in fact that they bent out of shape under the slightest pressure.

Bernard Smith, the engineer of today's launch attempt, had proposed balsa wood. Thicker metal, though stiffer, added too much weight. Balsa seemed a logical substitute. It was inexpensive, more rigid than metal of comparable weight, and easier to work. But unlike most metals, it was highly flammable. Smith tried to minimize this deficiency by making the balsa at least partially resistant to flame with coatings of metallic paint.

As the designated "lighter," Alfred Best mentally rehearsed the tasks he was to perform. Upon hearing the command, he must quickly light his torch, dash to the launching rack, maneuver between the guy wires, apply the torch to a fuse near the combustion chamber, wait to be sure it ignited, and then scurry back to cover in the dugout. The typewritten description of his duties concluded with the comment: The lighter "will have about one minute to accomplish this—plenty of time." Best sincerely hoped so. In a much larger command dugout seventy feet from the launching rack, Laurance Manning called out the elapsed time: "Two and a half minutes!" Best swallowed hard. Thirty seconds to go. Squinting over his right shoulder, he tried to catch a glimpse of G. Edward Pendray, the member in charge who would shout the order to send Best on his way.

Some five minutes earlier, Pendray and Bernard Smith had hovered over the launching rack as Pendray poured liquid oxygen into one of the tanks. Nearly half of the contents of his two-liter can had vaporized and wafted upward from the funnel Smith was holding before the valve sealing the tank was tightened in place. Then, at a signal from Pendray, Manning had begun counting. Pendray and Smith had then directed their attention to the other tank. One and a half pints of gasoline, previously loaded into the second cylinder, had pressurized from a supply of nitrogen gas. Smith then had lifted the motor case into place and attached the guiding finds to the aft ends of the tanks. Next he had assembled the detachable lever for remote opening of the valves and connected the cord leading back to Best's dugout twenty-five feet away. With these preparations completed, Pendray had hurriedly returned to the large dugout and Smith had joined Best in the smaller one.

Manning shouted: "Three minutes!" By now, pressure in the liquid oxygen tank had risen to nearly three hundred pounds. Pendray called out, "Lighter!" Best fumbled with his matches, lit the torch, and scrambled over the edge of the dugout. He reached the rack a few seconds later, ignited the wick below the motor, and scurried back. As soon as Best was safely under cover, Bernard Smith, crouching beside him, yanked the cord to open the valves. Until now, the experiment had proceeded like clockwork. At the most critical moment, however, with the fuse sputtering and pressure building in the oxygen tank, the valves did not open. Smith could see that the detachable lever had worked loose and fallen to the ground before turning the valve key. There were no emergency measures to cope with a situation such as this, so Smith dashed to the launching rack and replaced the lever. Pendray, in a report to the society's members a few days later, described Smith's next move: "In his excitement, or perhaps because of necessity, [Smith] then opened the valves before he had regained the shelter of the dugout . . . he was fully exposed at the time the rocket started."

There's no doubt about that. A photographer for Acme News Pictures recorded the moment for posterity. Smith, erect and at the edge of the dugout, is seen looking over his shoulder as motor, cylinders, and fins—scarcely thirty feet away—roar up off the beach. The launching rack, tilted five degrees toward open water, failed to control the direction of flight. Instead, the fins struck the top of the rack, veering the device into the wind at right angles to the intended course. Gathering speed rapidly, it climbed nearly a hundred yards before the oxygen tank exploded with a loud pop and yellow flames engulfed it. The guiding fins fluttered down while rocket motor and cylinders sped on for several hundred feet before plummeting into the sea. Two boys in a small boat, who were the first to reach the remains, promptly retrieved them from the gently rolling swells. The fins splashed into the surf and were fished out by Bernard Smith, who waded in after them.

To the hundred or so observers, including representatives of the New York City Fire Department's Bureau of Combustibles, this attempt by Pendray and his friends to become the Wright Brothers of interplanetary travel was a humorous fiasco. Amid chuckling and shaking of heads, the crowd, watching from a vantage point about a thousand feet from the launch site, quickly dispersed. But to members of the experimental committee, the test was not a failure. In his report to the monthly meeting of the society on May 19, Pendray captured their upbeat mood: "After firing a trifle more than two seconds . . . the flight was brought to an end by the bursting of the oxygen tank. Despite this mishap, the experiment must be considered a success. It proved without doubt the efficacy of [our] motor . . . and gave us our first experience with the firing of a liquid fuel rocket. The accident proves the need [to place] the oxygen tank well beyond the reach of the flame." An examination of the oxygen tank revealed a rupture along a vertical line closest to the exiting hot gases. But melting metal was clearly not the main cause of the fissure. Intense heat, exacerbated by the tank's proximity to the exhaust nozzle, elevated pressure within the tank too rapidly for the safety valve to relieve. The consequent buildup forced a blowout through the most vulnerable section of the surface, that exposed to the most heat. This finding opened up an entirely new avenue of development. Beyond an obvious remedy—the isolation of fuel tanks from nozzle flame—evolved a greater awareness of the need for better cooling techniques and pressure control.

As Pendray and his friends forged ahead on the design of three new rockets, there were fewer wild guesses and more well-reasoned decisions. While space travel was still the goal of the visionaries gathering periodically on the beach at Great Kills, prospects for realizing it receded further into the distant future. Yes, theory and dreams were important. But so were propulsion fuels, pumps, and stabilizers. Suddenly the word "interplanetary" in the organization's name sounded strangely out of touch with reality. Many asked, why not identify ourselves directly with our work now? The answer, though controversial at the time, was obvious. Shortly thereafter, the little band at Great Kills became known as the American Rocket Society.

9

Justice Derailed

AN ARROGANT SEIZURE of the reins of government launched a new dark age in Germany. Through bribery and false promises, the National Socialists, a minority political party, had won a stunning victory in the Reichstag. Passed by a vote of 441 to 84, the Enabling Act of March 23, 1933, conferred enormous dictatorial powers on Chancellor Adolf Hitler. For freedom-loving citizens, this was the first in a long, frightening series of nightmarish catastrophes. For opportunists such as Rudolf Nebel, it was a rare stroke of good fortune.

Although Nebel was in trouble with the law, the volatile political environment enabled him to thwart two efforts to put him behind bars. The first was initiated by the good burghers of the ancient city of Magdeburg; the other by the chief prosecutor of Berlin.

The root of Nebel's troubles in Magdeburg was his penchant for promising more than he could deliver. Having learned his way around town during an earlier fund-raising foray selling wireless radio sets door-to-door, he saw an opportunity to raise big money quickly. Magdeburg, he decided, suffered from an "inferiority complex." He was determined to exploit this weakness by appealing to civic pride. Three hundred years earlier, Otto von Guericke, a leading citizen, had gained fame through his experiment with the evacuated metal globe in the town square. When air was pumped out of two half spheres fitted together, atmospheric pressure on the exterior surfaces was strong enough to prevent two teams of horses, pulling in opposite directions, from separating them.

Nebel concluded that a comparable scientific "first" would surely put Magdeburg permanently back on the map. Putting his plan into motion, he told his startled companions at the *Raketenflugplatz* that he was going out of town on important business. A few days later, a postcard arrived announcing: "Greetings from Magdeburg. Negotiations progressing nicely. Hope to have money soon." This terse message was followed shortly by Nebel's triumphant return. Driving through the main gate with horn blaring, Nebel gleefully shouted that the *Raketenflugplatz* was back in business. His visit to Magdeburg, where he had conferred with the lord mayor and leading businessmen of the town, took place in December 1932. At that time, he came back with the initial payment on a 25,000-mark commitment. For this handsome fee, he and his associates were to launch a rocket from Magdeburg airport on June 11, 1933.

But this was not to be any run-of-the-mill rocket, such as those routinely demonstrated by Nebel. It was to be twenty-five feet high, larger than any ever built by him and his friends, and meant to deliver a thrust of nearly 1,300 pounds. Yet there was an added feature which, if implemented, would unquestionably ensure a prominent place for the Magdeburg rocket in the history of science. It was to carry a human passenger! The passenger, who was to ride in a tight little cabin in the aft section, was scheduled to exit at the peak of the trajectory (about three thousand feet) and float back to earth by parachute. The rocket motor and shell, also equipped with a parachute, were to come down at the same time. Before any of this was to be accomplished, however, experience must be acquired with a working prototype. This smaller version, which did not include a passenger cabin, was fifteen feet high with a power plant providing 440 pounds of thrust.

Despite misgivings, more than a dozen members of the inner circle at the *Raketenflugplatz* worked feverishly at their assigned tasks. Throughout January and February, Klaus Riedel and Herbert Schaefer, another experienced associate of von Braun, labored night and day, never less than sixty hours per week, on combustion chambers. Others helped fabricate a huge test stand that had enough stability to accommodate power plants much larger than any previously assembled. In the welding shop, some worked on motors while a few fashioned plates for the rocket's bullet-shaped shell. And Kurt Hainisch, who had won the prestigious assignment, drove daily to a distant airdrome for lessons in parachute jumping.

By late March, the new test stand was ready for use and the first of eight identical motor assemblies, made by Riedel and Schaefer, was bolted into place. On ignition, it exploded with such force that the

eyeballs of everyone within a hundred yards of the mishap ached
severely for hours. A few days later, a second motor was installed in
its place, but it, too, disintegrated in smoke and flames the instant fuel
entered its chamber. This far from auspicious beginning was followed
by three more successive failures. In each one, hot gases burrowed
holes through the throat of the exhaust nozzle. Satisfactory burns
were achieved in twenty subsequent tests, but the power generated
was disappointing—only half the required thrust for lift-off.

Throughout this period, delegations from Magdeburg arrived un-
announced with increasing frequency. Tempers flared and the officials, fearing that their sponsorship of this potentially disastrous failure would shower ridicule rather than glory on their fair city, voted to
permit substitution of the prototype rocket for the larger passenger-
carrying version. A cow pasture on the outskirts of Magdeburg was
selected for the launching and a sharply inclined wood ramp, thirty
feet high, was erected there. The first attempt was made on the
morning of June 9. When fired, the rocket moved slowly up the
incline, stopped, and slid back to its starting point. Another try two
days later failed because a leaky gasket diverted the flow of fuel to the
combustion chamber. More troubles followed in frustrating succession. Vent screws popped. Valves froze shut. Ignition capsules blew
prematurely. Fuel-line diaphragms burst. Then the rains came. When
the sun reappeared on June 29, no one noticed that days of dampness
had warped the wood framing. On the final attempt later that morning, a roller, slightly out of alignment, derailed and stopped. The
rocket, deflected from its vertical heading, took off on a horizontal
course. A few seconds later, it struck the ground and slithered thirty
feet through tall grass. For the Magdeburg councilmen, this was the
last straw. Convening in emergency session, they voted to file charges
against Nebel. They were too late, however. Before a warrant could
be issued for his arrest, the entire council was swept out of office and
replaced by a Nazi henchman.

Nebel's problems with the authorities in Berlin stemmed from
evidence of a legal maneuver he had planned and carried out when he
was secretary of the Society for Space Travel. Three years earlier, he
had secretly filed a petition of bankruptcy on behalf of the VfR. His
sworn testimony before the Court of Registry in February 1930
resulted in the dissolution of the organization in the eyes of the law.
As a consequence, he was no longer constrained by any legality or
audit of subsequent financial deals he conducted in its name. When

this deception was accidentally discovered by Willy Ley and Major Hans-Wolf von Dickhuth-Harrach (Hermann Oberth's successor to the presidency of the now officially defunct VfR), they immediately notified the authorities. Ledgers and correspondence were seized and Nebel was ordered to appear and answer charges of perjury and misappropriation of funds. On the appointed day, he arrived in court wearing a Nazi swastika armband on his coat sleeve. The prosecutor, shaken by the prospect of seeking punishment for an apparently favored follower of Adolf Hitler, quickly dropped the charges.

10

Empty Pockets

June 1933
Washington, D.C.

HURRYING ACROSS THE mall west of the Capitol, Professor Robert
H. Goddard glanced ahead at the towers adorning the roof of the
Smithsonian Building. He calculated that his destination, the stately
office of Smithsonian secretary Charles Greeley Abbot, was at least
ten minutes away. Fearing the embarrassment of a tardy arrival, he
quickened his pace, for he had pressed hard to secure this appointment. In a letter to Abbot ten days earlier he had written: "There are
some matters I would like to discuss with you before you leave for the
west, and I would appreciate it very much if you would let me know
how long you expect to be in Washington." Abbot had replied that
because he planned to remain there "except for brief intervals," he
would be glad to see Goddard anytime. Seizing the opportunity,
Goddard wired back: "May I see you next Monday? Please reply
collect." Abbot's affirmative answer had prompted Goddard's arrival
in Washington that morning.

Pacing briskly along a path on the mall, Goddard took stock of his
changing fortunes. On this day three years earlier, he had been
preparing for the move to New Mexico and Ivy Lee had been drafting
the announcement plan for the initial Guggenheim grant. Goddard
subsequently had received $25,000 for his work from July 1930
through July 1931 and a comparable amount for the succeeding twelve
months. Near the end of the second year, on May 25, 1932, the
advisory committee had issued a glowing endorsement, concluding
with the recommendation that "the investigations under way should
be continued for at least an additional year and, if possible, for the full
four years originally planned." Reeling in the wake of severe financial
reverses, Harry Guggenheim's response was short and to the point:

"Impossible!" In a later letter to Goddard, Guggenheim attorney Henry Breckinridge was more diplomatic: "It is a cause of very deep regret to me that the Guggenheims [cannot] continue their support of the rocket experiments this year. I hope next year things will be better."

Then had begun the sorry business of packing up and shutting down. Working with his crew, Goddard had scrapped parts, crated tools, and carted boxes to a warehouse in Roswell. In the evenings, he had sat disconsolately on the veranda, sorting and burning papers. By the end of June 1932, the last piece of scrap had been buried and all equipment and usable materials safely stored. Back in Worcester, the ensuing year had been indeed a lean one from the perspective of his research. Saddled with a full teaching schedule, he had had much less time and scarcely any money for rocketry.

Climbing the steps before entering the Smithsonian, Goddard ruefully concluded that any hope of continuing his research lay largely in the hands of C. G. Abbot. When the Guggenheim funds had been cut off a year earlier, it was Abbot who had kept the spark alive. Returning from California late in the summer of 1932, he had responded to a desperate appeal from Goddard: "[I have received] your letter of August 15th [requesting funds] for making tests to determine further the conditions necessary for [reducing the weight] of a high altitude rocket. While the income of the Institution has suffered somewhat from the general depression I [take] pleasure in approving [a grant] of $250."

For nearly seventeen years, Charles Greeley Abbot was Goddard's mentor and supporter. Their association began in 1917 when Abbot, then assistant secretary of the Institution, had energetically advocated a positive response to Goddard's first appeal for help. In a lengthy letter to the Smithsonian, Goddard claimed that he had worked for years on a method for "raising recording apparatus to altitudes exceeding the limits of sounding balloons." His entreaty ended with the rather grave conclusion that he had reached his limit. Without money and manpower, he could not go on. Abbot persuaded his superior, Smithsonian secretary Charles G. Walcott, to write to Goddard asking him to name the amount of money needed and how he proposed to spend it. Goddard's response estimated the cost of a one-year program to be $5,000. More correspondence flowed between Washington and Worcester, which culminated in the approval of a grant and a ringing endorsement by Abbot: "The character of Goddard's work is so high that he can well be trusted to carry it on to practical operation in any way that seems best to him."

From time to time, maybe. But not always. During the years that followed, Abbot was sometimes out of step with Goddard's way of doing things. The consummate scientist, Goddard was frequently tempted to pursue intriguing, though irrelevant problems that cropped up during his research. Sometimes he would succumb to the challenge and dash off on a tangent, leaving work on the main objective at a standstill. This troublesome habit was a thorn in Abbot's side during his tenure on the Guggenheim Advisory Committee. Knowing that other members were looking for significant achievements, Abbot was continually exhorting Goddard to press on: "I urge you to bend every effort to a directed high flight. That alone will convince those interested that this project is worth supporting. Let no side lines, however promising, divert you from this indispensable aim."

Goddard's failure to achieve a high flight during his two years in New Mexico preyed on Abbot's mind as Goddard was ushered into his office. He greeted his visitor warmly and they both sat down. Goddard quickly came to the point. He needed help. Reminding Abbot that a year had elapsed since operations had been terminated in New Mexico, he expressed his fear that flight experiments would continue on hold for another twelve months unless he secured a commitment for new funding soon. The matter was urgent because the drafting of final plans for the fall semester were under way at Clark. Wallace W. Atwood, the university president, had put the matter bluntly. He had to be advised, and quickly, whether Goddard would be in Worcester for the coming year or intended to apply for a leave of absence to resume experiments in the west.

Abbot listened but said nothing. Sensing that his strongest ally on the advisory committee harbored doubts about a resumption of funding, Goddard resorted to a repetition of observations offered in a letter written May 8, 1933, to Colonel Charles A. Lindbergh. At that time Goddard had directed Lindbergh's attention to the increasing public interest in scientific advances in the upper atmosphere. These embraced a broad spectrum of activities, ranging from the more precise measurement of cosmic radiations to establishment of new altitude records by balloons and high-flying aircraft. To document this trend, Goddard had even compiled a scrapbook of newspaper clippings that he thought Lindbergh might want to see. From the premise of a growing base of scientific inquiry, Goddard then drew a remarkably self-serving conclusion: "In spite of the depression, there are a number of scientific projects still going forward . . . many of which seem . . . to be of no greater interest and fundamental importance than the work I was carrying on in New Mexico."

In his letter to Lindbergh, and now in this meeting with Abbot, Goddard emphasized that not only were many of these projects much more costly than his experiments in Roswell, but few of them offered any contribution to national defense. Rockets, however, he continued, were well suited for antiaircraft applications. Citing his achievement of speeds exceeding five hundred miles per hour, he intimated that radio-controlled rockets might exhibit promising potential as future ground-to-air weapons. Also, work on such a project could be "well camouflaged" in New Mexico while still providing "easy access to Government officials through the New Mexico Military Institute, which is situated in Roswell, and is under [the control] of the U.S. Army."

Goddard then rested his case. Abbot sat silently for a few moments and shook his head slowly. Operating with a curtailed budget and a restricted spending program, the Smithsonian was unable to provide even a small stopgap grant. The best he could do would be to write a letter to the secretary of the navy. Would that be of any help? Goddard, desperate enough to clutch at any straw in the wind, said yes. Abbot called in an assistant and, dictating a brief note to navy secretary Claude A. Swanson, outlined Goddard's "very promising" progress during previous years of sponsorship by the Smithsonian and then the Guggenheim family. Now that funds from these sources had been temporarily discontinued, Abbot suggested: "with the great developments in naval affairs and aviation which have been authorized under the Industrial Recovery Bill, you may find Dr. Goddard's special knowledge very helpful, and I therefore venture to recommend him to you."

Clutching this endorsement in his hand, Goddard hurried over to the Navy Department. Lacking an appointment, he was turned away from navy secretary Claude Swanson's suite and managed to see only "an under officer in aviation." Early the next morning, he returned. This time he was granted an audience with George W. Lewis, a member of the National Advisory Committee on Aeronautics. Lewis was skeptical about one idea floated by Goddard, questioning the feasibility of installing turbine rockets on aircraft, yet warming to another Goddard scheme involving their use as power plants for torpedoes. On the strength of approval by Lewis, Goddard's name was sandwiched between two other appointments on the morning calendar of Rear Admiral Ernest J. King, chief of the Bureau of Aeronautics. When Goddard finally met King, the interview was brief. King listened politely for a few minutes, then, excusing himself, referred his visitor to an assistant, Commander Charles A. Pownall. Intrigued by Goddard's exposition on the merits of a rocket anti-aircraft weapon, Pownall gave assurances that a request for more detailed information on rocketry was likely to arrive shortly from the secretary of the navy.

A request was issued, but not by Secretary Swanson. On June 23, 1933, Hall L. Roosevelt, the acting secretary and brother-in-law of President Franklin D. Roosevelt, wrote that "subject to the unqualified approval of the Guggenheim [family], the Navy Department would be glad to receive the report of your work to date in rocket research." That message, pregnant with possibilities, precipitated a complicated exchange of correspondence. Goddard's reply suggested that Acting Secretary Roosevelt should contact Harry Guggenheim seeking permission to see the report. This communication was answered not by Roosevelt, but by the secretary himself. Swanson informed Goddard that he was writing to Harry Guggenheim, expressing the navy's interest in evaluating data relating to experiments in New Mexico and Worcester. Guggenheim's response to Swanson granted full access to the research findings compiled under the private sponsorship of the family and the foundation.

Then the anticlimax. On August 29, Admiral W. H. Standley advised Goddard that he found the report "very interesting" but "the Bureau of Ordnance considers [adaption of the rocket principle to projectiles and bombs] too expensive." Moreover, use of rockets for propulsion of aircraft "requires extensive development, with success probably very remote." Another dead end. Another cruel reminder that the most formidable obstacles were not those encountered in his experiments. With perseverance and hard work, they would be overcome. But hidden prejudices and false assumptions harbored in the minds of men were barriers far more difficult to breach.

No one, not even Dr. Edgar A. Fisher, the beloved family physician, was immune to this weakness. Goddard had fought a lifelong inconclusive battle against chronic tuberculosis. In 1912, at the nadir of his illness, he had been forced to leave his post as instructor of physics at Princeton University and spend much of the following year in bed recuperating. Long bouts of intense work always exacerbated his condition, and thereafter he paced himself carefully. During a periodic examination in May 1933, Dr. Fisher, noting an enlargement of a lung lesion, scolded him: "If you had lived as you ought to have when in the West the last two years and taken advantage of the opportunity, you might be well now." Goddard said nothing, but that night he wrote his reaction in his diary: "Dr. Fisher apparently thought the $50,000 grant was made to go West and take a rest cure on."

In another related entry, he philosophically noted the similarities between the technique of rocket propulsion and those who levitate themselves to high places in business and government: "The rocket is very human. It can raise itself to the very loftiest positions solely by the ejection of enormous quantities of hot air."

11

The Trouble with Willy

January 1935
Crestwood, New York

Pendray was puzzled. The correspondence on the desk before him offered no clues about Willy Ley's present state of mind. Unlike his earlier letters, which were filled with colorful descriptions of rocket experiments, Ley's commentaries now were uncharacteristically circumspect. The first evidence that something was amiss had surfaced two months earlier in a letter from Philip A. Cleator.

Writing from his home in Wallasey, in the historic county of Cheshire, England, Cleator confided that he had received "a rather mysterious communication" from Ley. Smuggled out of Germany and mailed from Holland, Ley's letter revealed that all his mail was opened and examined before delivery to his apartment in Berlin. Urging Cleator to exercise extreme caution in the future, Ley also directed that this warning be relayed to Pendray along with the admonishment that the word "rocket" not be mentioned in any communication from either of them. An odd request, indeed. Rocketry, after all, was the glue that held their international triumvirate together. Using their common interest in future space travel as the catalyst, Ley had forged the links bonding the Englishman, the American, and himself into a flourishing three-way information exchange.

Cleator's interest in rocketry dated back to school days ten years earlier when, at the age of fourteen, he had fashioned a "rocket pistol." The rocket, actually a small firecracker, was inserted into the gun's steel barrel, and when ignited, its cardboard casing shot out "at quite a fair speed." Cleator's infatuation with rocketry persisted into adulthood. Voraciously reading reports about Goddard's experiments, the lectures of the French space enthusiast Robert Esnault-Pelterie, and accounts of rocket launch attempts in Germany, Russia, and elsewhere in Europe, Cleator was troubled that no scientists of comparable stature had raised the standard in England. He ultimately decided to drum up interest in rocketry by writing about it himself. At first, his essays were rejected by, in Cleator's words, "almost every editor in England." Then, gradually, the climate changed. Some of his pieces started appearing in print, and finally, by the time he was corresponding with Pendray about the mysterious change in Willy Ley, the tables had turned and now editors were coming to Cleator for commentaries and reports on this or that aspect of rocketry.

Pendray, riffling through recent letters received from Cleator, selected and reread one dated November 2, 1934. It described a request Cleator had received from Ley that morning: "[Our friend] wishes to see the world a bit, particularly England and America. But as you know, Germans are not allowed to bring money out of the country. Herr Ley wonders—and he asks the same question of me—if you can think of any way he could earn some money during his stay in America." Cleator then candidly confessed that there was no way for Ley to generate personal income in England. In fact, Cleator added, he was still "trying to figure out a way to make money myself."

Pendray and Cleator were unaware that, for a while at least, Willy Ley harbored some unusual ideas about making money on his own. One of his more bizarre schemes concerned the introduction of the postal rocket in America. Friedrich Schmiedl, an Austrian engineer, had proposed setting up such a service in his own country between two villages on opposite sides of a high mountain range. His rockets, six feet long and powder burning, were to zoom over the precipice and eject a mailbag, which descended by parachute on the other side. Ley thought that such a technique might also be profitably applied in sending mail onto an island surrounded by heavy surf or "where a mail steamer travels within sight of a coast for many hours before actually making port."

The credibility of anyone promoting the delivery of mail via rockets, however, was seriously damaged by the highly publicized fiasco engineered by one Gerhard Zucker. After ballyhooing his airmail rocket throughout England for two years, Zucker, in the summer of 1934, finally secured authorization to dispatch a mailbag across a small stream in Scotland. About fifty letters, from stamp collectors around the world, were placed in his rocket along with one from a member of Parliament addressed to the King of England. When

Zucker depressed the firing pin, there was a glorious explosion and the charred remnants of fifty or so letters wafted away in the breeze.

At first, Pendray and Cleator assumed that the messages coming from Germany meant what they said. The facts, according to words committed to paper by Willy Ley, were simple: he was winding up one job in late December, and before starting another he planned to enjoy a visit to the United States. Then, reading between the lines, Pendray suspected there was another message. Or was he just imagining things? In any event, Pendray proceeded on his hunch. On November 25, 1934, he advised Ley that if a holiday was planned in the near future, "I would like very much to have you stay at my house. We have ample room to keep you for an indefinite time and I could think of no greater pleasure than to serve as your host in America." On November 20, Pendray wrote: "Anticipating that you may wish to come, I am writing this week to the American Consul in Berlin, asking him to grant you a visa to this country."

Pendray's lengthy appeal tried to assure the American consul that "despite [Ley's] youth, he is a man of considerable linguistic and scientific achievement." In an attempt to legitimize his suspicion that Ley's proposed visit was not just a lark, Pendray went on: "It is difficult to tell from the veiled and careful letters sent to me by [Ley] and by others just what the nature of the trouble is or how soon and under what conditions he plans to leave Germany. I believe, however, that he will call upon you for a visa before leaving, and I am writing this letter to urge you to give him a visa which will permit him to emigrate to this country and settle here permanently, if he desires to do so."

When Ley finally appeared at the American consul's office, his request for an immigration visa was turned down on two counts. According to Consul General Douglas Jenkins: "[It] cannot be granted to Mr. Ley because of his serious physical defect. He is practically blind in one eye." Also "he has practically no personal resources and no definite assurances guaranteeing his livelihood in the United States." But on the strength of Pendray's assurances that Ley would be his personal responsibility, a tourist visa was issued. Getting to America, the biggest hurdle, was overcome. Once established, Ley would secure visa extensions and, eventually, United States citizenship.

12

A Decision for von Karman

Spring 1935
Pasadena, California

AFTER THE THREE young men left his office, Professor Theodore von Karman mulled over their proposal. If one of the three had not been Frank J. Malina, a bright young student whom von Karman admired, he would have rejected it without hesitation.

Six months earlier, after graduating with honors from Texas A&M, Malina had come to Pasadena to accept a scholarship at the California Institute of Technology. Shortly thereafter, he landed a part-time job in Caltech's Guggenheim Aeronautical Laboratory, working on the crew that operated the wind tunnel. His keen analytical mind soon attracted the attention of von Karman, who, despite Malina's apprentice status, elevated him to the post of graduate assistant in the laboratory.

With a generous endowment from the Guggenheims and the inspired leadership of von Karman, the lab at Caltech had earned a worldwide reputation as a leading center of aeronautical education and research. Spurred on by von Karman's intellectual curiosity, the staff was continually breaking new ground in aerodynamics, fluid mechanics, and structures, while also blocking out solutions for the endless array of problems that surfaced as more became known about the dynamics of high-speed flight.

Into this fertile environment walked two unlikely newcomers. Neither John W. Parsons nor Edward S. Forman had been conditioned by the discipline of a university education. Their lack of formal training, however, was partially offset by their intuitive grasp of modern science. This attribute and their youthful enthusiasm impressed Malina when he met them for the first time. The events leading up to Malina, Parsons, and Forman's visit to von Karman's office were initiated by a lecture delivered by William Bollay of the

Guggenheim staff. Bollay had been intrigued by a technical report on rocket-powered aircraft by Eugen Sanger that had been published in Vienna in December 1934. After replicating some of Sanger's experiments, Bollay presented the findings before one of the regular weekly seminars conducted for Caltech's students and faculty. A news reporter in the audience, interpreting Bollay's comments as the precursor of a new Caltech research program, filed a story announcing the entry of the Guggenheim Laboratory into a new field of research: liquid-propelled rockets.

Parsons, a self-educated chemistry buff, and Forman, a skilled mechanic, had been drawn together by their mutual interest in rocketry. Having dabbled in powder propellants, they were now anxious to try their luck with the liquid variety. On the day that the Bollay story appeared, Parsons and Forman scurried over to the Caltech campus, found the Guggenheim Lab, and asked to see the manager of the rocket research group. There is no rocket research here, said the receptionist. Then she remembered that Frank Malina was planning a doctoral dissertation on the problems of rocket propulsion. "See Malina," she said. And they did.

Malina, schooled in the traditional scientific methods, was obviously not on the same wavelength as Parsons and Forman. Confirmed pragmatists, with no interest in the abstract, both wanted to quickly begin making and firing rockets. Since their early teens, they had shared the dubious distinction of being the wild kids in the neighborhood. The yard behind the Parsons house, once covered with green turf, was blackened and scarred, the aftermath of scores of powder-rocket explosions. Now they were ready for the more advanced liquid propellants, they told Malina. Because the newspaper said that Caltech was about to work on them too, they wanted to help.

At first, Malina was appalled at the prospect of permitting Parsons to run amuck in the Guggenheim Laboratory. Yet, if kept on a tight rein, he and Forman could be useful. Malina told them that he might be able to work something out but it had to be on his terms. This meant that in order to win von Karman's approval a project must be oriented toward a goal that was realistic and achievable. Even a venture as far out as rocketry had to be tied to something practical. To Malina, that something practical was a high-altitude sounding rocket that would carry instruments to heights unreachable by balloons. After discussing the details with Bollay and persuading Parsons and Forman to go along, Malina believed that he had a salable package.

Then, accompanied by Parsons and Forman, he went to von Karman and laid his cards on the table.

A high-flying rocket that could bring back data on the upper atmosphere, Malina began, would be an invaluable research tool. He further assured von Karman that his thorough reading of the literature showed that no existing engine design was powerful enough to break the altitude records set by balloons. Having defined the problem, Malina went to the heart of the matter: "I propose that the laboratory sponsor a series of theoretical studies which address the thermodynamic problems of the reaction principles and the flight performance requirements of a sounding rocket." The studies, he added, would be carried on in conjunction with static tests of liquid-propellant rocket engines. Parsons and Forman, whom he had introduced at the beginning of the presentation, would assist him in the experimental work.

After a few questions, all of which Malina fielded adroitly, von Karman fell silent. Finally, pursing his lips and steepling his fingertips, he indicated that the interview was over. As Malina stood up, von Karman smiled and said, "I'll think this over and give you an answer in a few days."

PART TWO

The Innovators

13

Money to Burn

April 1936
Kummersdorf, Germany

Colonel Walter Dornberger was ecstatic. And for good reason. Luftwaffe General Albert Kesselring, smiling affably from his place at the head of the conference table, had just agreed unconditionally to the plan presented to him.

Dornberger's initial contact with the air service had occurred more than a year earlier, when a junior officer in the technical command had come to Kummersdorf on a special mission. Major Wolfram von Richtofen had been assigned to investigate the potential of liquid-fuel rockets as a power source for aircraft. With no comparable expertise in the research and development groups of the Luftwaffe, von Richtofen turned to the artillery experimental station for help. The first phase of his program, von Richtofen explained, would be an evaluation of rocket boosters on conventional aircraft. Should results of those experiments show promise, a second, more comprehensive phase would be undertaken—the design of a fighter plane powered exclusively by rockets.

Dornberger did not need to think twice about cooperating. Von Richtofen, after all, offered that most effective of all persuaders, a seemingly limitless supply of money. Von Braun, with Dornberger's blessing, enthusiastically went to work with a group of aircraft engineers who had arrived a week after von Richtofen's visit. Their assignment: install a rocket booster on the underbelly of a Heinkel 112. Static tests of that device, conducted in the summer of 1935, were sufficiently impressive for von Richtofen to urge development of a rocket-powered plane immediately. At the same time, he authorized more work on a prototype of a jet-assisted takeoff booster for heavy bombers.

Von Richtofen wielded an unusually large measure of influence for an officer of his rank. At forty-one years of age, he was ideally positioned to exploit opportunities for promotion in the fast-growing Luftwaffe. With adequate maturity to remain untainted by the high-spirited recklessness of fliers ten years younger, he was nevertheless youthful enough not to be burdened with the hidebound stubborn-ness and antipathy to change frequently attributed to those over forty. Then, too, thanks to the illustrious exploits of his cousin, Baron Manfred von Richtofen, he benefited from the recognition accorded to the relation of a national hero.

Wolfram, like his famous cousin, was a scion of a family of gentle-men farmers who, when not overseeing their huge estates, were hunting game, shooting ducks, or riding prized specimens from their stables of thoroughbreds. In 1913, at the tender age of eighteen, Wolfram had been awarded an officer's commission in a hussar regi-ment of the German Imperial Army. Four years later, he transferred into the air service. After flight training, he was assigned to the fighter squadron commanded by his cousin Manfred, who, having downed eighty Allied aircraft, was the toast of all Germany. On the morning of April 21, 1918, in search of his eighty-first victory, Manfred led the flight of five companions, including Wolfram, over Allied lines. Man-fred did not return. Chasing a fleeing English Camel, he himself was gunned down from behind. Wolfram, however, survived the remain-ing seven months of hostilities and was credited with eight kills before the armistice in November 1918. After his discharge, Wolfram stud-ied engineering, received a doctorate, and returned to military service in 1923.

When von Richtofen approached Dornberger with his request for help, the modest experimental station at Kummersdorf was bursting at the seams. Static test stands, engineering and drafting sheds, and machine shops were crammed into a few crowded acres between two artillery firing ranges. The proximity to other ordnance development was enormously distracting, too. Von Braun frequently complained to Dornberger about the unnerving intermittent chatter of machine guns fired from a dugout only a few yards away from his test pit. Another frustrating complication was the need to conduct rocket launches many miles away, at sparsely populated areas along the Baltic. In addition, these critical experiments could only be performed during late fall, winter, and early spring. At most other times, the adjacent seashore was crammed with tourists and vacationers.

Dornberger, painfully aware that a much larger site with ample space for development, static testing, and launch facilities was desperately needed, responded to von Richtofen's plea for support with a proposal of his own. "Let's form a partnership," said Dornberger. "Our combined resources, funded by both army and Luftwaffe, can be a most effective way to serve the rocket development requirements of the two services." Von Richtofen was won over and he submitted a recommendation along these lines to General Albert Kesselring, then the chief of Luftwaffe aircraft construction.

General Karl Becker, the army's chief of ordnance, was determined to put on a first-class show for the subsequent visit of General Kesselring. Early in April 1936, he came to Kummersdorf and was thoroughly briefed with the aid of elaborate maps, plans, and diagrams by General Becker, Colonel Dornberger, and von Braun. It was a comprehensive plan because von Braun had even selected a site for the new, larger experimental facility. While enjoying the previous Christmas holidays with his family, he had talked about the difficulties at Kummersdorf and the need for a more isolated testing ground. His mother, recalling her father's hunting forays through the forests on the island of Usedom, suggested that he look at an area at the mouth of the Peene River. At the first opportunity, von Braun went there and was completely captivated by a wilderness of dunes and marshland overgrown with ancient oaks and pine trees. He returned a few days later with Dornberger, who readily agreed that this pristine vastness was the ideal solution.

The enthusiasm of General Becker, Dornberger, and von Braun, as well as his own deputy, Lieutenant Colonel von Richtofen, persuaded Kesselring to grant his approval on the spot. As he walked to his staff car with a handsome leather greatcoat thrown casually over his shoulders, he turned to an aide and gave instructions for him to acquire the land. That very night, a senior official of the Air Ministry telephoned General Becker. He had been sent to Usedom by high-powered car, where he purchased several thousand acres of land near the village of Peenemünde. Dornberger and von Braun were surprised, delighted—and impressed.

14

In Quest of a High Flight

August–September 1936
Roswell, New Mexico

DRIVING DOWN THE road into town, Robert H. Goddard ruefully acknowledged to his wife, Esther, that if the request had come from anyone other than an advisory committee member, they might now be enjoying a quiet evening at home. They needed the rest. Only a few hours ago, at 3:30 that Sunday afternoon, he and Mrs. Goddard had returned from a two-week auto trip to California. Their "home base" was Roswell again, thanks to a renewal of the Guggenheim funding a year earlier.

Shortly after their arrival at the Mescalero Ranch, Goddard had found a message from Robert A. Millikan among the letters retrieved from the mailbox. It was dated August 15, two weeks earlier. In June 1930, Millikan's prominence as a planner and builder of the famed Mount Palomar telescope, winner of a Nobel Prize, and director of the physics laboratories at the California Institute of Technology, had prompted his recruitment to help oversee Goddard's use of the Guggenheim grants. Since Millikan was a holder of the purse strings, his influence on Goddard's future was too crucial to ignore.

Now Millikan was asking a favor Goddard dared not refuse: "One of our students in aeronautics, Mr. Frank Malina, is working on some aspects of jet propulsion at the Institute, and as he is going east at the end of August for a short vacation, I have thought that it would be profitable for him, and might be interesting for you, if he stopped off at Roswell and saw what the status of the problem is from your angle. He is an able, scientifically minded chap of good judgment, who would not abuse any confidence that you may repose in him." Reading further, Goddard had been startled to discover that Malina's train from Los Angeles was scheduled to arrive in Roswell in a few hours.

The pleasant prospect of an early start on a good night's sleep quickly evaporated as they prepared for the impending appearance of this unexpected visitor. With no time to restock the larder after their two-week absence, Goddard agreed to his wife's suggestion that they take Malina to the Nickson Hotel for supper. Later, as the Southern Pacific streamliner stopped at the station in Roswell, Malina spotted Goddard, whom he had met briefly once at Caltech, and went over and introduced himself. During their drive to the Nickson, and throughout their meal, Malina briefed Goddard on his work with gaseous oxygen and gasoline and his efforts to design a reliable motor capable of handling this combustible combination. Goddard said little, and at the conclusion of dessert and coffee, he asked Malina to excuse their early departure, explaining that the many miles driven earlier in the day had exhausted them. The next morning Goddard returned and drove Malina back to the Mescalero, where, as he stated in a letter to Millikan on September 1, "I showed him through the shop . . . and also took him out to the testing field, where the tower for the flights is located."

But merely viewing some machine tools in a shop and walking fast around a launching tower were hardly a substitute for the guidance Malina had been led to expect. Goddard tried to defuse any negative reactions Malina might voice on his return to Caltech by pointing out to Millikan that "the subject of [Malina's] work, namely the development of an oxygen-gasoline motor, has been one of the chief problems of my own research work, and I naturally cannot turn over the results of many years of investigation, still incomplete, for use as a student's thesis." In his acknowledgment of Goddard's letter a few days later, Millikan agreed that it is unwise to talk much about what one is trying to do before one is reasonably certain that it can actually be done. But then Millikan parted company with Goddard: "That does not prevent us, however, from having constant intercourse with men who are working in the same field and from getting a lot of good from a mutual interchange." And there was a trace of annoyance in Millikan's response to Goddard's refusal to deal with a student: "[We have] a group of pretty able men at the Institute, working on the problems in which you are interested and I . . . thought that this contact might be mutually helpful here just as it has actually proved to be in every preceding case . . . in which it was tried."

Perhaps Goddard's viewpoint in this matter was more difficult for Millikan to accept because this was not the first time that Goddard had failed to help a Caltech student. In July 1931, a year after he agreed to serve on the Guggenheim Advisory Committee, Millikan had written to Goddard about a Mr. Agnew, a young graduate student who wanted to go to Roswell and work for Goddard during the summer. Millikan sweetened the request by assuring Goddard that the young man would work without pay and consequently there would be "no new demand on your budget."

Goddard, however, had politely refused. If he was uneasy about allowing an advisory committee member to monitor his day-to-day activities through the eyes of a surrogate, Goddard did not say so. Instead, he justified the rejection on the grounds that the young man simply would not have anything to do: "My work at the present time is largely of a preliminary nature, and requires chiefly skilled machinists and instrument makers. . . . I have as large a personnel as I can handle under present conditions. I regret very much that I do not see a way to use a research man, such as Mr. Agnew." Then Goddard hastened to dispel any suspicion that he had little faith in the competence of Caltech's faculty: "A considerable number of students have written me requesting information concerning courses in rocket development and jet propulsion. I am suggesting to all of them that . . . their best plan is to take a course in mechanical engineering at the California Institute of Technology or the Massachusetts Institute of Technology."

The first day of September marked the end of the 1935–1936 grant period. An accounting was therefore due. The Guggenheim Foundation required submission of a detailed report to the treasurer of the Clark University Research Corporation, the legal agent that held and disbursed funds as needed. Goddard had nothing to fear from the auditors at Clark. It had been a good year. He was within budget, using slightly less than was authorized. The $2,174 remaining on deposit in the Roswell Bank was slightly more than the previous year's balance. Of the $18,000 budgeted, Goddard had spent $17,947.41. The $12,000 payroll was by far the largest single debit item, representing 68 percent of the total. Next was "Materials." Piping, sheet metal, wire, and all of the other paraphernalia that went into building and testing rocket components accounted for $3,791.21, about 21 percent of the authorized funds. Miscellaneous operating expenses, legal fees, patent filing costs, insurance, and fuel made up the remaining 11 percent.

Goddard's technical accomplishments, however, were a mixed bag. In a letter to Charles Lindbergh accompanying his yearly report, he imparted this good news: "I do not think that there has been a year of the entire research when I have accomplished as many important things." Important, maybe. Earthshaking, no. And there was the rub. More than $80,000 had been poured into Goddard's research since 1930. Yet there was not a single giant leap upward that Harry Guggenheim could point to with pride.

Goddard himself freely acknowledged that all the work he did was "of an unspectacular nature." No one, of course, could single out any single development and call it a waste of time. On the contrary, a strong case could be made for the view that every project, in some measure, had helped to improve the probability of success in future rocket flights. During the year, for example, Goddard fabricated and tested the large chambers required for lightweight rockets. These were studied at length in a wide range of operating conditions in order to determine the precise amount of pressure, rate of flow, and the spraying method to generate the maximum thrust. He had also designed a strong, reliable turbine and thoroughly tested several construction approaches for medium and lightweight tanks.

But Charles G. Abbot's repeated admonition to "bend every effort" to a directed high flight had gone unheeded. Goddard had resisted these pleas in the past because firing rockets to "make an impression" was diametrically opposed to his scientific posture. Yet now he had a sound reason. He informed Lindbergh that he was ready to embark on an ambitious schedule of launches "not for the purpose of creating an impression . . . but because I believe that either the problems in making a rocket to exceed heights attainable by balloons have been solved or the means of solving them is known."

Remembering Goddard's penchant for dragging his feet, Lindbergh could hardly believe the words he was reading. When the letter bringing this news was delivered on September 15, 1936, Lindbergh shot off a fast reply: "A record-breaking flight would be very advantageous . . . for the effect it would have on the morale of everyone who is interested in the project."

Goddard, at last, seemed poised and ready for an impressive demonstration, a tour de force to dramatically dispel any unspoken doubts lurking in the minds of his generous and patient financial backer. On September 14, he confidently dispatched this message from Roswell to Harry Guggenheim in New York: "We are planning to attempt a flight next Saturday, the nineteenth and we would be glad to have you come. If it is more convenient for you, we could postpone until the following Monday." Guggenheim wired his regrets. Luckily for Goddard, a speaking commitment at the *Herald-Tribune* forum required Guggenheim to remain in New York.

Logistics—the host of little details required to move matériel to the right place by an appointed time—has a nasty capacity for confounding even the best-laid plans. In this case, the problems started with an overdue shipment of liquid oxygen. An equipment failure in the plant of Goddard's supplier, the Linde Air Products Company in El Paso, held up the delivery of fifty liters for twenty-six hours. Expected to arrive early on the morning of the eighteenth in plenty of time to be transported to the site for the Saturday launch, the large container of oxygen was not trucked into the ranch compound until 10:30 on the morning of the nineteenth. This pushed the proposed launch into Sunday. At 5:30 A.M., Goddard and his men drove the ten miles out to the tower. But the planned attempt at noon was scrubbed because it started to rain. The next day, the twenty-first, they went to the site at noon but were forced to pack up because of the weather. On the way back, the large trailer used to transport the rocket to and from the shop became mired in mud. Pulling it free took half the next morning, delaying another attempt until Wednesday, the twenty-third. Rain again. Meanwhile the liquid oxygen, evaporating as it aged, needed replenishment. A can of fifteen liters came from El Paso later than requested because of "compression trouble." By the twenty-sixth, little of the oxygen remained in the larger fifty-liter tank delivered six days earlier. Goddard wired Linde Products requesting more and then shipped the near-empty fifty-liter tank back to El Paso. More delays.

On the morning of October 3, Goddard and his crew left for the tower at 5:30 A.M. Installation of controls took longer than anticipated and the first test of circuits was not begun until four hours later. When the switch was thrown, the lever of one of the igniters froze in place. Nearly two more hours passed before Al Sisk returned from the shop with a replacement. They were now ready for the big moment. Despite a strong wind, Goddard opted to make the attempt. Huddling in a shelter a thousand feet from the launch tower, the crew watched as Goddard, beside them, turned the control keys. The rocket rose rapidly on the guide rails. Clearing the top of the tower, it climbed another two hundred feet. Then the combustion chamber burned out, causing the rocket to rotate in midair. An instant later, it started falling, crashing to the ground seconds later about twenty feet from the tower.

In a letter to Harry Guggenheim, a few days later, Goddard reported: "The large chamber is giving us trouble by burning out. I am hoping to have the trouble remedied within the next few weeks, and after we have had a flight in which things work satisfactorily, I shall let you know and arrange to [delay our next attempt] until you can come here, as I am anxious for you to see a good flight." Not nearly as anxious as I am, Guggenheim thought as he put the letter aside.

15

Down in the Arroyo

May 1937
Pasadena, California

JACK PARSONS SHIFTED into second gear as his battered Chevrolet sedan negotiated a bumpy dirt road in the foothills of the San Gabriel Mountains. Two more hours of driving lay ahead before arrival in Pasadena. Having taken this route frequently in the past, Parsons knew that his estimate of the time needed to traverse the remaining distance was reasonably accurate. For most of the week, he had worked a double shift in an explosives manufacturing plant in the Mojave Desert. A hazardous way to make a living, but the pay was good. On weekends, or any other time he could get away, he hurried back to Caltech to join in Frank J. Malina's experiments.

For Parsons, at home behind the wheel of any vehicle, driving was a relaxing diversion. Consequently his mind was free to dwell on other things. While morning sunlight shone through the rear window, he reflected on events that had transpired since his visit to Professor Theodore von Karman's office with Malina and Ed Forman two years earlier.

Though skeptical at first, von Karman had eventually sanctioned Malina's proposed inquiry into the practicality of using rockets to gather meteorological data at high altitudes. Unfortunately, von Karman's blessing was the only support they received. Apart from access to a workbench, Malina and his friends had to forage elsewhere for anything else they needed. Reduced to buying essentials with money from their own pockets, they were constantly strapped for cash. Parsons added funds to the kitty regularly, but contributions by Malina and Forman were neither as large nor as frequent. Malina's income was minimal. Nearly all of it came from work in the wind tunnel for which he was paid eighty cents an hour. This modest stipend was supplemented occasionally by earnings from odd jobs such as drafting illustrations for a textbook von Karman was writing or drawing exhibits for the professor's prolific output of technical papers.

Free time was precious. Too little was available for productive work on the rocket project. When not driving around Los Angeles negotiating deals for secondhand measuring instruments and other supplies, Malina and Parsons were concocting schemes for making money. They even started to write an antiwar novel. Many hours were invested in fleshing out a plot featuring the machinations of some evil rocket scientists and a jingoistic foreign dictator. For a fat fee, they planned to sell the outline to a nearby Hollywood studio for conversion into a movie script. Yet when they ultimately came into a substantial sum of money, the catalyst was not a wild scenario but Malina's own research.

Early in 1937, Malina had not yet won von Karman's approval to make rocketry the theme of his doctoral thesis. Trying to convince the learned professor that there was ample evidence to justify a study, Malina began a lengthy theoretical analysis of rocket-motor propulsion. Concern about initial findings was expressed in a letter to his parents on March 7: "Together with a fellow named Apollo Milton Smith, I have made a series of calculations on rocket performance. Without air resistance, the rocket soared 500,000 feet [on paper] but made a measly 35,000 feet when air resistance was accounted for. . . . I should be sad as these calculations may force me to find a new subject for my Ph.D dissertation." A few days later he wrote that prospects appeared brighter: "Am feeling more hopeful with my research. Made another analysis of altitude flight and found very encouraging results possible, at least so it seems on paper. The calculation was quite exciting especially toward the end when the rocket reached several hundred thousand feet. I wouldn't believe my calculations so had Smith rework the problem. He obtained the same answer."

Malina was so fired up by this mathematical confirmation of his views that he persuaded the committee in charge of Caltech's weekly seminars for engineering and science students to grant him a place on the program. Shortly thereafter, standing before an audience attracted by bulletin-board announcements touting a potential breakthrough in meteorological data gathering, he presented his case. While his arguments were received with moderate interest, there was enough enthusiasm among a few to keep him in animated conversation for more than an hour after the end of the program. A Pasadena daily news-paper story was marred by "only a few misquotations," and a day or two later, a photographer for the *New York Times* arrived, an event that made him uneasy: "I wouldn't mind pictures being taken if they would leave me out of them. To say I feel silly . . . is putting it mildly."

Malina's presentation and the subsequent publicity prompted Weld Arnold, a student assistant in the astrophysics laboratory, to come to him with an offer he could not refuse. Captivated by the excitement he sensed in rocket work, Arnold asked to join Malina's team. If accepted, Arnold was prepared to contribute $1,000 to the cause! Five hundred now and the balance the following month. Malina was thunderstruck, then skeptical. But true to his word, Arnold returned within a few hours, dropped a package wrapped in newspaper on Malina's desk, and declared, "Here's the first five hundred." Inside were bundles of cash in one- and five-dollar bills. Arnold, who delivered the second installment as promised a few weeks later, never revealed where the money came from and Malina never asked. Neither did the authorities at Caltech. Malina turned the money over to the institute's comptroller, who obligingly established a "Fund for the Rocket Research Project."

Weld Arnold's largess immediately lent Malina's experimental work an aura of stability. True, von Karman's willingness to tolerate his young protégé's refusal to choose other, more promising avenues of aeronautical research should have been sufficient. Yet, until Arnold came along, the project's shaky financial condition had been a sword of Damocles. Malina was continually haunted by a fear that, despite frugality and careful planning, he would be forced to terminate ex-periments on the brink of a breakthrough. Now, happily, such a calamity seemed less imminent. With money in the bank, there was also less need to continue his and Parsons's effort on the novel. Their decision to shelve that project conveniently reduced the time Malina had to be inside of Parsons's house. Going there was making him jittery because Parsons, who intended to earn extra money man-ufacturing explosives on his own, was accumulating a supply of tetranitromethane in his kitchen.

Although the rocket research fund was instrumental in reducing Malina's anxiety, it did little to improve his image. Most of his peers viewed rockets as dangerous toys and those who played with them hopeless lunatics. When Malina and the few zealots daring enough to

join him assembled the gear for their frequent expeditions to the
Arroyo Seco, onlookers bombarded the "suicide squad" with wise-
cracks and catcalls. As they loaded cylinders of oxygen, methyl
alcohol, and other apparatus onto a requisitioned Caltech truck, Malina steadfastly ignored the taunts. The reactions of his companions
varied. Weld Arnold was indifferent. Apollo M. O. Smith also said
nothing, reasoning that silence was a more effective way to discourage
the abuse than responding in kind. Hsue-Shen Tsien, a brilliant
young student who had come from China to study under von Karman, was humiliated by these episodes but disguised his discomfort
with stoic detachment. Parsons and Forman, however, were less
inhibited. They retaliated with a barrage of exotic profanity that
continued unabated until Parsons climbed onto the driver's seat and
they drove off.

Malina and Tsien usually rode in the cab with Parsons. Arnold,
Forman, and Smith stood on the open bed of the platform truck
holding on with one hand and restraining the jostling cargo with the
other. Their destination was a deserted area along the Arroyo Seco
about three miles north of the Rose Bowl. Some thirty minutes after
their departure from the Caltech campus, Parsons customarily maneuvered the truck to the edge of a gully behind Devil's Gate Dam.
Malina and Tsien then jumped out and guided Parsons with hand
signals as he jockeyed back and forth, finally stopping in the best
position for unloading. Then followed the backbreaking chore of
lugging tanks and other equipment down onto the floor of the dry
gulch.

Setting up was a tedious process. After holes were dug and numerous sandbags filled, the test stand, fuel lines, and instruments were
placed in position. Because these experiments were static burns, not
launch attempts, the motor was inverted on the stand. With exhaust
nozzle aimed skyward, thrust was directed downward. Propulsion
force was measured by a diamond-on-glass recorder under the motor
chamber and buffered from it by a shaft-and-spring mechanism. Four
hose lines ran to the motor chamber. One supplied oxygen, another
fuel, the third water for the cooling jacket, and the fourth monitored
pressure inside the chamber.

When all lines were connected and thoroughly tightened, and
appropriate flow meters, pressure gauges, and check valves were in
place, Malina and his team positioned themselves behind the sandbag
barriers. The moment of truth had arrived. In the next few seconds,

they would learn whether the many days, sometimes weeks, of preparation were a step forward or wasted time. There were disappointments—and moments of terror. In one instance an oxygen hose
split, ignited, and lashed about crazily, prompting the entire party to
take off down the arroyo. But for the most part, results were good,
even better than anticipated. Like the time a motor ran flawlessly for
forty-four seconds, maintaining a consistent chamber pressure of
seventy-five pounds per square inch. When that happened, all jumped
up, cheered, and embraced each other joyfully.

Malina, however, was determined that the experiments be more
than fun and games. In response to his prodding, some members of
the team were persuaded to document key aspects of the work.
Parsons's contribution was an analysis of the relative merits of various
types of fuels. Smith collaborated with Malina on a mathematical
study of the influence rocket shell design exerts on performance of a
constant-thrust engine. And Tsien examined the effects of changing
exhaust nozzle angles on motor thrust. These papers, along with an
introductory piece by Malina outlining potential future fields of investigation, a description of an ideal laboratory for this work, and a
comprehensive summary of all experiments undertaken thus far, were
incorporated into what Malina dubbed their "Bible."

This bulky loose-leaf volume was a testimonial to the fact that their
pilgrimages to the Arroyo Seco were not boondoggling junkets, as
many suspected, but truly legitimate research. Troubled by nonpro-
ductive time consumed each weekend to transport and set up equipment, then tear down and truck all gear back to the campus, Malina
sought permission to conduct a few small-scale experiments within
the Guggenheim building itself. Claiming that some design theories
can be adequately tested using miniature components, he built a tiny
motor with an extremely small nozzle, only an eighth of an inch in
diameter. Maintaining that such a little device represented no threat to
life or property, Malina persuaded a sympathetic von Karman to go
along.

One Saturday morning shortly thereafter, Malina gathered his team
inside the nearly deserted Guggenheim Laboratory. The goal that day
was to demonstrate the efficacy of an oxidizer devised by Parsons—a
combination of nitrogen oxide and methyl alcohol. After briefing
Parsons, Forman, Tsien, and Arnold on the setup, Malina, accompanied by Smith, went to the Gates Chemistry Building. There they
obtained a cylinder of N_2O_4, which they carried out to the front lawn.

Intending to draw about a liter for the experiment, Malina turned the valve, but it jammed. A moment later, there was a tremendous spout of N_2O_4. Before they got it under control, the N_2O_4 saturated a large patch of carefully groomed turf, rendering the tainted grass brown and dormant for weeks to come. A bad omen.

When Malina and Smith returned to the Guggenheim, the setup was almost complete. Following Malina's instructions, the others had suspended a line from the ceiling of a gallery, extending fifty feet to the pump room in the basement. Attached to the lower end of the line, the motor and an accompanying canister of fuel functioned as the bob of a giant pendulum. By measuring the deflection of the motor-driven bob, Malina expected to calculate the force generated by the fuel mixture. But there was a misfire. Instead of igniting, the motor emitted a tremendous red cloud, which eventually covered any exposed steel in the entire building with a coating of rust. When he discovered the mess the following Monday, von Karman shouted, "Out!" After the "suicide squad" finished the cleanup (which required scrubbing all exposed surfaces with oily rags), a chastened Malina and his companions installed their pendulum from a davit on the downwind side of the building.

16

Pied Piper of Peenemünde

July 1937
Peenemünde, Germany

Wᴇʀɴʜᴇʀ ᴠᴏɴ Bʀᴀᴜɴ replaced the telephone handset in its cradle and hastily added a new name to his list of potential recruits. These were the cream of the old *Raketenflugplatz* crowd. Although Dornberger's cadre had grown to nearly ninety, a personnel freeze had prevented hiring many von Braun wanted. But now the restriction was lifted. With laboratories, tool shops, and assembly buildings rising from the wilderness around Peenemünde, scientists and technicians must be found to man them—men like Hans Heuter, Kurt Hainisch, Klaus Riedel, and Helmut Zoike.

When Rudolf Nebel's tangles with the law abruptly halted their work at Reinickendorf, these four, aided by an influential industrial benefactor, were hired by the aircraft instrument division of the Siemens Company. All were exceptional men. Hans Heuter, however, best personified the experience and youth von Braun sought to recruit. At thirty-one years of age, he was a seasoned manager but still young enough to adapt easily to direction by the twenty-five-year-old von Braun.

In 1927, having completed his education and unable to find employment as an engineer, Heuter signed on as an assembly mechanic for an iron-bridge maker. In six months he was promoted to the drafting department and given various design assignments. Then, in the summer of 1929, he switched to a better-paying job: assistant manager in a coke manufacturing firm. Soon after, he was named director of the night shift, responsible for operation of the entire plant. Regrettably, like the sales for most capital goods in a worldwide depression, coke oven sales nose-dived in 1931 and the company folded the following year. Finding no work anywhere, Heuter, in desperation, joined Nebel's group at Reinickendorf. Committed to long hours in exchange for bed and board, he labored on a series of projects until the ill-fated Magdeburg rocket destroyed the last semblance of Nebel's credibility.

Stimulated by a recent decree establishing the Luftwaffe as a sister service equal in stature to the army and navy, the aircraft-related businesses of Siemens were booming. Heuter, enjoying a job security unknown to him before, was understandably reluctant to pitch it all away when von Braun came knocking on his door. To be sure, building rockets was fascinating, at times even exciting. But to Heuter, turning away from a promising career in a flourishing company for an unknown future in rocketry seemed foolhardy. To dispel Heuter's doubts, von Braun needed facts and figures, not pie in the sky. Yet that was all he had to offer. Progress thus far in development of liquid-fuel motors was encouraging but by no means earthshaking. With no other choice, von Braun turned to the only strength worth talking about: the high-caliber talent already at work on the army rocket program.

Dr. Walter Thiel, for example. This gifted researcher repeatedly devised ingenious strategies to breach apparently impenetrable technological barriers. His studies were the basis for selecting optimum fuel mixtures, unraveling the mystery surrounding incomplete combustion, and designing the most efficient motor configurations. Unassuming, in appearance, with a sallow complexion, an average build, and light brown hair brushed severely back in pompadour style, Thiel nevertheless commanded immediate respect with his piercing dark eyes staring through thick black-rimmed spectacles.

Or Arthur Rudolph. Not the scholar Thiel was, Rudolph ended his formal education in 1936 after earning a bachelor's degree in mechanical engineering. A confirmed pragmatist, he believed that continued exposure to a structured academic curriculum was senseless if it did not provide a sharper perspective on things he wanted to know. At the time, Rudolph's obsession was space travel, a subject that no university was inclined to explore. And so, when not at work in Berlin, helping co-workers at the Heylandt plant fabricate storage tanks for liquid oxygen, Rudolph dedicated all his spare time to learning more about rockets.

At first, much of this self-education was acquired in the company of Max Valier, the celebrated driver of rocket-powered racing cars. Rudolph made himself useful, and Valier, needing a good engineer, had come to rely more and more on his young protégé's expertise.

Their relationship was ended abruptly, however, by the explosion that took Valier's life. In March 1934, nearly four years after Valier's death, Arthur Rudolph succeeded where Rudolf Nebel had not. In the isolated clearing between two artillery firing ranges near Kummersdorf, Rudolph successfully launched a rocket of his own, fulfilling all of the prescribed conditions for a smiling Walter Dornberger. Rudolph was subsequently hired, joining Dornberger's section in the army weapons department.

Von Braun, applying his considerable persuasive powers, then identified several more who had opted to work for the army's fledgling rocket group. To the wavering Hans Heuter, von Braun offered a choice. Stay in a "safe" job and vegetate or follow others who were living out their dream. Heuter succumbed to the lure of the dream. So did Kurt Hainisch and Helmut Zoike. But Klaus Riedel was deterred by a loyalty to Rudolf Nebel, the one *Raketenflugplatz* alumnus whom von Braun adamantly refused to hire. Von Braun saw Nebel, now also employed by Siemens, as an "unscrupulous salesman with little technical and no scientific background." Under the circumstances, von Braun would also undoubtedly have endorsed the opinion offered by Willy Ley in a letter to G. Edward Pendray after discovering Nebel's hanky-panky with VfR funds: "[Nebel's] name means mist or fog in English and that's what he is and what he does always."

While agreeing that Nebel was unsuited for service at Peenemünde, Riedel was reluctant to leave him "empty-handed." Nebel, after all, had enabled Riedel to amass the experience that made him a valuable prospect for von Braun. In Willy Ley's mind, however, Nebel owed more to Riedel. That conviction was expressed in a letter to Pendray three years earlier: "[Nebel] is the typical bluffer [who] buffaloed us all with the great oratories of his and ruined the VfR by contracting personal debts of I don't know how many thousand marks. Though he actually founded the *Raketenflugplatz* and allowed no God besides himself, all work was done by Klaus Riedel."

Conceding that perhaps Nebel deserved some compensation, von Braun devised a ploy that released Riedel from his supposed obligation and also deprived Nebel of any legal grounds for future claims. The medium was an old patent, held jointly by Nebel and Riedel, protecting their rights to an aluminum rocket motor featuring fuel injection "opposite to the main flow." This technique had long since been abandoned and the patent was therefore worthless. But von

Braun induced Dornberger to authorize a payment of 75,000 marks (about $30,000) to the co-owners. This huge windfall put Nebel in the right frame of mind to sign the agreement relinquishing rights to the patent. The contract also barred Nebel from seeking any future compensation and included a clause requiring Riedel to become a member of the Peenemünde establishment "in order to make their knowledge [of the patent] fully available."

The charisma that extinguished doubt and inspired talented people to follow von Braun was complemented by a shrewdness that enabled him to get things done despite a slow-moving, nit-picking bureaucracy. One of many instances where his decisiveness and wit routed pompous adversaries began with the purchase of Christmas sparklers for an experiment during the summer of 1933. The sparklers offered a convenient way to ignite the first drops of oxygen and alcohol squirted inside the throats of a few experimental motor chambers. A year later, an auditor in the budget bureau insisted on knowing why winter holiday sparklers were bought in midsummer. Von Braun sent back the terse reply: "For experiments." Eight weeks passed, then a request for clarification: "What kind of experiments?" Von Braun answered: "Secret experiments." The matter was dropped.

On another occasion, von Braun came into his office to find his deputy, Eberhard F. M. Rees, laboring over a detailed response to an objection raised by the purchasing department. A requisition for a gold-plated instrument mirror, signed by von Braun, had been rejected because of "insufficient justification." Rees was trying to compose a lengthy technical explanation, citing reasons why the mirror was needed and where it was to be used. After telling Rees that it was useless to reason with those blockheads, von Braun issued a simple instruction: "Just tell them we want a gold-plated mirror because a *solid* gold one is too expensive." Rees sent that one-sentence rejoinder and the requisition was promptly approved.

17

First Try with a Barograph

April 20, 1938
Roswell, New Mexico

AL KISK SUPPRESSED his frustration as the rubber clasp slipped from his fingers again. These were far from ideal working conditions. Crowded and hazardous, the narrow scaffolding creaked under the weight of Kisk, Charles Mansur, Major John E. Smith, and Captain Howard Alden. Their four pairs of hands groped through a narrow port in Rocket L28, trying to mount a small boxed instrument in place.

The task would have been easier were it not for one condition. The National Aeronautic Association decreed that the barograph must be calibrated, sealed, and installed in the presence of their official observers. Smith and Alden were two of a trio representing the NAA. Minutes earlier, at the base of the tower, Colonel D. C. Pearson had affixed the NAA seals and handed the box to Smith, who had then climbed the extension ladder with Alden.

By cooperating with the National Aeronautic Association, Goddard was finally responding to the pleas of advisory board member Charles E. Lindbergh. A few weeks earlier, writing from England, Lindbergh urged: "I have not in any way changed my feeling about the importance of obtaining a reasonably high and authenticated flight as soon as possible." Nor did Lindbergh hesitate to restate his conviction that, at this point, a practical demonstration was a more critical need than further scientific study: "I suggest that you concentrate upon [achieving a validated] flight and after that on whatever research you consider most advisable."

Although Lindbergh prevailed, Goddard, the quintessential scientist, refused to squander weeks of preparation solely on an "exhibition." Standing with Colonel Pearson and Mrs. Goddard at the base of the tower, he waited patiently to begin his twenty-eighth test in the

"L" series. While ostensibly conforming to Lindbergh's admonition to put first things first, Goddard surreptitiously equipped the rocket for experiments: an in-flight evaluation of his movable tailpiece steering mechanism and a tryout of a new nitrogen-pressured fuel-feed system. Since initiating the "L" series on May 11, 1936, he had conducted thirteen test stand burns and fourteen flight attempts. Altitudes achieved ranged from a few shots barely clearing the tower to one reaching eight or nine thousand feet. But telescopes and other ground-based instruments used to corroborate that high flight only permitted estimates: "The altitude [reached was] uncertain because of haze remaining from dust storms."

With the National Aeronautic Association now monitoring a flight, more precise measurements seemed assured. Considering the NAA's unsullied reputation, this was by no means an unreasonable assumption. Never relying on the judgment of human observers alone, the NAA also validated altitude claims with the incontrovertible record of an on-board barograph. Because no "L" series rocket was designed to accommodate one, Al Kisk was forced to struggle with the jury-rigged mounting devised at the last minute. It was a tight fit. The interior diameter of the rocket in the area where he was working was only nine inches. The largest exterior dimension of the boxed barograph was six inches; the smallest, four inches, leaving insufficient space for any lateral or angled supports. Instead he affixed four strips of rubber, previously sliced from a discarded automobile-tire inner tube, to the top and bottom of the instrument case. These were to dampen longitudinal shock. Side-to-side motion was cushioned by several pieces of sponge rubber wedged between the barograph and the interior wall of the rocket.

Kisk moved aside as Major Smith and Captain Alden threaded a wire through a fixture in the barograph case and around a strut inside the rocket. After joining two ends of the wire with a seal, Smith and Alden followed Kisk and Mansur down the ladder. Then Goddard's two assistants quickly completed final preparations for the launch. After filling the fuel tanks, they and the rest of the party climbed into two cars and a truck and immediately drove toward the control shack, about a thousand feet from the tower.

Minutes saved not walking were precious. Time wasted after topping off the tanks unnecessarily depleted the liquid oxygen available for the flight. Kisk slowed the truck enough to permit Mansur to jump safely onto the road when they neared the control shack and then continued on for about a mile, stopping by a theodolite erected on a tripod. Meanwhile, the NAA observers, Mansur, and Mrs. Goddard stationed themselves behind the shack. Goddard stood in the doorway, peering through a telescope focused on an instrument panel at the base of the tower.

Three telegraph keys, mounted on a waist-high shelf, were at his fingertips. Mrs. Goddard, a movie camera in her hand, moved back from the group to gain an unobstructed view. Her husband turned, looked around briefly, and then resumed his monitoring of the instruments through the telescope. A few seconds passed. Suddenly Goddard broke the silence: "Ready . . . go!" At that instant, he pressed the first of the three keys. Flame and smoke gushed from the base of the tower accompanied by a roar that Major Smith likened to the sound of "a hundred safety valves on boilers all let loose at once." Then Goddard pressed the second key, which released the rocket from its moorings. The long thin cylinder rose, cleared the top of the tower, and accelerated rapidly. Happily, the third, "stop," key remained untouched. Depressed only in emergencies before launch, it shut down pumps and closed fuel valves.

Climbing higher, the rocket veered off the vertical a few degrees and then, responding to gyroscopic correction, nosed back in the opposite direction. This undulating behavior continued for several seconds until the fuel was exhausted. Reaching its zenith, the shiny cylinder, now barely visible to the naked eye, leveled off. Knowing that if unchecked, a precipitous fall to earth would follow, the observers vented their anxiety by begging the descent parachute to open. But it did not. Describing a graceful arc, the rocket nosed over and plummeted from the sky into the sagebrush about a mile away. Before the sound of the crash reached them moments later, Goddard looked up from a stopwatch in his hand and announced: "Twenty-nine and three-fifths seconds." Only a half minute had elapsed since he depressed the second telegraph key, starting L28 on its journey.

Kisk noted the angle on the theodolite and then loaded the instrument aboard the truck and returned to the control shack. By this time, everyone had begun a trek across the barren plain toward the crash site. Major Smith arrived there first but touched nothing until Goddard and the others joined him. Standing near the point of impact, Smith surveyed the wreckage around him. Nothing was salvageable. The nose of the rocket had blasted a cavity fourteen inches deep and some eighteen inches wide. Remnants of the barograph were discovered a short distance away. Goddard could not understand why the parachute had failed to open. The release mechanism, geared to activate when the rocket's axis turned from the vertical to the horizontal, had functioned perfectly on five previous launches.

Sifting through the sand, Goddard was unable to find any evidence to support his suspicion that the last-minute installation of the barograph below the fuel tank, instead of in the nose cone as originally planned, was responsible for the devastating finale. The change was necessary because the barograph case was larger than Goddard had been led to believe in earlier correspondence with the NAA. Possibly an electrical circuit had been disturbed during the mounting of the instrument. Or maybe some other flaw—errant grains of dust in a valve, perhaps—had gone undetected, thus immobilizing the release mechanism. Almost as difficult to endure as the failure were the gnawing doubts about the cause. Goddard, his wife, assistants, and the NAA observers hiked back to the control shack in silence. That elusive goal, an authenticated high flight, still remained beyond reach.

18

Parley at Falaise

September 18, 1938
Sands Point, New York

PROFESSOR THEODORE VON KARMAN was unable to size the man up. To the distinguished and learned aviation scientist, observing was as essential as listening. A gesture, a frown, an unguarded arching of the eyebrows conveyed more than words. But these clues were denied him because a huge floral arrangement, gracing the center of the table, blocked his view. Both von Karman and the man obscured by the centerpiece were among the nearly dozen guests at a sumptuous Sunday luncheon hosted by industrialist and philanthropist Harry F. Guggenheim.

Liveried footmen moved about noiselessly, serving cold beef and hot vegetables from silver platters onto blue, gold, and white Minton ambassadorial china. The delicious repast and exquisite procelain symbolized, in a unique way, facets of the man who was the lord and master of Falaise. Independent? Self-sufficient? Of course. Even the beef was fattened in the fields surrounding the manor house. Nor were the vegetables delivered by an exclusive purveyor. All had been grown, as were the fresh flowers on the table, in the estate's own gardens. The fine china displayed the Great Seal of the President of the United States and was a not-so-subtle reminder that Harry was an experienced statesman, too. Appointed ambassador to Cuba by President Herbert C. Hoover in 1929, he had carried out the administration's noninterventionist policies throughout the tumultuous years of rule by the despotic Gerardo Machado. Near the end of his first and only term in office, Hoover wrote a letter of appreciation to Harry, including this encomium: "We may get through our particular term without any great disturbance in your territory, for which I am undyingly grateful."

Now Harry was applying his considerable diplomatic skills, so effective in mirroring Hoover's do-nothing stance in Cuba, to the embryonic science of rocketry. From his place at the head of the table, he thoughtfully surveyed his guests. On his left were Clark Millikan, representing his father; Caltech president Robert A. Millikan; Theodore von Karman, head of the aeronautical laboratory endowed by Harry's father, Daniel; and three representatives of the National Advisory Committee for Aeronautics. On his right were a colonel in the research and development command of the United States Army; a navy commander with comparable responsibilities; an aide to the chief of the army's air service, General Henry H. Arnold; and the beneficiary of many generous Guggenheim grants, Robert H. Goddard, and his wife, Esther.

Harry Guggenheim had not convened this gathering to knock heads together, though he would have been justified if had chosen to chastise them. Instead, he opted to take the high road. Diplomatic persuasion. Maybe some gentle arm twisting. Harry clearly held the upper hand, for all of his guests were in his debt—Goddard certainly more than the others, by this time the recipient of well over $100,000 in grants. Von Karman, too, owed much to Guggenheim's philanthropy, having found a welcome haven from the deteriorating situation in Germany by accepting Robert Millikan's invitation to become director of the aeronautical laboratory at Caltech. The military and NACA representatives were also aided by available expertise and new ideas emanating from Guggenheim-funded research centers at New York University, the Massachusetts Institute of Technology, and the University of Michigan.

Von Karman finally gained his unobstructed view of Goddard when the entire party adjourned to the mansion's huge reception hall for coffee. The two had met briefly six years before during one of Goddard's visits to the West Coast, and again that morning, when Guggenheim's chauffeured limousine had picked up the Goddards, Millikan, and von Karman at the Commodore Hotel in midtown Manhattan. The hour-and-a-half drive to Sands Point was filled mostly with chitchat about the Goddards' recent vacation trip to Europe, which had ended a few days earlier. Von Karman, who sat in a jump seat next to Millikan and in front of the Goddards, was only able to establish eye contact with either of them for brief periods when he turned awkwardly and looked over his shoulder. Now, in the great hall of Falaise, von Karman sat directly opposite Goddard in one of the two huge sofas flanking the fireplace.

After everyone was comfortably settled with coffee, sherry, or a cordial, Harry Guggenheim walked over to the fireplace, turned, and with his back to the softly glowing embers and hands clasped behind him, started to tell his guests about a problem that had been troubling him. Von Karman knew what was coming, for he had been briefed in advance. So did Goddard, who had dined with Guggenheim on the evening of September 15, 1938, shortly after disembarking from the *Normandie*. The notation in his diary concerning that event is short and noncommittal: "Went to Mr. Guggenheim's on the 3:45 train. We had dinner on the outside veranda. Talked until 10:30. Mr. Guggenheim has a plan of speeding up a large, light rocket by 'farming out' some of the problems so that the results can be used together and a flight made in a year or so."

With an audience before him, however, Guggenheim embellished his thoughts on "farming out" problems into a sort of patriotic pep talk. Dark war clouds were thickening in Europe, he warned, and the right answers to questions about America's national defense must be developed quickly. The only way to assure success, he went on, was through "teamwork," planning in concert rather than independently. These remarks were aimed at Goddard more than anyone else. But they fell on deaf ears. Goddard was not persuaded to divulge his secret research to strangers. He was a loner and ever fearful that any findings he "shared" might be stolen and later claimed by others as their own. Sentiment, however, was lining up solidly behind Guggenheim. Goddard was forced to make a face-saving concession by offering something. Considering the limited manpower at his disposal (only three mechanics to work on a score or more precision components going into every rocket), Goddard suggested that von Karman might lend a hand on a troublesome liquid-oxygen pump. Leaving this small offering on the table, he then begged to be excused, explaining that he and his wife had to depart for Washington because of an important appointment the next morning with Charles G. Abbot at the Smithsonian Institution. Assuring von Karman that details on the pump would be sent to Pasadena as soon as they returned to Roswell, the Goddards thanked Harry Guggenheim for his hospitality, said their good-byes to the others, and left.

To his credit, Goddard did not conveniently forget his promise to von Karman. Performance specifications, blueprints, and other relevant data on the pump were dispatched to Caltech as soon as he reached Roswell. But he refused von Karman's subsequent request for information on combustion chamber and nozzle design, which von Karman believed he legitimately needed to solve the "problem." Finally, in a letter to von Karman on December 5, 1938, Goddard severed the tenuous bond that had been forged three months earlier in Sands Point: "Since our talk in September, I have considered carefully the plan of cooperation which we discussed on the chamber problem in connection with this year's rocket project. My conclusion is that the various factors of the problem are interrelated to such an extent as to make it practically impossible to have these factors studied as separate research projects." Then, amazingly, he let slip that contrary to Guggenheim's wishes that he "farm out" the pump problem to von Karman, Goddard had been working on it all along anyway: "During the past two months, we have been able to develop a pump which will, I believe, serve as a starting point for high pressure tests with chambers. It will therefore not be necessary for me to come to California, at least for the present, so I must forego [sic] the pleasure of the lecture which you were so kind to suggest. . . . It was a great pleasure to talk my troubles over with you and Dr. Clark Millikan, and it may be that something along the lines we discussed can be arranged at a later time."

Realizing that additional overtures to win Goddard's cooperation were useless, von Karman then composed a letter to Harry Guggenheim, asking to be released from the commitment made at Falaise, summing up his feelings with the comment: "I cannot work on anything unless I have the whole picture."

19

Demonstrations for the Führer

TIRES SQUEALED AS a military motorcade slowed and turned abruptly off the autobahn. Led by a dozen steel-helmeted soldiers on powerful motorcycles, four large Mercedes sedans snaked their way around the curves of a narrow road seventeen miles south of Berlin. Ensconced on handsomely upholstered cushions in the first vehicle, Colonel General Walther von Brauchitsch tried to fathom the thoughts of the man seated beside the chauffeur. Von Brauchitsch saw only the back of his head. Had he been able to observe his face, particularly the eyes staring vacantly at the passing landscape, von Brauchitsch would have no doubt correctly surmised that the führer's attention was far removed from the purpose of this journey into the countryside.

Adolf Hitler was indulging a personal preference. He liked the front passenger seat. The view was better. More importantly, he was also freed from any obligation to converse with the person beside him. On this rain-drenched blustery morning in March, he was in no mood for talk. There was too much on his mind. The turmoil in Czechoslovakia, for one thing. The separatist movement there, orchestrated by agents of the Nazi Foreign Ministry, was threatening to tear that small sovereign nation apart. If the Slovaks, responding to the fiery Dr. Vojtech Tuka, succeeded in achieving independence, Hitler planned to use the revolution as a pretext for marching into Prague. On the other hand, if the central government prevailed over the separatists, he intended to exploit the opportunity presented by the conflict to occupy Prague anyway. The question was, when? While waiting for Czechoslovakian president Dr. Emil Hacha to make his move, it was important for Hitler to assume a posture of detached indifference, to maintain a routine schedule. This sojourn was a brilliantly deceptive business-as-usual activity, lulling the spies in the Chancellery, back in Berlin, into reporting that the führer apparently had no designs on Czechoslovakia. Also, it put an end to the tiresome pleadings by von Brauchitsch for Hitler to visit the original rocket development station at Kummersdorf.

Until the ascendancy of von Brauchitsch to the supreme command of the *Reichswehr*, the army officer corps had been courted and coddled by the Nazis. For while Hitler's power remained unchallenged as long as professional soldiers maintained their disdain for politics, there were limits on how far he dared to go. With the army firmly in the hands of the military elite, arousing the ire of this sleeping giant was too risky to contemplate. A year earlier, however, Hitler and his cohorts had seen a way out of this frustrating impasse. In February 1938, Field Marshal Werner von Blomberg's unfortunate liaison and later marriage to a woman of questionable character sufficiently alienated the amorous war minister from his aristocratic colleagues for Hitler to cashier him. With the disgraced von Blomberg consigned to limbo, Heinrich Himmler, the head of the infamous secret police, went after Colonel General Baron Werner von Fritsch, the army chief of staff. Using the perjured testimony of underworld characters, Himmler concocted false morals charges against von Fritsch, who was forced to resign.

Hitler then consolidated his position by personally assuming the duties of war minister and finding a compliant candidate for von Fritsch's former post. He found a man of impeccable standing in the officer corps over whom he, as führer, could exert complete control. This rare combination was discovered in the person of Walther von Brauchitsch. Throughout the higher echelons of the army, von Brauchitsch was regarded as a distinguished example of the Prussian aristocratic tradition. He had recently commanded the East Prussian military district and, at the time von Fritsch was deposed, was in charge of the armored group of the German ground forces. The crack in his own armor, however, was his entanglement with the divorced wife of a brother officer. Von Brauchitsch's wife would not yield to his request for a divorce without first receiving a handsome cash settlement. It was here where Hitler was to be of service. From his own huge personal fortune (amassed through tax-free royalties from the publishers of *Mein Kampf* and fees for the use of his likeness on German postage stamps), Hitler gave von Brauchitsch the money to satisfy his wife's demand.

After elevating von Brauchitsch to the top command, Hitler used him to systematically purge the general staff of many who professed less than blind loyalty to the regime. The unfortunate chief of the army, though ostensibly wielding enormous power and finally married to the vivacious Charlotte Schmidt-Ruffer, was nevertheless handicapped by a deep personal obligation to Hitler and the consequent loss of independence in the conduct of military affairs. His vulnerability was difficult to conceal, prompting his own chief of staff to observe that he often stood before Hitler "like a little cadet before his commandant." Nor was his obeisance unmarked by the diplomatic corps. In a memorandum written August 9, 1938, Britain's Sir Robert Vansittart commented that "Hitler has a stranglehold on von Brauchitsch of some private and discreditable kind."

As Hitler and his top general rode on in silence behind their motorcycle escort, an occupant of the second sedan in the motorcade grew increasingly anxious. He was General Karl Becker, now chief of the army weapons department, whose reputation was on the line today. Becker had convinced von Brauchitsch that the extraordinary progress achieved by Dornberger's team clearly merited a visit by the führer. But as Hitler's entourage arrived at the gates of the Kummersdorf Rocket Experimental Station, Becker fretted that he may have been overzealous in his description of Dornberger's achievements. When his Mercedes rolled to a stop, Becker could not wait for the driver to come around and open the door for him. Instead, he jumped out, paced rapidly to the lead sedan, and waited for Hitler and von Brauchitsch to emerge.

Arrayed before them was a small welcoming party. Dornberger, in front, tight-lipped and standing ramrod straight. Two paces behind him, von Braun and Dr. Walter Thiel, the motor expert. Von Braun was relaxed and slightly amused by Becker's agitated state. Thiel, wide-eyed behind his thick glasses, was unabashedly enthralled at being a part of this historic visit. The only ranking member of von Braun's staff still stationed in Kummersdorf, Thiel remained there because motor test stands at Peenemünde were not yet completed. Behind von Braun and Thiel were several army and civilian section chiefs. Their job was to pair off with members of Hitler's retinue and brief them throughout the visit.

Becker made a great show of presenting Dornberger to Hitler and von Brauchitsch. Dornberger saluted smartly and clicked his heels. Hitler responded with a laconic raising of his forearm, his traditional

Nazi greeting. Dornberger, unprepared for such diffidence, described his reaction in his memoirs many years later: "I immediately had the impression that [Hitler's] thoughts were elsewhere . . . his eyes seemed to look through me to something beyond. His remarkably tanned face, with the unsightly snub nose, little black moustache, and extremely thin lips, showed no sort of interest in what we were to show him."

The first stop on their walking tour was Kummersdorf's oldest test stand. On a signal from Dornberger, a horizontally mounted combustion chamber was ignited, developing a thrust of some three hundred pounds. Hitler watched impassively as a pale blue jet of gas roared from the exhaust nozzle. Thick wads of cotton, pressed into everyone's ears, failed to dampen the throbbing pressure on eardrums, yet Hitler seemed not to notice. At the next test stand, a vertically mounted motor generated a thrust of over two thousand pounds. Again, no reaction from the führer, who watched through a slit in a protective wall only thirty feet from the flame. As they walked toward the assembly towers at the third test stand, Dornberger, expecting to be peppered with questions and comments, was not, forcing him to continue his monologue.

But he was running out of subject matter. Rather than trudge along in silence, Dornberger opted to talk about Peenemünde. He spoke of how the huge assembly building, development works, and tests stands—larger than any at Kummersdorf—were transforming the wilderness into an impressive military-industrial complex. And, of course, the rockets. He proudly told Hitler that they had progressed well beyond the earlier experimental models, the A-1 and A-2. Now they were near the end of testing on the A-3 series. Soon all rocket research would be conducted on a more sophisticated experimental model, the A-5. Meanwhile, as new components and techniques proved successful, more were incorporated into the design of the A-4, the first operational missile.

Entering the assembly tower, Dornberger gestured toward a cutaway model of the A-3. Valves, tanks, piping, and motor chamber were easily visible through slits cut in the outer skin. While Hitler peered through one of them, von Braun gave a rapid-fire description of each component's function. Hitler, impassive, looked through another slit at a maze of small pipes, painted in different colors to facilitate identification of the various control and propellant subsystems. Finally, he turned away, shaking his head slowly.

Later, at lunch in the officers' mess, Hitler sat between Becker and von Brauchitsch. Dornberger was too far away to hear what was said when the führer turned his head and talked to Becker. He hoped that at last some interest was being expressed in the demonstrations just witnessed. Hitler then turned from Becker and, looking at Dornberger, asked when development work on the A-4 might be completed. Hedging, Dornberger cited the long-drawn-out peacetime schedules then in effect, venturing no opinion on how they might be accelerated if accorded top priority. Hitler nodded, said nothing, and focused attention on his mixed vegetables. Near the end of the meal, he looked up and asked Dornberger another question. Thinking about the scarcity of lightweight metals needed for the expanded Luftwaffe aircraft construction program, the führer wondered if the rocket outer skin might be sheet steel instead of aluminum. Such a substitution might be feasible, Dornberger replied, but changing now will surely stretch out the development schedule. Hitler listened quietly and said no more until taking his leave at the main gate. Looking absently into the distance, he smiled wanly and said, "*Es war doch gewaltig,*" an idiom that translates roughly into a bland rendition of the English "Well, it was grand."

Dornberger was devastated. All had gone well. Better than planned. Yet nothing had captured the führer's fancy. Not the massive jets of gas spewing from the nozzles at unprecedented speeds. Not the dazzling array of luminous colors dancing in the flame. Not the thundering roar of the motors. As the motorcycle guard escorted Hitler and his retinue down the road and into the forest, Dornberger turned, looked briefly at those standing with him, and walked silently back through the gate.

20

Parsons Packs a Punch

Summer 1939
Pasadena, California

SEATED IN A tiny shack on the edge of the Arroyo Seco, Theodore von Karman winced at the unnerving boom of another explosion. He did not want to be here but he had no other choice. Whenever there were urgent matters to discuss with Frank Malina, he could not instantly summon his young protégé because telephone service was not yet available along the barren arroyo. Now, because he must have immediate answers to questions about some experimental data before dispatching a report to General Henry H. Arnold in Washington, von Karman reluctantly came to this remote site for a conference with Malina.

The meeting was a consequence of a speech Malina had delivered at the annual luncheon of the Caltech chapter of Sigma Xi eight months earlier. Promoted as a discussion of "Facts and Fancies of Rockets," the talk debunked widely held myths while offering exciting projections based on findings from the Arroyo Seco experiments. Before the applause died down at the end of Malina's presentation, two members of the audience put their heads together and nodded in agreement. Caltech president Robert A. Millikan and Professor Theodore von Karman then went over to Malina and told him that he was to go to Washington, D.C., to give expert testimony to a National Academy of Sciences committee on which they both served.

At the time, General Henry H. Arnold, then the commanding general of the army air corps, faced many troubling technical problems. They ranged from a search for ways to prevent the icing of aircraft windshields to the endowment of heavily laden bombers with additional lift on takeoff. Responding to Arnold's appeal for help, the National Academy of Sciences created a special committee that included Millikan and von Karman among its distinguished members. Because he believed Malina's rocket know-how might be the key to boosting overloaded aircraft off the ground quickly, von Karman persuaded other members of the committee to hear his young assistant. Malina's testimony, scheduled for a meeting that convened on December 28, 1938, was supported by a comprehensive written report. It opened with an overview of fundamental concepts, then an exploration of various propulsion techniques. The third part went into the possible use of these propulsion methods. The fourth section was an assessment of the current "state of the art," and finally, there was a research plan for developing an appropriate propulsion system.

Ironically, the report's most perplexing component, over which von Karman and Malina agonized for days, was not a sticky technical question but mundane terminology. For many prominent scientists of the 1930s, the word "rocket" was a turnoff, more suited to pulp fiction magazines than serious research. Von Karman, therefore, finally opted to expunge all references to rocketry from the text. Wherever the term appeared, a euphemistic "jet propulsion" was substituted.

Parsons and Forman were elated when Malina returned from Washington with the happy news that the National Academy of Sciences was recommending that the army award a research contract to Caltech. Almost overnight the "suicide squad" gained respectability. With an initial $10,000 payment deposited in Caltech's coffers, von Karman had no trouble persuading the trustees to authorize leasing several acres on the west bank of the Arroyo Seco from the city of Pasadena. Malina and his crew were now legal tenants, not trespassers. There was money, too, for temporary structures on the site; a workshop, storage space, and a small office for record keeping and other paperwork.

The contract enjoined Caltech to develop jet propulsion systems for the "super-performance" of aircraft. The types of super-performance to be addressed had been personally described by General Arnold during a secret meeting with von Karman in a blacked-out limousine parked behind a darkened aircraft hangar. Von Karman, driven to this late-night rendezvous, heard Arnold express deep concern about the need to get his bombers airborne in less time from shorter runways. He also desperately wanted an auxiliary power source that might push his pursuit planes into steeper climbs and provide extra bursts of speed in level flight.

Although work was authorized on liquid- as well as solid-propellant engines, von Karman concluded that for the intended applications a solid-fuel device was the best choice. The problem created by this decision was that no one had ever made a long-burning dry-propellant rocket. All black powder in single-charge skyrockets, for example, usually burned in two seconds or less. The air corps, however, wanted power bursts of at least ten seconds or more. For performance of that caliber, von Karman needed a less progressive burn, similar to glowing tobacco in a cigarette. Through employment at the explosives factory in the Mojave Desert and many hours of experimenting on his own, Jack Parsons had amassed more know-how with dry propellants than anyone else. He, therefore, was the obvious choice to spearhead the research. Parsons shouldered this new responsibility with enthusiasm and, in von Karman's view, reckless abandon. Week after week, as the shock of rocket explosions thundered up from the floor of the arroyo, the genial professor began to doubt that Parsons would ever master the optimum mix.

After many nights of mulling over possible ways to retard the burn rate, von Karman resorted to an approach that had gotten him out of trouble several times before. Late one evening, he composed four differential equations that amply covered the parameters of the problem. The next morning he handed his jottings to Malina and said, "Let's work out the implications of these equations. If they show that the progress of restricted burning is unstable . . . we'll give up." Then looking knowingly at Malina, he added, "But if they show that the process is stable, we'll tell Parsons to keep on trying."

Malina went to work. Eventually, he developed enough solutions to convince von Karman that it was indeed possible, in theory at least, to harness the power of a slow-burning solid propellant. The word was still go. Parsons, exuberant and relieved, returned to his experiments. The air around the arroyo continued to reverberate with explosions, announcing to all within earshot that he had not yet discovered the right combination. But with persistence, luck, and what von Karman described as a "rich talent for chemistry," Parsons finally landed right on the money. Into a paper-lined cylinder, he packed one-inch layers of a compressed black powder propellant that he had concocted. When a small charge ignited one end, the burning surface progressed smoothly through the length of the cylinder. Everyone was jubilant. But not for long. Stockpiling the new formula was its undoing. If kept on the shelf for a few days, the mass would expand and become riddled with tiny cracks. When ignited in this condition, rather than deliver the desired slow burn, the rocket blew up.

Disappointed but not discouraged, Parsons and his associates went back to their improvised laboratory. After experimenting with a variety of combinations, they started over again on a new approach. This time Parsons proposed combining an oxidizer (potassium perchlorate) and fuel (common roofing tar) in the same mixture. Years later, in his memoirs, von Karman lauded the expertise of the young self-educated chemist: "Parsons' method of making the charge was quite clever. First, he heated the roofing tar to the liquid point in a mixer, then added the granular perchlorate, and cast the mixture in the rocket chamber where it was allowed to cool to a hard solid . . . it is just this development [casting propellant into large charges] that has made possible such outstanding rockets as the Polaris and Minuteman and has helped the United States [maintain] its excellence in large solid-propellant rocket engines."

21

The Washington Merry-Go-Round

September 1940
Washington, D.C.

IT WAS ONE of those rare occasions when Robert H. Goddard felt at ease in the company of a bureaucrat. This man was different. He was certainly not one of those pompous windbags who dictated obtuse memoranda, keeping countless other civil servants busy deciphering their foggy pronouncements. No, Dr. C. H. Hickman was a scientist, a clearheaded rational thinker who happened to be on loan to the federal government. More importantly, he was an old friend and colleague.

Goddard's association with Hickman dated back to 1918. At that time, Hickman was assisting Goddard in the development of a single-charge rocket that the United States Army believed had promising military potential as an antitank weapon. Because Worcester, Massachusetts, lacked the seclusion appropriate for secret ordnance experiments, C. G. Abbot of the Smithsonian Institution suggested using the shops at the Mount Wilson Solar Observatory near Pasadena, California. After Major General George Squeir granted War Department approval, Goddard and two assistants departed early in June 1918 on their transcontinental rail journey. To save time and avoid delays after arrival, Goddard took several suitcases loaded with rocket propellant aboard the train with him. Earlier, he had expressed discomfort about this arrangement in a note to Abbot: "Concerning taking certain things with us . . . I do not wish to do this entirely on my own responsibility and would be glad if it were possible that I could have assurance of backing if any difficulties should arise." Abbot, however, refused to endorse the transport of combustibles on a civilian passenger train. His terse telegraphed reply indicated that if apprehended Goddard would twist slowly in the wind alone: "DESIRED AUTHORIZATION IMPRACTICABLE YET PLAN

SHOULD WORK." In a confidential memo to the War Department the following day, Abbot defended his position: "While we could not direct [Goddard] to carry his propellant to Pasadena in suitcases, we saw no danger in it and in view of the urgency advised him to do so."

Abbot, as it turned out, was right. Goddard and two companions arrived safely in Pasadena five days later. Hickman, who was then a member of the solar laboratory staff, agreed to assist Goddard in his rocket experiments. In retrospect, it was a costly move. Three weeks after Hickman joined the rocket team, Goddard wrote to Abbot: "While Mr. Hickman was removing the paper cap from the blasting cap on a 10-gram cartridge, the cartridge exploded, and necessitated the amputation on the left hand, of the thumb to the first joint, and the first two fingers to the second joint; and on the right hand, of the first finger to the first joint." Fortunately, his other injuries, small cuts on the face and chest, were minor. The urgency that prevailed during the summer of 1918 dissipated with the signing of the armistice in November. Soon after, Goddard received a letter from the army ordnance department advising him that "no further experimenting will be done on this matter at present. . . . [Your] data which is very interesting to us will be without doubt a valuable guide for future reference."

Hickman and Goddard then parted company, but throughout the ensuing years they kept in touch with each other. In May 1938, writing from Roswell, New Mexico, Goddard tried to induce Hickman to collaborate with him again: "It would be a great help if there were a real physicist here. . . . I am wondering if you would care to get a year's leave of absence from Bell Telephone Laboratories, and work with me." Hickman's reply intimated that he "would like the climate and as to the work, it could not be more fascinating," but nevertheless he turned down the proposition because he had just been promoted. No longer in research, he now headed a new mechanical-apparatus design section and therefore "could not ask for a leave of absence at this time." Hickman remained with Bell Telephone Laboratories until the summer of 1940, when he was finally persuaded to take that leave of absence by Dr. Vannevar Bush, chairman of the National Defense Research Committee. Bush named Hickman chairman of a section organized to investigate the military potential of "single charge" rockets. He barely had time to meet his fellow committee members before he was writing to Goddard for help: "We are anxious for you to come to Washington to discuss various phases of this work with us. . . . Both Commander [John] Hoover and the Chief of the Bureau of Ordnance think it would be desirable for you to come as soon as it is convenient for you to do so."

Less than ten days after Hickman dispatched that appeal to New Mexico, Goddard was sitting in Hickman's office in the Munitions Building in Washington, D.C. Goddard's willingness to drop everything and go east had not been prompted solely by Hickman's need for advice and counsel. He had worries of his own. Alarmed by his inability to win a government research contract, Goddard jumped at the chance to use Hickman's influence to open some doors. The Guggenheims, to be sure, had kept him going for more than six years. Yet these were annual grants that might be terminated at any time. Adding to his concern were the vigorous, though still unsuccessful, efforts by Harry Guggenheim to associate the government with his experiments in New Mexico. The fact that Goddard's sponsor was petitioning the military to step in and take over the reins did little to increase Goddard's peace of mind about his future.

One high-level meeting, arranged by Harry Guggenheim, was to take place in the office of General Henry H. Arnold on May 28, 1940. Goddard arrived in Washington the night before and readied himself, reviewing notes and other data, for his presentation the following morning. At 8:30 A.M., he was expecting to be ushered into Arnold's inner sanctum to meet the one man who, at the stroke of a pen, could open a floodgate of resources. But General Arnold was not there. Nor was Harry Guggenheim, who was still airborne over the Chesapeake Bay after bad weather had delayed his flight from New York. The meeting was then relocated to the office of Brigadier General George Brett, who also, at the moment, had more important things to do. Goddard was escorted to a seat at General Brett's conference table, joining Commanders F. W. Pennoyer, W. S. Diehl, and R. S. Hatcher of the navy, Captain C. A. Ross of the army air corps, and several other junior army officers.

With no designated chairman, the meeting soon degenerated into a random exchange of opinions and irrelevant comments. A representative of army ordnance ventured that his department saw no potential in rocketry. If any funds were budgeted for this purpose, he predicted, his unnamed superiors would use the money for "improvement of trench mortars." One of the navy men revealed that his superiors might be willing to subsidize research on "very-high-speed plane propulsion." Guggenheim's overdue flight from New York eventually landed in Washington, and upon entry into General Brett's office, Guggenheim announced that he would be glad to turn over Goddard's operation to national defense work for the duration of the emergency. Brigadier General Brett, the absent senior officer, then arrived and, after sizing up the situation, uttered the first constructive comment Goddard had heard that morning. Reiterating primary objectives on General Arnold's technical agenda, Brett asked Goddard to write a response to Arnold's previously expressed need for an auxiliary propulsion device that would accelerate aircraft briefly during takeoff and flight.

Sitting in Hickman's office exactly three months later, Goddard recounted how he had promptly answered Brett's request, submitting a comprehensive plan for development of an aircraft rocket booster less than two weeks after their meeting. After recapitulating the conditions presented to him—to provide an additional one thousand pounds of thrust for at least one minute—Goddard outlined his recommendation for positioning rockets on a test aircraft, described the rocket chamber design, listed ignition methods, and then offered an ingenious plan to increase fuel efficiency through use of a turbine propeller driven by the rocket motor. Goddard, however, wanted bigger fish to fry, closing with an appeal to be asked to undertake a much wider range of applications research because: "Enough has been shown by rocket performance in directed flights in New Mexico to prove that the subject is ready for intensive development."

Hickman nodded sympathetically when Goddard told him that General Brett's response gave little encouragement—merely a terse acknowledgment that his "preliminary calculations have been studied at Wright Field and interest has been expressed in them." Therefore, Brett suggested, it would now be in order for Goddard to write "a more concrete proposal for actual application of jet propulsion methods to the assisted-take-off problem." But that was all. No comment on Goddard's wish to broaden the study to include other potential military applications. Nor was there even a hint that a contract might be in the offing. Telling this to Hickman was made more painful by the knowledge that over a year earlier von Karman and Malina had generated sufficient confidence in high places to win a lucrative research and development grant.

Hickman's membership on the National Defense Research Committee provided access to secret scientific documents, including, of course, the periodic status reports from von Karman to army air corps headquarters in Washington, D.C. Leaning across the desk, he handed Goddard a copy of the most recent dispatch from Pasadena. Goddard glanced through the summary on the first page, looked up, and said, "They're now just about where I was fifteen years ago." Reading further about results achieved with black composition powders and some initial findings with liquid-fuel motors, Goddard caustically observed that the rocket chambers had "no adequate provision against heating and erosion." Hickman stirred uncomfortably in his chair. Finally, no longer able to contain his feelings about Goddard's failure to win a military research grant, Hickman spotlighted a deficiency that, until then, no friend had had the courage to express. "Discuss things more openly," urged Hickman. "Not enough is known about what you have done." Citing a paper written in 1936, which had been published in the *Smithsonian Miscellaneous Collections* and later condensed in *Scientific American*, Hickman maintained that if Goddard had been more candid, the full measure of his accomplishments would be more widely known, better appreciated, and fully acknowledged. Goddard listened but remained unconvinced. Complete openness was foolhardy, he retorted, because telling all only played into the hands of his enemies.

Hickman's point is difficult to refute. The sparse experimental data that had appeared in print was merely the tip of the iceberg. Although all major accomplishments were documented in written reports to Harry Guggenheim, Goddard's semiannual summations were confidential and not distributed to his peers in the scientific community. Only a favored few were privy to the scope of his work in New Mexico. Considering the modest resources available to him, the record is impressive. Scores of rocket motors, pumps and turbines were thoroughly evaluated in more than a hundred proving stand tests. Forty-eight flights were attempted with thirty-one achieving the primary objectives. In addition, with the aid of only four assistants, he designed, assembled, and successfully launched several "quarter ton" rockets at a time when Wernher von Braun, although producing much larger vehicles, was supported by hundreds of technicians at Peenemünde.

Goddard's passion for secrecy combined with his geographic isolation in New Mexico continued to handicap him in the madcap maneuvering that dominated the competition for research grants and contracts. A few days later, having participated in numerous conferences and meetings in Washington, he boarded a train and returned, dejected and empty-handed, to the Mescalero Ranch near Roswell. Any lingering hopes that Hickman, who had been "putting in some good hammer blows" for him, might still save the day were dashed when a letter from General Brett arrived in late September. Brett's rejection of Goddard's bids was as swift and decisive as a surgical air strike: "[Your proposals] have been carefully reviewed [but] while the Air Corps is deeply interested in the work being carried on by your organization, it does not, at this time, feel justified in obligating further funds for basic jet propulsion research and experimentation."

22

A Boost by JATO

CAPTAIN HOMER A. BOUSHEY, JR., waited in the small cockpit of a lightweight Ercoup. The motor was idling and he was ready to roll, but the people from Caltech wanted to make a final inspection of the twelve small powder rockets mounted under the fuselage. Boushey wished they would hurry. Yet, at the same time, he wanted them to be thorough, and not to cut any corners.

Two weeks earlier, Boushey had gone over to Pasadena to see a demonstration of a similar battery of rockets in the Arroyo Seco. Standing a safe distance away, he and Frank Malina watched Jack Parsons set up for the test. When everything was ready, Parsons retreated to a nearby shelter and, after a short countdown, threw the ignition switch. Each rocket was expected to deliver a steady thrust of about twenty-eight pounds for approximately twelve seconds. Instead, a spectacular series of explosions ensued, spewing a dozen jet nozzles high into the air. What had gone wrong? The answer was obvious to Parsons. These rockets had been "on the shelf" too long. Because those used in other successful tests were less than a day old, Parsons concluded that fresh mixtures averted failures. Acting on that premise, he and his associates pressed powder into rocket casings early in the morning of the March Field flight test. Then they raced this fresh batch to the air base in a Caltech truck and mounted them on the Ercoup.

Boushey may have been shaken by the explosions in the arroyo, but his faith in the potential of auxiliary rocket power was stronger. A confirmed career officer, he had joined the army shortly after his graduation from Stanford University. He then had entered the air corps flight training program, earned his wings, and served seven years as a commissioned pilot. Also a rocket buff from the start of his romance with aviation, Boushey read everything in sight on the subject, including Goddard's famous 1919 Smithsonian report. He was a dreamer, too. In June 1940, while stationed at Scott Field, Illinois, he wrote to Goddard seeking advice: "I hope that you may be interested in an invention of mine whereby the efficiency of a rocket, or more specifically a rocket-propeller combination, is increased at relatively slow speeds through the air." Suggesting that Goddard might want to "use, develop or adapt" his invention, Boushey, who was planning a flight to the West Coast ten days later, sought permission to stop over at Roswell for a "short talk." By return mail, Goddard asked Boushey to come to dinner on Friday evening, June 28, but confessed that "I do not know how much help I can be, beyond some theoretical considerations, as rocket propellers are new territory to all of us."

Boushey eagerly accepted the invitation. Goddard's gracious hospitality unexpectedly generated a handsome dividend. Learning that deliveries of liquid oxygen by the Linde Air Products Company were becoming more costly and less reliable, Boushey intimated that he might find a better alternative. After returning to Scott Field, he scouted around for a portable liquid-oxygen machine that he remembered had been built several years earlier to supply oxygen for air crews on high-altitude flights. Advancing technology, however, spurred development of pressurized-oxygen tanks, rendering liquid oxygen obsolete. Mothballed and almost forgotten, the apparatus eventually had been located in a storage depot about five miles from Wright Field, Ohio. It was huge. Oxygen-liquefying machinery and associated gear were bolted onto the bed of a five-ton Marmon Harrington truck. The vehicle's 175-horsepower engine supplied the energy to operate the equipment when power was not required for locomotion. Goddard, while profusely grateful for Boushey's detective work, nevertheless made no attempt to acquire the system. Writing to Boushey on July 27, 1940, he said: "I have submitted a proposal to the Army Air Corps on the program of work I mentioned when you were here, and until I receive word as to what will be done, I shall of course not be in a position to negotiate regarding the oxygen plant, as I shall not know until then under what auspices I am to work next year."

Although the oxygen liquefier was left on the back burner, Boushey nevertheless performed yeoman service for Goddard as a bird dog on other matters. For one thing, he was an important unofficial source of information in air corps procurement operations. At first, the intelligence he gathered sounding out support for rocket development was not encouraging. Writing from Scott Field on June 25, 1940, Boushey reported: "Concerning your proposal on the augmented take-off project I was able to learn little. . . . Jet propulsion is merely one of three or four possible solutions and frankly Captain [Bernard R.] Fink thought liquid oxygen and gasoline 'too risky.'"

At Wright Field the mood was no better. Flying there the following week, Boushey contacted Captain J. W. Sessums. Four years earlier, Sessums had visited Goddard in Roswell to discuss the possibility of propelling gliders with rocket power. At the time, gliders were towed as targets for antiaircraft artillery training. For tow-plane pilots, such duty was extremely hazardous, particularly when flying through the field of fire. Development of cost-effective power for drones soon became an important priority in military research. Goddard was convinced that gliders could be delivered safely to a target zone with liquid oxygen-gasoline rockets, and he said as much in a letter to Major General A. H. Sunderland three days after his meeting with Sessums. Sunderland took the matter up with General Henry H. Arnold. Arnold, however, threw cold water on the idea, calling it "impracticable." Sunderland, who had hoped that the air corps would share development costs, regretfully wrote to Goddard that "one of the War Department agencies has reported adversely on the use of rocket-propelled targets. That report will remain the final decision until such time that I can show that a self-propelled plane can be developed."

When Boushey was ushered into his office at Wright Field in early August 1940, Sessums was cordial but no more encouraging than Captain Fink. Reflecting the bias against volatile liquid fuels shared by many air corps officers, Sessums denied knowledge of any rocket project then sponsored by his branch of service. He was pessimistic about future prospects, too. Commenting on his conversation with Sessums, Boushey later reported to Goddard that "money for any radically new development, or pure research grants, would be most difficult to obtain at this time."

But what a difference a year makes. Sitting in the Ercoup cockpit waiting for Parsons to complete his inspection, Boushey recalled the welcome accorded to Goddard's bid for a JATO contract by Colonel Paul H. Kemmer three days earlier. Kemmer, who was chief of experimental aircraft programs at Wright Field, had come to southern

California to oversee an important new project at the Northrop Aircraft Company. Having read a copy of Goddard's earlier proposal that was summarily rejected by General Brett, Boushey told Goddard that "it failed to present your case in a favorable light." Urging him to "write an entirely different type of presentation," Boushey hammered away about the need for more specifics: maximum thrusts obtained with powder and liquid oxygen-gasoline fuels; oxygen and gasoline consumption in pounds per pound of thrust per second; top temperatures in firing chambers; and gas ejection velocities at maximum thrust. Goddard complied, and the very afternoon the revised proposal was delivered Boushey took it to Kemmer's hotel. Thumbing through the pages of data, Kemmer expressed satisfaction with Goddard's numbers, leaving Boushey with the clear impression that he was "quite receptive to the whole idea."

Crawling from beneath the belly of the Ercoup, Jack Parsons made a circle with his thumb and forefinger indicating that everything was in order. Boushey lifted the hand microphone from its cradle and called the March Field control tower, requesting permission to taxi to a runway. Within moments, the small plane was rolling across the tarmac and onto the edge of a strip of concrete that stretched into the haze a half mile away. Boushey revved the motor and the Ercoup shuddered under the strain. Satisfied with the response, he released the brakes and the plane moved off, slowly gathering momentum. It had gone less than a hundred yards when Boushey kicked the ignition switch. Rockets fired and smoke billowed from beneath the tail. An instant later, he pulled back hard on the control column and the plane accelerated upward as if it had been propelled from a giant slingshot. Climbing sharply at a near fifty-degree angle, the Ercoup leveled off at an altitude of seven hundred feet, circled the field, and landed.

Boushey emerged from the cockpit, a wide smile illuminating his face as he shook hands with the jubilant von Karman, Malina, and Parsons. That first jet-assisted takeoff, and others to follow, proved beyond doubt that the von Karman–Malina theory was valid. A slow burn was indeed possible. Rocket power could be controlled and used to achieve a defined goal. If anything, theory erred on the conservative side. The result was far better than the prediction. Takeoff distance had been shortened by as much as 50 percent. General Henry H. Arnold's big bombers would now fly from hundreds of airfields too small for them in the past.

23

Speer Encounters the A-4

June 13, 1942
Peenemünde, Germany

CIRCLING SLOWLY OVER the island of Usedom, a Heinkel 111 descended on its final approach. The north runway of the Luftwaffe air base at Peenemünde West lay dead ahead. Inside the passenger cabin, Albert Speer, minister of armaments, gazed through his window at the green fields surrounding the small village below, and then toward the Baltic, at the rocket test emplacements, assembly buildings, army barracks, and civilian residence compounds stretching back from the shoreline.

Privately, Speer still marveled at the circumstances that had propelled him into his present situation. Ten years earlier, as an aspiring young architect, he had won a modest assignment to redecorate the Berlin headquarters of the National Socialist party. Adolf Hitler, the party's leader, had been pleased with the transformation. A succession of increasingly significant commissions followed and finally, in 1938, he was delegated to assist the Munich architect, Paul Ludwig Troost, in a renovation of the chancellor's residence in Berlin. His skill in enabling Troost to cope with the complex work rules of the Berlin construction trades helped to assure completion of the assignment in record time.

After Troost's death, Speer's star rose quickly. Through Hitler's addiction to building and architecture, Speer was drawn into the führer's private circle of intimates. The morning after a plane crash killed Minister of Armaments Fritz Todt, Speer was summoned to an audience with Hitler. Todt had been responsible for all road building, navigable waterways, and power plants in addition to his duties as minister of armaments. Speer was flabbergasted when Hitler solemnly announced that he was to take over all of Todt's assignments. Believing that the führer had failed to express his intentions accurately, Speer replied that he would try to be an adequate replacement for Todt in overseeing construction. Hitler, growing impatient, retorted, "No, in *all* capacities, including Minister of Armaments." Speer protested, doubting his competence to manage this totally unfamiliar jurisdiction. Hitler was adamant: "I have confidence in you. Besides . . . I have no one else."

Five months after the extraordinary meeting with Hitler, Speer was heading this delegation, representing the three armed services, to witness the launch of an A-4 rocket. When wheels of the Heinkel 111 touched down gently on the airstrip, he and his fellow passengers tried to conceal their relief that the flight from Berlin had ended without incident. As Speer negotiated the narrow steps onto the tarmac, Colonel Walter Dornberger saluted and Wernher von Braun, standing beside him, smiled broadly. Speer was followed by Luft-waffe Field Marshal Erhard Milch, Navy Admiral Karl Witzell, and Army General Friedrich Fromm. After handshakes all around, Dornberger escorted the party to a line of staff cars that were waiting with motors running.

Passing beyond the airport's perimeter, the caravan entered a pine forest. Within minutes, they arrived in a clearing, the site of Test Stand Number Seven. Speer and the others were startled when they saw the A-4 looming above them. Although briefed in advance, they were nevertheless unprepared for the ominous presence of this tower-ing hulk, nearly as high as a five-story building. Clouds of vapor curled upward around its circumference as liquid oxygen was pumped into the fuel tanks. This, by necessity, was the final step. Despite intensive efforts to design an efficient seal for the liquid oxygen section, nearly five pounds evaporated during every minute that elapsed between topping off the tanks and launch. With a 19,000-pound capacity, losses were negligible and therefore tolerable in short intervals. But long delays, resulting in a depletion of hundreds of pounds, inevitably required additional refueling.

Dornberger hurried the party toward the observation bunker at the edge of the clearing while the voice of the launch director, booming over a loudspeaker, ordered all personnel out of the area. Test vehicle 2 of the A-4 series was poised and ready. Another voice: "Two minutes to lift-off." In less than a quarter of an hour, by noon, the success—or failure—of the preceding weeks of round-the-clock prepa-rations would be known to all.

The prelaunch "fine tuning" had been more extensive than Dornberger cared to admit. Nearly seven weeks had elapsed since the first arrival of vehicle 2 at Test Stand Number Seven on April 19, 1942. During the first three days, equipment was trucked in and assembled for fuel-injection tests. Eight were conducted using an auxiliary steam generator. Then, after the rocket's own steam generator (which supplies power for turbopumps in flight) was installed, the sequence was repeated. Next came static firing tests. Three separate ones, to prove the reliability of the propulsion and steering units, went according to plan. But during the fourth, a combustion chamber screw failed, damaging the steering cable mechanism. This seemingly minor glitch precipitated a major overhaul. Tail and nose sections were dismantled to gain access to the steering system. The combustion chamber was also replaced and the motor carefully inspected. This was followed by flow measurements throughout the liquid oxygen and alcohol fuel systems. Then, with nose and tail sections remounted, the entire rocket was transported to the assembly plant for oscillation tests. Not until June 8 was it back in place and ready for launch.

Dornberger, following the countdown in the bunker with Speer at his side, silently hoped that the considerable time and effort invested in vehicle 2 would reap a rich return, not the disastrous fireball that had engulfed its predecessor. Wincing as he recalled that ill-fated rocket's destruction on the launchpad three months earlier, he ruefully reminded himself that a repetition of that debacle would dissolve Speer's support like a wisp of smoke in the wind.

The voice of the loudspeakers counted off the final seconds: "Four . . . three . . . two . . . one. . . . Fire!" Crowded around small viewing slits in the wall of the bunker, all focused their attention on the base of the rocket. Suddenly smoke spewed out intermingled with showers of sparks. The smoke dissipated, replaced by a golden red flame darting around diverter plates embedded in the concrete slab. The flames grew larger and, almost imperceptibly, vehicle 2 vibrated on its base. The umbilical cable—the only remaining physical link with the power plant and control center—swung free as the launch director threw the main-stage switch. Instantly the liquid oxygen and alcohol supply systems began to feed thirty gallons of fuel per second into the combustion chamber. The tail flame brightened to white-heat intensity. Slowly at first, the sheathed metal column rose from its base.

Fifty-six thousand pounds of thrust. Speer and his party watched in wonder as the rocket climbed above the rim of treetops. They rushed out of the bunker, craning their necks, as it zoomed upward.

Wernher von Braun beamed broadly at everyone. Dornberger, relieved, managed a smile, too. Then, turning to Speer and his party, von Braun began a rapid-fire description of the rocket's acceleration, velocity, and trajectory during the next few minutes of flight. Moments earlier, at the launch site, ears had been ringing with the thundering lift-off, followed by the howling ascent. Now there was only a distant rumble, diminishing slowly in intensity. Exhilaration reigned. A mood of foreboding, however, descended on the observation posts along the coastline and nearby islands. Monitoring progress with the aid of binoculars, cinetheodolites, and cameras, the remote lookouts were more aware of the true state of affairs. Early in its ascent, they saw the huge rocket begin to twist from right to left along its long axis. The movement was easy to discern from their vantage points by watching the black-and-white stripes on the sides and the different colors painted on the stabilizing vanes. A moment later, the twisting stopped. Then a turn briefly in the opposite direction before a resumption of the right-to-left spin. As it disappeared into the cloud ceiling, the huge rocket was rotating an alarming 360 degrees every two seconds. Though visible no longer, vehicle 2 continued to be monitored by radio. Thirty seconds after launch, it was still climbing through an altitude of 15,000 feet when the onboard transmitter shut down. Air speed, according to the last telemetered data, was 750 miles per hour. Not nearly fast enough. Acceleration, too, was sluggish— more than 10 percent under the precalculated minimum.

At the launch site, fifty-two seconds into the flight, the rocket's engine was barely audible. The festive mood at Test Stand Seven continued unabated with von Braun and the others engaged in animated conversation until they were distracted, some forty seconds later, by a new sound, a piercing melancholy whine, directly overhead and growing louder. Speer and the others exchanged puzzled looks, but before anyone had a chance to question von Braun or Dornberger, a technician shouted, "It's coming back!" Bewilderment mixed with terror gripped everyone. Speer's first inclination was to run. But where? Frozen in his tracks, he tried to peer through the cloud cover but was unable to divine the direction of the rocket's plunge. Then suddenly it emerged, wobbling while falling in a horizontal mode. Air rushing over the exposed wide surface became increasingly audible. An eerie howl grew in intensity until it was silenced by a splash into the sea less than a mile away.

During the brief drive back to the airfield, Dornberger desperately sought to cast favorable light on an awkward situation. Trying to accentuate the positive, he adamantly maintained that a significant goal had been achieved. Successfully lofting twelve tons of metal and fuel into the clouds was clearly worth something. Speer remained unmoved. Today's performance, the armaments minister replied dourly, would in no way dispel Hitler's skepticism. Meanwhile, in the second car of the cortege, General Fromm, chief of *Reichswehr* armament, sat in embarrassed silence as Luftwaffe Field Marshal Milch and Navy Admiral Witzell quietly rejoiced in not being a party to this humiliating failure. When they arrived at the airfield and walked toward their waiting transport, it was Milch's turn to be red-faced.

The object of Milch's discomfort was a new HE-177, the brainchild of the eminent Professor Ernst Heinkel, taxiing along the tarmac preparing for takeoff. Originally billed as a heavy bomber and long-range reconnaissance aircraft, the HE-177 had been demonstrated first for the Luftwaffe, amid great fanfare, in November 1939. By June 1942, over two and half years later, fewer than a hundred of the much ballyhooed model had been produced, and less than a third of those accepted for operational use. Engine fires, wing fractures, and a dismally long list of other defects had prompted Luftwaffe inspectors to order over a thousand engineering changes following initial flight trials. Delays were exacerbated by Professor Heinkel's policy of allocating the lion's share of available resources to the profitable HE-111. Consequently, the modifications of the HE-177 that were ordered by the Luftwaffe were implemented with "catastrophic lethargy."

Hoping that this symbol of a failed procurement would pass unnoticed, Milch tried to divert Speer's attention until they were aboard their own aircraft. He had compelling reasons for not wanting the HE-177 to be the subject of a conversation now with the armaments minister. As state secretary of the Air Ministry, Milch bore prime responsibility for the condition and performance of every aircraft in the Luftwaffe inventory.

The ploy failed. Distracted by the noise of its engines, Speer stopped and watched as the HE-177 maneuvered into position on the runway. As the bomber gathered speed, Speer remembered Hermann Göering's rage earlier that year when the Luftwaffe reich marshal had discovered that Heinkel had perpetrated an enormous deception. Göring, who had been under the impression that the HE-177 was a four-engine bomber, learned that there were indeed four engines— but only two propellers! In a flagrant violation of the engineering maxim that holds that simplicity, not complexity, should be the Holy Grail, Heinkel coupled two engines together driving a single prop. As a result, basic maintenance—even replacing spark plugs—was a mechanic's nightmare. Despite frequent crashes, Heinkel's staff persisted in their belief that the four-engine, two-propeller design was the most efficient configuration for the bomber's primary mission.

Noting Speer's interest in the departing aircraft, the commandant of the Luftwaffe establishment at Peenemünde went over to the armaments minister and informed him that the HE-177 was conducting a test flight with four tons of bombs aboard. All watched as it lifted off the runway, banked sharply to the right, then suddenly sideslipped downward and out of sight from a height of five hundred feet. The crash, which could be heard but not seen by Speer and his party, killed the entire crew. Speer preceded Milch onto their HE-111 with the wry comment that he had witnessed enough disasters for one day.

Later, while presiding over a postmortem of the ill-fated A-4 launch, Dornberger ordered von Braun and his team to find a plausible explanation. Evidence was needed to support Dornberger's conviction that the A-4 concept was fundamentally sound and that the aborted flight was caused by an aberration unrelated to the design. Photographs and telemetered data ultimately focused attention on the triaxial guidance system's failure to halt rotation after lift-off, which deprived the rocket of an opportunity to steer from the vertical onto the programmed parabolic course. Dornberger's subsequent report emphasized this conclusion, but Hitler was not swayed. Shaking his head, the führer continued to harbor the "gravest doubts" about the Peenemünde program.

24

Goddard and the Flying Boat

September 23, 1942
Annapolis, Maryland

SMALL RIPPLES LAPPED at the hull of a PBY "flying boat," tethered to a mooring near the mouth of the Severn River. Throughout the two previous days, mechanics from the Naval Engineering Experimental Station clambered in and about its tail section, installing a maze of tanks and feed lines. On the afternoon of the second day, their job completed, they stepped onto a waiting launch to enable three civilians to climb aboard and inspect their handiwork. Charles Mansur was a machinist and Lowell Randall and George Bode were test assistants who had come east from the Mescalero Ranch to help Dr. Robert H. Goddard conduct this test for the navy.

Work on the project had begun in Roswell ten months earlier. But the eighteen months preceding the signing of the navy contract were a period of frustration and considerable difficulty for Goddard. He was convinced that government bureaucrats were giving him a colossal "runaround." As recently as two months before Army Captain Homer Boushey told him that Colonel Kemmerer was "quite receptive" to the revised JATO proposal, Goddard was informing Harry Guggenheim that he was "still not expecting much from Wright Field." Wondering who was helping whom, Goddard complained: "We are calling upon the Army and the Navy for engineering assistance and yet at the same time they are both seeking help here." He also viewed Guggenheim's behind-the-scenes maneuvering to influence assignment of government scientists to Goddard's New Mexico operations as more hindrance than help. Recognizing that neither the army nor the navy had done significant work on liquid-fuel rockets, Goddard correctly surmised that the military was not equipped to offer him competent support, "because anyone coming [to Roswell] would have to be instructed in liquid-rocket technique before he could contribute anything of engineering value."

The appalling naïveté of those in high places when circumstances ultimately forced them to deal with rocket matters was another cross that Goddard was destined to bear. Rear Admiral J. H. Towers, for example, who was chief of the navy's Bureau of Aeronautics in July 1941, responded to Goddard's JATO proposal with an offer to fund "part-time consulting services" to be rendered by Goddard for up to 120 days at a maximum rate "as allowed by law of twenty-five dollars a day." Goddard, however, was not seeking employment. On the contrary, he was offering a finished product: a prototype JATO engine incorporating tested and proven components. Goddard graciously declined the admiral's offer, saying that it was an honor he deeply appreciated and adding that, although he would be glad to assist the navy in a consulting capacity, he preferred an arrangement where the continued operation of the Roswell laboratory was assured. To reinforce the latter point, he enclosed a second, more detailed proposal for a JATO system, which included layouts of pressure-tank and pump-type rockets and drawings illustrating how they might be mounted under the wings of two-engine aircraft.

Unwilling to rely solely on his own persuasive powers, Goddard sought to enlist Harry Guggenheim's clout in punching home this message. Having dispatched a practically identical proposal to Air Corps General Henry H. Arnold, Goddard wrote to Guggenheim asking that he "telephone General Arnold . . . and suggest that he give his personal attention to the proposal . . . submitted to his office." Goddard hastened to add that this was not his idea but "was suggested by Captain Boushey who appears to be familiar with such matters." Boushey, it seems, also tried to orchestrate any conversation Guggenheim might initiate with General Arnold. In his letter to Guggenheim, Goddard said that Boushey urged several points be emphasized. Among them was the rather cavalier conclusion that "we have the only *liquid-fuel* rockets in existence in the United States and probably elsewhere." Having crawled far out on a limb, Goddard hastened to inch back to a more reasonable position with a bracketed addendum that "it is not known whether or not Germany has them."

Goddard also proposed that Guggenheim pursue a similar strategy in dealing with the navy: "If you think it worth while, you might also telephone Admiral Towers, and suggest that he give his personal

Dr. Robert H. Goddard on the campus of Clark University, Worcester, Massachusetts, with rocket chamber used in his 1915–1916 experiments. (NASA)

Dr. Goddard standing beside his first rocket to fly with liquid propellants at Auburn, Massachusetts, March 16, 1926. (NASA)

Klaus Riedel (on ladder) and Rudolf Nebel make final adjustments on a small rocket at the Raketenflugplatz, *circa 1930. Wire pulled from a safe distance turned the bicycle wheel that activated the rocket.* (G. Edward Pendray Collection, Princeton University Library)

Rudolf Nebel and eighteen-year-old Wernher von Braun with two of the original Oberth rockets at the Raketenflugplatz *near Berlin, Germany, circa 1930.* (G. Edward Pendray Collection, Princeton University Library)

Rudolf Nebel (left), Willy Ley, and Klaus Riedel before a rocket-motor proving stand at the Raketenflugplatz, *circa 1931. Operation of the stand was remotely controlled by the overhead cables.* (G. Edward Pendray Collection, Princeton University Library)

H. F. Pierce (left) and G. Edward Pendray with the American Rocket Society's initial design in a field near Stockton, New Jersey, circa 1932. (G. Edward Pendray Collection, Princeton University Library)

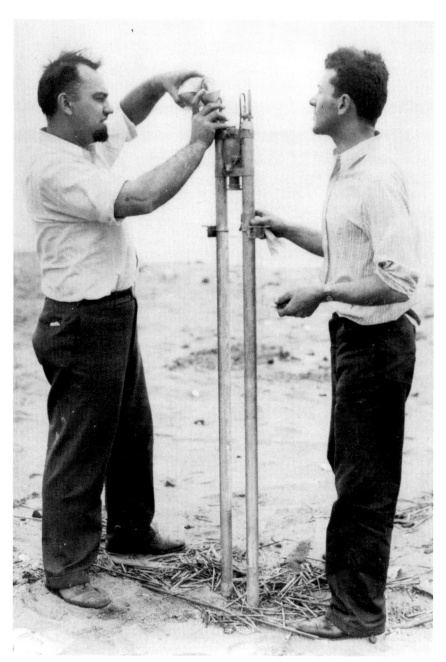

Bernard Smith (right) helps G. Edward Pendray pour gasoline into the tank prior to a rocket launch at Great Kills, Staten Island, New York, May 14, 1933. (G. Edward Pendray Collection, Princeton University Library)

G. Edward Pendray (center) watches Bernard Smith rehearse pulling the lever that opens the pressurized tanks on the rocket. Meanwhile, the "lighter" Alfred Best arranges his equipment, May 14, 1933. (G. Edward Pendray Collection, Princeton University Library)

Harry Guggenheim and Charles Lindbergh visit Dr. Goddard's rocket launch site near Roswell, New Mexico, September 25, 1935. Left to right: Al Fisk, Guggenheim, Goddard, Lindbergh, N. T. Ljungquist. (Goddard Collection, Clark University)

Dr. Robert Goddard monitors prelaunch conditions at his New Mexico test site with the aid of a telescope, circa 1937. The keys on the shelf controlled the firing sequence. (Smithsonian Institution)

Resting while waiting for additional fuel to arrive between tests at the Arroyo Seco are (left to right) Rudolph Scott, Apollo M. O. Smith, Frank J. Malina, Ed Forman, and Jack Parsons, circa 1937. (Archives, California Institute of Technology)

Robert H. Goddard (on ladder, right) directs assistants who are preparing rocket for launching, circa 1940. (B. Anthony Stewart, copyright National Geographic Society)

A corner of Robert H. Goddard's workshop near Roswell, New Mexico, circa 1940. Goddard (left) adjusts pressure lines aided by N. T. Ljungquist, A. Kisk, and C. Mansur. (B. Anthony Stewart, copyright National Geographic Society)

While two assistants check launching tower and rocket, Robert H. Goddard (lower left) reads pressure levels in ground support equipment, circa 1940. (B. Anthony Stewart, copyright National Geographic Society)

Theodore von Karman (center) completes last-minute calculations on the wing of a convenient aircraft before a JATO test under the watchful eyes of (left to right) Clark Millikan, Martin Summerfield, Frank Malina, and army pilot Homer A. Boushey, Jr., circa 1941. (G. Edward Pendray Collection, Princeton University Library)

A jet-assisted takeoff device, built by Robert H. Goddard, is tested on a PBY flying boat on the Severn River, near Annapolis, Maryland, in September 1942. (Nimitz Library, U.S. Naval Academy)

Frank J. Malina and WAC CORPORAL at White Sands Proving Grounds, New Mexico, circa 1945. (Archives, California Institute of Technology)

Theodore von Karman and H.-S. Tsien were members of an Allied scientific research team that interrogated Dr. Ludwid Prandtl of the Kaiser Wilhelm Institute, following occupation of Göttingen, Germany, May 1945. (The Johns Hopkins University)

A former barbershop in a Los Angeles suburb was the initial home office of the fledgling Ramo-Wooldridge Corporation. Left to right: Dean Wooldridge, Simon Ramo, and new employees Aimee Joy and Frank Clement, circa 1953. (TRW Space & Defense)

Wernher von Braun and Willy Ley (right) frequently reminisced about their days at the Raketenflugplatz *and also discussed plans for the future, including a small rocket-powered passenger aircraft, circa 1954.* (Smithsonian Institution)

Maj. Gen. Bernard Schriever (center left) congratulates Dr. Simon Ramo at the dedication of their first joint headquarters, in June 1956. (TRW Space & Defense)

Hermann Oberth (left) with Wernher von Braun, following presentation of the first Hermann Oberth Award to von Braun by the Alabama section of the American Rocket Society, circa 1956. (Smithsonian Institution)

Krafft Ehricke was awarded the Loesser Prize by the 1956 International Astronautical Congress in Rome, Italy, for his pioneering work in rocketry. (Smithsonian Institution)

Dazzling successes achieved by Simon Ramo and Dean Wooldridge earned them the recognition of a Time *cover on April 29, 1957.* (Copyright 1957 by Time Inc. Reprinted by permission)

Posing with an early model of the Saturn are (left to right) NASA Administrator T. Keith Glennan, Maj. Gen. John B. Medaris, Wernher von Braun, and Brig. Gen. John Barclay, ABMA's deputy commander, circa 1959. (Smithsonian Institution)

Lt. Gen. Bernard A. Schriever amid a display of operational and proposed U.S. Air Force launchers, circa 1963. (Smithsonian Institution)

attention to the Navy proposal." No evidence has been found of Guggenheim's reaction to this plea for him to overtly pitch Goddard's case to the top brass. Nor is there any record that such calls were actually placed. There are, however, plausible theories to support a case for and against his involvement. On the positive side, there is his well-documented campaign, initiated early in 1940, to have the military take over sponsorship of Goddard's work in New Mexico. On the other hand, because Guggenheim was also a member of the navy's inactive reserve, it is doubtful that he was willing to jeopardize his chances for recall to active duty by associating himself so blatantly with such a controversial matter as rocketry.

In August 1941, with or without Harry Guggenheim's help, Goddard was suddenly transformed from a wallflower into the most sought-after swain at the ball. On August 4, Captain D. C. Ramsey, assistant chief of the navy's Bureau of Aeronautics, wrote: "[Your proposal] has been read with interest. In order that the details of a possible contract may be discussed [we are sending] a representative of the Bureau [to] visit you. . . . Lt. C. F. Fischer, USNR, plans to arrive in Roswell about August 11th." Fischer actually came a day early, on Sunday the tenth. Goddard drove down to the Hotel Nickson that afternoon and brought him back to the ranch. They talked on the veranda until supper. Later, Goddard showed movies of earlier flights and some pump tests. The next day he picked Fischer up at midmorning and took him to the shop, where they talked over the proposal letter. Then, after lunch, they went out to the tower. Having spent almost two days in Roswell, Lieutenant Fischer took his leave on the morning of the twelfth. Two weeks went by and then came welcome news from Fischer. The Navy Department had accepted Goddard's proposal. A letter of intent was to come shortly, followed by a contract within three weeks.

Meanwhile Boushey was tramping through corridors and knocking on doors, also touting Goddard's proposal. On August 31, he jubilantly wrote to Goddard that, finally, the army was expressing serious interest. The matériel division was drawing up a contract to be dated September 15. Of equal significance, the issuance of an "authority to purchase"—the document that triggered payment of funds— seemed imminent. Knowing that Goddard needed a continuing source of support, Boushey had also influenced inclusion of a provision that ensured regular monthly payments following submission of periodic progress reports. Then he summed up this obvious good news with the comment that "everything seems to be going smoothly."

For the navy, perhaps. But not for Boushey's vigorous campaign on Goddard's behalf. The navy's letter of intent, which arrived before the army acted, constituted a binding agreement with the government. The army's tardily expressed interest in Goddard, however, was not to be ignored. A duplicate of the JATO system that Goddard proposed to develop for the navy was to be built later for the army. Navy Captain D. C. Ramsey voiced no objection to this arrangement "provided the work [does] not interfere with or delay delivery of the first motor to the Navy . . . and that demonstration and delivery to the Air Forces is made subsequent to delivery to the Navy." The implications of these conditions were obvious. Goddard's rocket work was to be strictly a navy show.

Boushey, devastated, wrote to Goddard in October 1941: "I don't know what sort of contract you have with the Navy (and I certainly wish it was with the Air Forces instead) but I hope you have the best of luck and the success you so richly deserve." Trying to boost Boushey's morale, Goddard replied with praise for the flier's adroit footwork: "A contract [was granted] by the Air Forces for something along the lines you suggested, which we can put down as a miracle of sorts which you helped bring about."

Slightly more than a year after this exchange, Goddard's crew was checking out the rocket in the tail of the navy PBY. Ten months of development work had been invested in the device prior to the transfer of operations to the western shore of Chesapeake Bay in July 1942. Before packing and moving east for flight tests, Goddard, in an upbeat mood, wrote to Lieutenant Fischer: "I feel sure it will make you feel much better . . . when I tell you that we made a run with the takeoff unit which gave an average of 800 lb for 22 seconds." The significance of this noteworthy achievement was enhanced by the absence of any melting or erosion within the metal firing chamber. Also, the "velocity efficiency" was 44.1 percent, higher than the best performance noted until that time. At first, Goddard was tempted to share this happy news with Boushey, but then, possibly recalling Captain D. C. Ramsey's admonition, decided to defer any revelations to an army representative until a prototype was delivered to the navy.

Charles Mansur, Lowell Randall, and George Bode, who helped Goddard conduct numerous static tests of the JATO motor behind the workshop in Roswell, were on hand to ensure that "Little Nell" lived up to her advance billing. Inside the tail section, Mansur gripped the fuel cylinder with both hands, testing the rigidity of the mounting struts. No movement. Silently, he saluted the skill of the aviation mechanics who had installed the tank and associated piping. Outside, Randall and Bode, balancing themselves in a dinghy, studied the orientation of the thrust chamber and nozzle. Both were aligned, within allowable tolerances, with the longitudinal axis of the fuselage. Satisfied that no bugs had been created during installation, Mansur crawled forward to a hatch in the waist of the hull and signaled to the others that he had completed his inspection.

In less than an hour, the PBY was fueled, liquid oxygen loaded, and a motor launch made ready for Goddard, Lieutenant Fischer, and two other observers. Initially, a few runs were to be made on the surface without attempting takeoff. In the first test, the JATO unit was activated while the PBY taxied slowly toward the mouth of the Severn. Five seconds later, a thermostatic cutoff switch, apparently sensing above-normal temperatures near the liquid-oxygen tank, shut down the combustion chamber's fuel supply. After Goddard's boat came alongside, he climbed aboard, crawled aft, but found no evidence to support a discontinuance of the tests. Suspecting that vibration may have triggered the cutoff switch, Lieutenant Fischer directed a mechanic to increase the distance between the contacts.

The second test went much better. According to Goddard, when the plane was moving "about five knots [it] underwent a substantial increase in speed during the fifteen-second thrust period." A third test, also taxiing, went smoothly. Then, in a fourth test, engines were revved up to near takeoff speed, but a cap that closed a nozzle opening in the hull washed off, dislodging the igniter before it was fired. During the fifth test, with the nozzle cap now well tightened, combustion began on cue but mysteriously shut down two seconds into the burn. Fischer, suspicious that the thermal cutoff switch was the culprit, ordered that it be bypassed. The sixth test, which was the third takeoff attempt, was a success. The JATO unit delivered the required amount of thrust for a period of fifteen seconds. The PBY lifted off the surface, climbed steadily, leveled off, circled around, descended, and skimmed along the water to a rendezvous with the launch. Another brief examination inside the tail section revealed that everything seemed to be in good working order.

Fischer then called for one more takeoff attempt. He and Goddard, in the launch, watched the PBY gather speed. When the JATO unit fired, the color of the flame spewing from its nozzle indicated an oversupply of oxygen. The pilot, however, did not abort. He took off because a radio aboard the launch failed and the observers were unable to warn him. In a subsequent report, Goddard explained: "At this moment . . . the chamber opened up, causing a sudden rise of pressure in the rear compartments of the plane, and the shock broke the liquid oxygen line between the main oxygen valve and the strainer, allowing liquid oxygen to pass into the hull under pressure until the oxygen tank was automatically vented, requiring about three seconds normally." In this supercharged atmosphere, anything flammable started to burn. Flames consumed insulation on wires, components in the control box, even portions of fabric on the tail surfaces. Fortunately for pilot and crew, the fire was brought under control by one of the gunners wielding fire extinguishers.

A disaster was averted, but confidence in Goddard's work was at a low ebb by nightfall. How was he to refute a finding that in its present form, his liquid-fuel rocket was more a hazard than a help? There was no way to blunt the negative impact of the experiments than to claim, quite legitimately, that he was a victim of circumstances. Disablement of the thermal cutoff switch, a move Goddard opposed but was powerless to countermand, eliminated the one safeguard that may have saved the day. Far more satisfactory results might also have been achieved if radio communication between the observers on the launch and the PBY pilot had been maintained. In his report summing up the day's events, Goddard stressed that if the radio had not failed, "the last test could have been stopped at any time . . . and certainly before the chamber had become seriously heated."

25

A Time to Remember

A CELEBRATION? OF course. After disappointments, failures, and doubts expressed in high places, after successfully resisting countless temptations to abandon the pursuit of an "impossible" goal, this was a time to rejoice.

In the morning's bright light, an A-4 rocket rose majestically into the sky, arched over the Baltic, and soared faultlessly downrange. Perched on rooftops and other vantage points, hundreds witnessed this feat and saw the huge, yet graceful, bullet-nosed cylinder thunder straight up and then, seconds later, begin an almost imperceptible tilt to the east. Technicians manning the observation posts along the Pomeranian coast followed its course. They had the data, the documented records, the telemetered transmissions and radar plots proving beyond doubt that this A-4 had performed like no other before it. And finally there was the visual confirmation. General Walter Dornberger waited expectantly on the tarmac of the Luftwaffe airfield at Peenemünde West as Captain Ernst Steinhoff climbed from the cockpit of an ME-109. He was smiling. Dornberger smiled, too, upon hearing Steinhoff say he had spotted the bright green dye marker in the water. The rocket had plummeted into the sea within two miles of the targeted longitude and latitude.

Sipping a dram of schnapps in his suite a few hours later, Dornberger prepared to don the full-dress uniform that his orderly had laid out for him. A festive mood prevailed throughout the officers' compound. The commander of Peenemünde listened impassively to the laughter and banter from the courtyard below, reflecting the universal exuberance that this first successful launch of an A-4 had unleashed. Dornberger, however, was beset by a strange melancholy. His thoughts dwelt on the past, particularly on the doubts of a former immediate superior, General Karl Becker. Becker's death in the summer of 1940 now denied Dornberger the satisfaction of hearing the venerable army weapons chief disavow his earlier lack of faith in the rocket project. Although Becker, persuaded perhaps by Dornberger's unshakable confidence, always went along when the chips were down, he had nevertheless harbored deep misgivings. His ambivalence was evident during their last meeting when, looking somberly at Dornberger, he had said, "I only hope I have not been mistaken in my estimate of you and your work."

Becker's worries about Peenemünde had no doubt been exacerbated by more serious problems elsewhere. Caught in a bind between Hitler, who made extraordinary demands to increase armament quotas, and industrial leaders who resented being told how to manage their business, Becker found himself in a no-win situation. Field Marshal Wilhelm Keitel, who obediently transmitted Hitler's orders to Becker, had first warned the führer that the unrealistically high production goals might jeopardize quality and reliability. But when Hitler bluntly rejected that argument, Keitel reverted to his customary servile flattery. The field marshal, therefore, did not take kindly to Becker's insistence, in a conference held in early 1940, that he was unable to comply with an order issued on December 12, 1939, which literally doubled the previous program's figures. Becker pointed out that even if the millions of shells demanded were actually manufactured, Germany's chemical processing plants were then not large enough to supply the explosives to arm them. Keitel, refusing to be the bearer of bad tidings, said nothing of this to Hitler. A month later, when Becker's production figures landed on Hitler's desk, the führer's rage reached apoplectic proportions. Instead of going up, output of the most important weapons had gone down. Incredible! But wait, there was more bad news. Becker's projections showed that the new higher quotas would not be achieved anytime within the foreseeable future.

Barely able to contain his fury, Hitler demanded that something be done immediately. Obviously an expert troubleshooter was needed. Someone suggested Dr. Fritz Todt. Hitler agreed and Todt was summoned. Endowed with excellent credentials, Todt had earned Hitler's respect through his skillful handling of two mammoth construction projects: the network of autobahns that had become the showpiece highways of all Europe and the vast defensive complex facing the French border known as the Siegfried Line, Germany's answer to the Maginot Line. After a quick look at the situation, he recognized that General Becker's tolerance of the martinets in the ordnance office had killed any chance of winning the cooperation of civilian managers. Get the army out of munitions making was the first advice Todt offered to Hitler. Be a partner of industry, not an overlord. To accomplish this, Todt urged the appointment of a civilian minister of armaments. Find someone, he told the führer, who will share planning responsibilities with the steel and chemical industries. After all, he reasoned, who knows their business better than they do? Coming from Todt, this was sound advice, for he had deftly proved the same strategy in expediting the building of the autobahns and the West Wall.

Hitler, impressed with these wise words, saw no need to look elsewhere and promptly named Todt the new minister of armaments and munitions. For Keitel, this surprise appointment was like a slap in the face with a dead fish. Watching Becker founder, Keitel had tried to persuade Hitler to consolidate all armaments under the field marshal's personal jurisdiction. But Hitler, too shrewd to commit such a blunder, rejected Keitel's overtures. While the selection of Todt proved to be a brilliant solution, it must be acknowledged that Todt was also given extraordinary powers—far greater than any conferred upon General Becker. Within a few months, by the summer of 1940, every critical component in Germany's war arsenal was on target or close enough to be tolerated. Todt's breathtaking success in so short a time was a humiliating indictment of Becker's failed leadership. Brooding for weeks, the disgraced former army ordnance chief, no longer able to face his fellow officers, finally locked himself in a room, took an automatic pistol from a desk drawer, and killed himself.

Sitting in his suite moodily contemplating Becker's downfall, Dornberger drained the last drop of schnapps, stood up, and took his dress shirt from a hanger. Becker was gone. Todt was, too. Speer now controlled their destiny. Fumbling with the studs on his shirtfront, he ruefully tried to cope with reality. Like it or not, there was a new Albert Speer. Before becoming chief of armaments, he had been a valued friend of the rocketmakers. When inspector general of construction, he frequently circumvented Hitler's wishes by secretly diverting more scarce resources to Peenemünde than was officially authorized. But after assuming control of all armament production, Speer had refused to be as lenient with allocations. Once, when they were alone, Dornberger confronted Speer on this point.

Speer's response was meant to soothe Dornberger's ruffled feathers: "It's one thing to help you with what resources I have, when I am Inspector General of Construction, carrying no responsibility for the conduct of the war, and quite another to do so as minister responsible for German armaments, with a thorough knowledge of the multiple needs of the armed forces." Considering this a weak excuse, Dornberger suggested that if Speer really believed in them, he would have found some way to continue helping after he became chief of the ministry. Unable to refute Dornberger's logic, Speer admitted that he had changed his mind about rocketry's potential. Defending his switch to an opposing view, he declared: "Is it to be wondered at? Right from the start, I had to listen to the experts. Apart from the Fuehrer's skepticism, it was my own most important colleagues, technicians with great industrial experience, trained in development and production, who always regarded your plans with incredulity and doubt."

Winding a white bow tie around his stiff high wing collar, Dornberger smiled as he thought how quickly Speer and every doubting Thomas at his ministry would change their tune when news of today's success reached them. He swelled with pride thinking about those who would gather around him to celebrate: Wernher von Braun, Arthur Rudolph, Walter Thiel, Klaus Riedel, Hans Heuter, and many more. Eagerly he looked forward to joining them, to raising his glass with theirs in a toast to the magnificent A-4.

26

A Summons to Wolf's Lair

July 7, 1943
Rastenburg, East Prussia

IN THE CABIN of a Heinkel HE-111 transport, with a fog-laden sky engulfing them, General Walter Dornberger and Wernher von Braun flew blindly eastward. Not once had they caught sight of the aircraft's wing tips since lifting off the runway at Peenemünde West. Captain Steinhoff, the young Luftwaffe pilot who regularly flew a fast "chase plane" to pinpoint splashdowns after an A-4 launch, was at the controls. Crouching behind him, a wireless operator anxiously called for weather reports whenever an airfield or observatory came within range of his radio. Every response was the same. Fog blanketed all of Pomerania from the shores of the Baltic deep into the mainland in the south.

As they crossed over the former Polish corridor to Danzig, the fog suddenly dispersed. Sunlight streamed through the windows and, below, the waters of the Vistula shimmered brightly. Ahead lay the black forests and glistening lakes of East Prussia. Rastenburg, their destination, was less than a half hour away. Dornberger was exhilarated and also apprehensive. A telegram from Armaments Minister Albert Speer had ordered his appearance at Wolf's Lair, Adolf Hitler's headquarters, on the afternoon of July 7. Told to bring a film of the successful launch of an A-4 on October 3, 1942, Dornberger, wanting to cover every possible contingency, also brought colored sectional drawings, organization plans, trajectory charts, several wooden models, and Wernher von Braun.

The summons to Rastenburg was another attempt by Hitler to establish priorities that should have been set six weeks earlier. Alarmed by the huge quantities of scarce raw materials consumed by two competing weapons systems at Peenemünde, Hitler directed that a "Long Range Bombardment Commission" designate the one offering the best chance of success. On May 26, 1943, Speer, Luftwaffe Air Marshal Erhard Milch, Navy Grand Admiral Karl Doenitz, Army Colonel General Friedrich Fromm, and a host of high-ranking officials from various ministries met at Peenemünde. The deliberations began with an evaluation of the Fi-103, a jet-driven air torpedo, and von Braun's A-4. Dornberger had overseen early development work on the Fi-103 at Kummersdorf, but in 1940, deciding to work solely on ballistic propulsion through airless space, he transferred the air-breathing jet drive to the Air Ministry, which he felt was better equipped to handle it.

In any competition with the A-4, the Luftwaffe's Fi-103 had impressive advantages. It was much smaller (wing span of slightly over twenty-five feet) and inexpensive to build. It was easy to handle and transport. Compared to the A-4, fuel consumption was low. Unfortunately, however, so was speed—only 350 miles per hour. Worse yet, its air-breathing apparatus limited flights to altitudes below six thousand feet. This was a serious limitation in the eyes of many commission members, who feared that enemy planes and antiaircraft would down many Fi-103s before they could reach a target.

On the other hand, the A-4, once on its way, was unstoppable. Accuracy, too, over long ranges was better. And unlike the Fi-103, which had to be guided initially by a long sloping ramp oriented toward a narrow target sector, the A-4 could be fired in any direction. But there was a high price to pay for this flexibility. A single A-4 cost as much to build as ten Fi-103s. Because both were designed to carry similar one-ton warheads, only two out of ten Fi-103s needed to get through to deliver more explosives than an A-4. Despite his vested interest in ballistic propulsion, Dornberger took the position that "in view of the difference in the two weapons and the tactical conditions of their employment, there would be no point in favoring one at the expense of the other. The disadvantages of the one would be compensated by the other's advantages. But if at last, it is really intended to make practical use of these long-range missiles, there had better be no limit to the strength deployed."

The commission carefully weighed the pros and cons—and did nothing. Like members of any committee charged with the responsibility of a difficult and painful decision, most were motivated more by their own parochial prejudices than a selfless recognition of the common goal. Aside from Dornberger, those with a vested interest in the army's dominance backed the A-4. Air Marshal Erhard

Milch and his retinue, sensing that a capitulation would diminish the Luftwaffe's future influence in rocket matters, lined up behind the Fi-103. Seizing the face-saving option of accepting a tie rather than risking a loss, both sides agreed not to agree. Instead of canceling one or the other, the recommendation drafted for the führer was precisely what he did not want to hear: "Put both types into mass production as soon as possible with top priority and maximum output."

To accomplish so little, one is tempted to ask why it was necessary to summon these busy and important personages to the remote and wooded reaches of the Baltic coast. Certainly the debate could have been conducted, and recommendation drafted, far more conveniently in some ministry's conference hall back in Berlin. The purpose of bringing so many so far was to enable them to witness tests of the Fi-103 and the A-4. Yet these demonstrations were held *after* the commission had already written and signed a report to the führer. Though meaningless, this part of the agenda was a triumph for Dornberger. Two A-4s were fired, flew flawlessly east over the Baltic, and plummeted into the target area 160 miles away. The Fi-103, regrettably, was beset by technical problems. Two were launched but each crashed ignominiously after a brief flight. Before departing, Air Marshal Milch, with nothing to lose, could afford to be magnanimous. Slapping Dornberger on the back, he smiled and said, "Congratulations! Two–nothing in your favor!"

Six weeks to the day after that joshing praise by Milch, Dornberger gripped the edge of his seat as the HE-111 nosed downward on the final approach to the airstrip at Rastenburg. When the transport's wheels touched the ground, Dornberger breathed a sigh of relief. An officer and two enlisted men from the führer's headquarters were waiting as he and von Braun stepped onto the tarmac. The soldiers clambered aboard to retrieve luggage, film, and exhibit materials while the officer escorted them to a waiting staff car. A half hour later, they were driven through the outer gate of Wolf's Lair and then to Hunter's Height, the army guest house. Once inside the attending adjutant informed them that the audience with the führer had been rescheduled. He would not see them until 5:00 P.M. With time to kill, Dornberger rehearsed his standard presentation, the little show he frequently staged at Peenemünde for visiting dignitaries. Satisfied that the timing of each sequence was appropriate for this occasion, Dornberger summoned two orderlies, who packed their paraphernalia into another staff car. Equipped with passes granting admittance to the most sensitive restricted areas, they drove to a clearing surrounded by oak trees, which helped conceal the concrete bunkers and adjacent sheltered structures comprising Hitler's headquarters. Because a film was to be shown, a building near the center of the compound that housed a projection room was the designated meeting place. Dornberger directed the setting up of his exhibits on wooden easels positioned on either side of the projection screen. Wooden models of a firing bunker and various types of transport and support vehicles were arranged on a table nearby. With everything in place, von Braun sat down while Dornberger paced back and forth. They waited. Five o'clock came and went. Another half hour. Then another. Finally, there was a flurry of activity outside. The door flung open and someone shouted, "The führer!" Hitler entered followed closely by Field Marshal Wilhelm Keitel, Generals Walter Buhle and Alfred Jodl, and their personal aides.

Dornberger, who had not seen Hitler since the visit to Kummersdorf four years earlier, was stunned by his appearance—hunched shoulders, pallid face, fatigue slowing his pace. Lack of sunlight and fresh air in the huts and shelters where he now spent his days were obviously taking their toll. While Hitler diffidently offered his hand to Dornberger and von Braun, an aide lifted a huge black cape from his shoulders. Then he sat down in the first row of a tier of theater seats facing the screen. Speer and Keitel took the ones to his right and left, and the others found places in the second and third rows.

Standing behind a lectern, Dornberger offered a few opening remarks and then the room darkened slowly. Von Braun stepped up to the lectern when Dornberger sat down and launched into a rapid-fire commentary as each new sequence flashed on the screen. First, there was awesome footage filmed on October 3, 1942, of the historic ascent of an A-4 rocket from Test Stand Number Seven. Then the great assembly hall's huge doors, nearly a hundred feet high, slowly swung open. Through the portal came an upright A-4 suspended in a huge mobile frame. Static tests. The A-4 was positioned over the concrete water-cooled blast tunnel that curved deep underground. Fire and smoke spewed from its exhaust nozzle. Fine, but could the rocket be moved easily? They watched the Meilerwagen—the custom-designed carrier—maneuver around curves, up steep grades, and, yes, even through the narrow twisting lanes of a mountain village. Next, a launch under field conditions—powerful hydraulic lifts on the Meilerwagen moved an A-4 deftly into place for firing. The camera zoomed in. Flames filled the screen as the A-4 majestically rose from an improvised pad, ascended on a perfect vertical course, and then, when almost out of sight, tilted slightly, beginning its arched trajectory to an intended target.

Von Braun's expert commentary on these scenes was delivered, according to Speer, "without a trace of timidity and with boyish sounding enthusiasm." The combination of breathtaking power displayed on the screen and the fast-paced authoritative description by von Braun appeared to win Hitler's undivided attention. When the film ended, the lights went up, and Dornberger began another discourse on logistics and other organizational matters: equipment and support-personnel needs, the option of firing A-4s from hardened concrete bunkers or from motorized batteries, industrial planning considerations, output figures, delivery dates, and technical training.

While Dornberger was talking, Hitler left his seat and went over to the table on which models of bunkers and transport vehicles were arranged. His eyes darted back and forth repeatedly, first at the replicas, then at Dornberger. Finally the presentation ended. The time for questions was at hand. Hitler, excited by what he had seen and heard, immediately engaged himself in a dialogue with Dornberger and von Braun. Minutes later, when Hitler's questions were directed mostly to von Braun, Dornberger detached himself and drew Speer aside. He reminded the armaments minister that during an earlier visit to Peenemünde Speer had promised to ask Hitler to recognize von Braun with a titular professorship, a high honor conferred only by Germany's head of state. Later, after Hitler had bid Dornberger and von Braun a cordial good-bye, Speer brought up the matter of the professorship. Hitler retorted, "Yes, arrange that at once. . . . I'll even sign the document in person." Then, looking up at Speer, he asked, "Weren't you mistaken? You say this young man is thirty-one? I would have thought him even younger!"

Von Braun's youth captivated Hitler. During the ensuing months, late at night and alone with his confidants, Hitler would frequently refer to this meeting in Wolf's Lair to support a favorite thesis: Most people waste the best years of their lives on accomplishments of no consequence. But rarely, very rarely, a great talent accomplishes much at a young age—Hannibal's early conquests of the Romans, for example, and Napoleon's early seizure of power. And now, in his lifetime, another young genius had reshaped the science of warfare.

27

Hanna Reitsch and the Flying Bomb

August 17/18, 1943
Peenemünde, Germany

Women envied her. She was vivacious, petite, attractive, and a celebrity. Tonight, as in many other places, men flocked to her like moths to a flame. Coquettishly flashing a smile at the circle of worshiping faces, Hanna Reitsch raised a glass to her lips. The champagne she sipped was the choicest served in the officers' mess. Because all places around her in the salon were occupied, several admirers stood behind their more fortunate comrades, savoring brandy and enjoying the repartee.

Famous throughout Germany, Hanna basked in the adoration of those now favored by her presence. Whether combat pilots or rocket builders, all maintained that her adventurous spirit made her one of them. Slightly more than a decade earlier, while still in her teens, she had startled glider instructors in her native province of Silesia by advancing faster than the young men in her class. Not long after, her considerable natural skill enabled her to breach the "male only" entrance rule for the prestigious Civil Airways Training School.

In 1937, she was selected to join the Luftwaffe's cadre of test pilots. Rising to an honored place in that elite group, she flew all types of fighters, bombers, seaplanes, and helicopters. Difficult and dangerous assignments were her specialty, prompting her selection, in 1942, to test the skittish, experimental Me-163B rocket plane. On one fateful flight, coming in for a landing, she crashed, suffering multiple skull fractures. While rescuers worked feverishly to free her from the wreckage, she stubbornly refused to lose consciousness until vital data was recorded in her notepad "so that the flight might not have been in vain." For that feat, after recovering from her injuries, she was summoned to a personal audience with the führer, who awarded her the Iron Cross First Class.

Hanna Reitsch was on temporary assignment to Peenemünde West to help the Luftwaffe unravel another knotty problem. Having won the approval of Armaments Minister Albert Speer to begin production of the Fi-103 "flying bomb," Air Marshal Erhard Milch was nevertheless frustrated by its sorry performance. Test flights were ending in an alarmingly high rate of failures. Only six out of ten launches achieved a cruising altitude of four thousand feet at speeds approaching four hundred miles per hour. After Hanna and seven other pilots were ordered to uncover the cause of the malfunctions, dozens of the flying bombs were refitted with small cockpits to accommodate the human observers. Then, suspended from the wing of a large aircraft, the Fi-103 would be released at a safe height, enabling Hanna and other fliers on the team to monitor aerodynamic stress and strain.

The hazards encountered during these flights did not faze Hanna, who was now enjoying a pleasant respite at day's end in the salon of the officers' mess. Nor did the rumble of distant aircraft coupled with the wail of sirens. Such sounds were commonplace as Allied bombers regularly came in over the Baltic and then flew south toward targets in central Germany. Mindful that all good times inevitably come to an end, Hanna reluctantly informed her companions that she had to leave to prepare for an early-morning test flight. Wernher von Braun escorted her to a car that was directed to take her back to her billet in Peenemünde West. Then he made his way on foot to the men's bachelor quarters, where he had a small apartment.

To night revelers remaining in the salon of the officers' club, the rumble of distant engines grew louder, suggesting that Royal Air Force night bombers were closer than usual. Yet the carefree mood prevailed even when lights flickered and glasses vibrated on tabletops. The banter and laughter were silenced, however, by a rapid series of explosions. Immediately everyone jumped up, rushed out of the building, and ran toward a large underground bunker, soon filled to capacity with nearly three hundred people. Included in the throng were Wernher von Braun and General Walter Dornberger.

Until he reached the courtyard outside his living quarters, von Braun assumed that the bombers were on their way to Berlin. But he quickly changed his mind when he saw a bright flash directly overhead. Then the sky came alive with target marker flares dropped by the lead "pathfinder" aircraft. Guns on the roofs of nearby buildings and in sandbagged entrenchments along the roadway opened up a rapid-fire barrage. Von Braun turned back and hurried to the shelter, where he encountered a grim-faced Dornberger, clad in tunic, trousers, and bedroom slippers.

Jolted awake by the pounding of antiaircraft guns, Dornberger had dressed hastily—his orderly had removed his shoes for polishing after he went to bed. He and von Braun huddled on a bench as bombs crashed above them for nearly an hour. Finally, the explosions diminished, then ceased, and the roar of engines overhead receded into the distance. The eerie wail of sirens signaled the all clear and everyone groped his way outside. A glow from flaming buildings and the light of a full moon illuminated the entire area.

Dornberger and von Braun ran several hundred meters to their headquarters office building. It had sustained severe damage and, like most others in the area, was burning. Drawing closer and peering through the main entrance, they could see that the stairway to the second floor, where important records and plans were kept, was still intact. Pressing against walls of the stairwell to minimize pressure on the weakened risers, Dornberger, accompanied by von Braun and a few others, climbed the single flight and retrieved the most vital documents. Back outside, after several hazardous forays up and down the stairway, Dornberger called to a lone soldier passing by and ordered him to guard the rescued stacks of papers until transport could be found to haul them away. Then, before rushing off to organize fire-fighting efforts, he told von Braun to meet him at the airfield at daybreak.

At dawn, Dornberger requisitioned a Storch observation plane. With von Braun at the controls, they started to reconnoiter the northern sector of Usedom Island. It soon became apparent that the Luftwaffe installation in Peenemünde West had not been the previous night's objective. No bombs had fallen on the airfield, hangars, or any buildings in the area. The launching site for the Fi-103 flying bombs on the western tip of the island was also undamaged. Their suspicions were now confirmed. The full force of the raid had been directed at the army's Peenemünde East. Flying toward the sun, slowly rising out of the sea, they soon reached the large and imposing launch site on the eastern shore of the island. Test Stand Number Seven, from which rockets in the A-4 series were being successfully launched with increasing frequency, was quiet in the early-morning light. But the launchpad and the high revetment surrounding it were pockmarked with a dozen bomb craters, and a large section of the roof of an adjacent hangar was burned through, exposing the steel support girders. After telling von Braun to circle the area a second time, Dornberger directed him to fly south along the shoreline.

Reaching the development works a minute or so later, Dornberger began counting the damaged buildings. Of the eighty structures there, over fifty had been struck by bombs and incendiaries. He drew some comfort in noting that the two large assembly halls appeared to have sustained minimal damage and the vitally important measurements building as well as the liquid-oxygen plant had come through the attack practically unscathed. Neither the foreign-labor camp nor the living quarters for German technical personnel and their families had fared as well. Eighteen of the thirty huts in the labor camp had been leveled and there was nothing to count in the civilian housing area. It was totally devastated. Dr. Walter Thiel, occupant of one of the residences, had told Dornberger a few weeks earlier that "never again" would he be separated from his family. That remark, prompted by Thiel's long-awaited success in arranging their move from Berlin, had been prophetic. For shortly after the bombers headed back for England and Dornberger began assessing damage, he learned that Thiel, his wife, and children were among the 735 casualties of the raid.

Reaching forward in the two-seater Storch, Dornberger tapped von Braun's shoulder and shouted above the engine noise that he had seen enough. It was time to go back. Von Braun steered in a northwesterly direction, and ten minutes later they were bouncing along the runway at Peenemünde West. Because no bombs had fallen there, it was business as usual at the airfield. Mechanics were servicing the engines of several Heinkel HE-111s drawn up on the tarmac, and an Fi-103 flying bomb was being fitted to the undercarriage of one of them. As she had been the previous evening, Hanna Reitsch was again the center of attention. A small group of pilots and ground personnel gathered around her were reviewing procedures for a test she was about to conduct. Once satisfied that she thoroughly understood the plan, Hanna strolled over to an Me-163B fighter while pulling on a leather flying helmet. Then she climbed up on the wing and slid her small frame into the cockpit. Hanna had volunteered to fly another model of the infamous rocket-powered plane despite her brush with death a year earlier. Fortunately this was not a repetition of the previous disaster for which she had been awarded one of Germany's highest decorations for valor. She executed all of the required maneuvers inside her reserved air sector over the Baltic and then, when the rocket flamed out, glided back for a perfect landing.

The rocket plane nevertheless remained a sideline for Hanna because Air Marshal Milch's growing embarrassment over the Luftwaffe's main bid for a presence in rocketry kept the Fi-103 on the front burner. The continuing poor performance prompted a call for a new series of tests with human observers aboard. During the ensuing weeks, she personally guided ten more flights of the pulse-jet-powered craft and became the only member of her team to finish the assignment unscathed. By the time the tests were ended in late October, two of the seven other test pilots had been killed and five seriously injured.

28

A Puzzle to Ponder

November 1944
Farnborough, England

FOR THE TWO Americans, this was a rare experience. Three challenges by British sentries in less than ten minutes. The first encounter was at the main gate of the Royal Aircraft Establishment. The second occurred as their staff car entered a high-fenced enclosure, and the final one barred access to a door at the end of a corridor in a darkened warehouse.

Frank Malina and his escort, U.S. Army Captain C. E. Martinson, waited patiently for a Royal Air Force officer to study their papers while the third sentry to stop them directed a flashlight over his superior's shoulder. After checking their names against a list on a clipboard, the officer turned and opened the door behind him. Malina and Martinson entered a large windowless expanse, lit dimly by a few bare incandescent bulbs hanging from the ceiling. On the floor before them were the remains of the eighty-ninth test rocket in Peenemünde's A-4 series. Nozzles, pumps, valves, and control elements were arrayed on wires and wood supports to simulate their probable positions inside vehicle 89 before it had disintegrated over Sweden five months earlier.

Two hours before noon on that fateful day, the rocket had stood majestically on a launchpad at Peenemünde East. Working high on an adjacent gantry, Ernst Steinhoff and two assistants had methodically checked voltages of each component in an experimental radio guidance system developed for use in a new antiaircraft missile. In this first airborne test, Steinhoff planned to evaluate responses to directional signals transmitted from a ground observation station. Although tail vanes responded accurately to commands radioed from remote vantage points while the rocket was sitting on the pad, no one knew whether spewing engine gases might distort communications in

flight. Finally satisfied that everything was in order, Steinhoff watched technicians bolt the hatch in place, then ordered the gantry removed.

A half hour later, Steinhoff joined the ground controller in an
observation post near the airfield at Peenemünde West. As vehicle 89
rose above the pine forest surrounding the launch site a couple of
miles away, Steinhoff, watching through binoculars, ordered the
controller to take over. A moment later, the rocket disappeared into a
small cloud. Unable to regain sight of it, the controller panicked and
instead of moving the control stick to the right for a few seconds and
then to the left, according to plan, did precisely the opposite.
Steinhoff, aghast, shouted, "You transmitted the commands with the
wrong sign!" There was no way to undo what had been done. Their
only salvation would be if, somehow, vehicle 89 fell harmlessly into
the sea. Hoping to confirm that remote possibility visibly, Steinhoff
commandeered an Me-109, took off, and flew away on a northeast
heading. Meanwhile, radar tracking data filtered in to the command
center at Peenemünde East. The reports were ominous. The rocket
had veered toward the Scandinavian mainland, but then the blip had
disappeared near the Swedish coast. Alarmed, the tracking officer
notified General Dornberger, who, after learning that Steinhoff was
in the air somewhere over the Baltic, rushed to a communications
post. Once contact was established via radio, Dornberger blurted,
"Steinhoff! Did you fire into Sweden?" For a few seconds, only the
crackle of static emanated from the earphones on Dornberger's head.
Then came Steinhoff's plaintive reply: "I must have."

Steinhoff was guessing, but he was right. A crater, five feet deep
and fifteen feet in diameter, scarring a field in southern Sweden,
corroborated Steinhoff's assumption. There was also physical evidence. Nearly two tons of fragments were gathered up by the Swedish authorities. The German ambassador dutifully conveyed an apolo-
gy while the British Air Ministry applied all of the diplomatic clout it
could muster to gain possession of the debris. Despite the declared
neutrality of Sweden, requiring internment of combatants and con-
fiscation of war matériel, the British were remarkably successful.
Vehicle 89 had violated Sweden's airspace on the morning of June 13,
1944, an intrusion that clearly warranted impoundment for the duration of hostilities. Yet by mid-July the recovered parts were on display
in a security-tight warehouse at Farnborough.

For the team of experts trying to rebuild the rocket, the four months of analysis preceding Malina's arrival on the scene had not been unlike assembling a three-dimensional jigsaw puzzle, rendered more baffling by an unknown number of missing pieces. Although placement of most components was guesswork, rather than the product of logical deduction, helpful hints were at hand. The United States Navy contributed data acquired in some of Goddard's experiments and access was also provided to various reports written by von Karman's group at Caltech. American aid, however, was not limited to documents. Thomas F. Dixon, a former production expediter for U.S. Navy solid-propellant rocket launchers, had been sent over to help. Dixon and his British hosts came to a significant conclusion early in their study. Limited ventilation within the warehouse left no doubt that many of the parts were saturated with a common industrial chemical. The assault on their olfactory senses was irrefutable. The Germans were using alcohol to power the A-4.

Additional conclusions were by no means as easy to reach. First there was the tedious process of trying to fit each piece in its proper place. Much debate usually preceded a consensus that qualified a fragment to be moved from the warehouse floor to the wire and wood supports. As weeks went by and unidentified components dwindled to a precious few, there was sufficient visible evidence to venture some educated guesses. The diameter of the rocket was estimated to be between five and six feet (straddling the actual five feet four inches). Distance from nose to tail was believed to be anywhere from thirty-five to forty-five feet (true length was forty-six and three-quarter feet). Weight, without fuel, was put between five and seven tons (reasonably near the actual four-plus tons). Other estimates were further off the mark. Propellant weight was thought to exceed twenty tons, more than twice the nine tons customarily loaded at Peenemünde. And imaginations wandered even further when confronting the question of explosive power. More conservative members of the team asserted that the rocket accommodated a warhead no larger than six tons while some claimed it ranged as high as eight. Had Dr. Joseph Paul Goebbels been privy to those figures, he might well have rubbed his palms with glee. Dedicated to instilling fear in the hearts of Germany's enemies, Hitler's propaganda chief would have been gladdened to know the British believed the A-4 delivered eight times the destructive power of the actual one ton of explosives.

A greater need for deception, however, faced Goebbels on the home front. During the summer of 1944, a daily average of three thousand tons of Allied bombs were falling on Germany and the Axis-occupied territories. The suffering populace, devoid of hope, was crying out for relief. Goebbels responded with macabre optimism. In a speech broadcast on July 20, he stridently predicted: "The war is about to change in a manner that will make our enemies choke on their own shouts of triumph." A month earlier, the first of thousands of Fi-103 flying bombs to eventually fall on London, Antwerp, and other Allied marshaling points, sputtered into the sky toward England. To Goebbels, the prosaic engineering identity, Fi-103, was a shameful waste of a valuable propaganda asset and so he decreed that this vanguard of the long-awaited "retaliation weapons" would be known henceforth as *Vergetlungswaffe-Eins*, the V-1. Similarly, when the A-4 was first launched against London on September 8, 1944, Goebbels's Propaganda Ministry jubilantly announced the addition of the "V-2" to Germany's arsenal.

By the time Malina viewed the V-2 debris at Farnborough, Air Marshal Erhard Milch's V-1 was virtually obsolete. The capture of channel-coast launch sites by Allied armies reduced the Luftwaffe to the awkward expedient of lashing a few V-1s to the wings of bombers that flew them within range of London under cover of darkness. Now that the number of these pulse-jet-propelled craft to reach England was severely curtailed, they became more nuisance than menace. As long as the familiar *pop-pop* sound was audible overhead, savvy Londoners went quietly about their business. Only when the onboard timer silenced the engine, and the loss of power enabled gravity's pull to take over and force the plunge to earth, did those within earshot scurry for cover.

The V-2, on the other hand, silently hurtling from the stratosphere, fulfilled its potential for destruction before anyone knew there was an imminent threat to life and property. Faced with the choice of living permanently in shelters or blithely ignoring the danger, most of the British populace adopted a fatalistic disdain for the V-2. Evidence of this determination to ignore blows against which no defense could be mounted was brought home to Malina during a subsequent visit to Fort Halstead, a center for British armaments research. Seated at a conference table with several ordnance experts during a meeting with J. E. Lennard-Jones, the chief superintendent, Malina was jolted from his chair by a tremendous explosion nearby. Rushing outside, he and the others encountered a cloud of dust rising from a huge crater, which, considering the absence of aircraft overhead, they quickly deduced had been gouged in the earth by a V-2. Malina later recalled that the experience "left me rather disturbed, but my colleagues continued the meeting as though nothing had happened."

A few days later, Malina and his escort, Captain Martinson, boarded a C-47 transport bound for Paris. In France they were met by two American ordnance officers, who during the ensuing week guided them on a tour of V-1 launching sites at Mizerne, Montreuil, and Sivacourt. The long narrow ramps, resembling mountain ski jumps, were obviously difficult targets and consequently had sustained minimal damage from Allied bombing raids. Malina, however, observed that the adjacent villages "were a shambles." After a sumptuous turkey dinner on Thanksgiving Day at the Hotel Plaza Athénée in Paris, he and Martinson returned to London. In mid-December, his mission completed, Malina climbed aboard a transport for the long flight to Boston. Reviewing his notes as the aircraft bounced through the buffeting winds of the North Atlantic, he found that he had conferred with eighty-two scientists and engineers on a diverse array of subjects. Liquid-fuel engines. Antiaircraft rocket missiles. Ramjet development. Hydrogen peroxide and nitromethane propellants. And, of course, numerous debates on the esoteric functions of various puzzling V-2 components. As the C-47 began to descend for refueling at Reykjavík, he suddenly realized that the objective set back in 1936—launching of a high-altitude sounding rocket—was now within reach. The means and the know-how were ripe for exploitation.

The prospect of lofting a package of sensitive measuring instruments high into the stratosphere monopolized Malina's waking hours during the remainder of his journey. After arriving in Union Station in Washington, D.C., two days later, he located a shuttle bus that took him across the Potomac to the Pentagon. Following a brief wait, he was escorted into the office of Colonel G. W. Trichel. Trichel, who was chief of the rocket development branch of army ordnance, listened attentively as Malina gave an oral summary of the report he planned to write covering the many meetings and interviews conducted during the previous eight weeks. When finished, he paused, took a deep breath, and began an impassioned pitch to win Trichel's backing for the development of a sounding rocket. Explaining that a small program could be mounted easily, Malina proposed a modest goal: lift a payload of approximately twenty-five pounds to an altitude of 100,000 feet.

With other more relevant priorities to address, the colonel was about to terminate the discussion when a remark by Malina recaptured his attention. Aware that ideas sell best when they appear to satisfy an existing need, Malina hinted that experience gained in launching a high-flying sounding rocket would be a valuable first step in furthering a major ordnance objective—the development of an antiaircraft guided missile. Trichel, snapping up the bait, asked Malina to prepare a written proposal. Malina smilingly agreed, shook Trichel's hand, and started back to Pasadena.

29

A Very Private Man

June 1945
Annapolis, Maryland

A PEACEFUL, EARLY-EVENING stillness settled over Tydings-on-the-Bay. Although only eight miles from the bustling activity in Maryland's state capital, the residence occupied by Dr. and Mrs. Robert H. Goddard was as distant from worldy cares as a remote island paradise. Perched on a bluff overlooking the Chesapeake, the house offered a panoramic view of the bay through broad windows in an expansive pine-paneled living room. Sitting there alone, Goddard watched light from the setting sun tint the sails of a fishing ketch sailing south toward the open sea. A bell buoy clanged in the gentle swells of the incoming tide and a pinpoint of brightness shot out of the dusk on the distant eastern shore. Now another beam farther down the coast was visible as more lighthouses along this seaway turned on their beacons to guide ships plying their way between Baltimore and the Atlantic.

While his senses drank in the sights and soft sounds of this quiet June evening, Goddard tried to ignore the irritation in his throat. The discomfort was chronic, prompting frequent visits to the office of Dr. Harry Slack, a Baltimore specialist. Two years earlier, Dr. Slack had advised Goddard to give his throat a complete rest by not using his voice. That respite provided some relief but was by no means a permanent cure. Everything prescribed after subsequent examinations worked for a time, yet the old soreness persisted. Upon his return from the most recent visit to Dr. Slack's office on May 16, 1945, Goddard had scrupulously followed the physician's instructions: "Get a complete rest and sit in the sun as much as possible." This was easy to do because his machine shop was closed for a two-week vacation. Every day he sunbathed in the mornings and napped in the afternoons. Yet tonight was a repetition of the familiar pattern. The pain had eased off at first, but now it was back.

Preparations for the future, however, could not be put off. Goddard's tenure as a director of aeronautical research for the navy was drawing to a close and he was soon to leave government service to work in private industry. The initial contact with his prospective new employer, the Curtiss-Wright Corporation, had been made three years earlier. Convinced that the future of aviation lay with jet propulsion, M. B. Bleeker, an executive in the Caldwell, New Jersey, plant, had urged the purchase of many Goddard patents as well as enlisting his expertise. Neither the Navy Bureau of Aeronautics nor Harry Guggenheim, who as a major supplier of funds for much of the early research could register a veto, voiced any objection to an involvement with Curtiss-Wright. At first, Goddard was authorized to work as a consultant "for a maximum of ten days per month," provided the affiliation did not conflict with navy interests. But that restriction had been lifted early in 1945. With navy experiments winding down and ties with Curtiss-Wright growing stronger, he was invited to move operations to Caldwell beginning July 1.

Adjusting to the customs of corporate life was difficult for Goddard. His academic and scientific background left him unprepared to cope with even the basic tenets of business practice. In June 1944, he had gone to Caldwell for a meeting with Robert L. Earle, a Curtiss-Wright vice-president. Back in Annapolis several days later, he mailed an expense report. Amazed by the small outlay for sustenance throughout the trip, Earle replied: "Upon seeing how much you spent for meals, I greatly wonder how you exist on so little food." Goddard responded that his sparse diet was more the consequence of timetables than voluntary fasting: "There is nothing more conducive to skipping meals than train delays which require changes to be made in a matter of seconds." Goddard added, however, that he resolved to remedy his tendency to ask for too little: "Being a professor for a number of years has [kept me] a novice in the technique of making out expense accounts. I will see to it that this fault is corrected in the future."

Goddard's move from pristine scientific research to the commercial sector was overdue if he expected practical benefits to accrue from his years of immersion in theory and experimentation. Others in similar situations were graced with a better sense of timing and had bridged the gap nicely. Von Karman, for example, formed the Aerojet Engineering Corporation with Malina and three other students, successfully applying the fruits of their combined research in the production of solid-fuel JATO boosters for army and navy aircraft. And a group of rocket enthusiasts in New Jersey started Reaction Motors, Inc., which was dedicated solely to the commercial development of jet propulsion systems.

Goddard's indecisiveness in this matter was not due to a lack of interest. Three years earlier he had flirted with the prospect of becoming a business partner of Curtiss-Wright. In a letter to Harry Guggenheim on August 7, 1942, he offered the opinion that "an arrangement with the Curtiss-Wright people might solve a number of problems . . . turning parts over to them to manufacture during the war [would enable them] to carry out work on my developments afterwards." He also saw advantages in having a large company to protect his interests "before the end of hostilities [rather than] wait until the war was over and then look around for someone interested in the patents."

The laissez-faire attitudes of businessmen were another lure, too. Being under contract to the government severely curbed his freedom to speak out as a private citizen. Theodore Adams, producer of the CBS network radio show "We the People," tried to persuade Goddard to talk on the program in the summer of 1944 when V-weapons were raining down on London. Stroking Goddard's ego, Adams wrote: "Because you are unquestionably the widest-known of all men in America who have given long study to this subject . . . comment from you on the use of self-propelled rockets, past, present and future would be of the utmost interest to our wide American audience." Goddard expressed appreciation for the invitation but declined: "I am considerably handicapped in discussing [rockets], particularly the present status because so much is in the confidential category. I [may] take the matter up with you at a later time when I am no longer working for the Government."

For Goddard, the banning of public comments on rocketry was intensely frustrating because he had attained several significant goals ahead of the Germans. He had kept correspondence confirming that Hermann Oberth had requested and received a copy of his 1919 monograph, "A Method for Reaching Extreme Altitudes," a year earlier than Oberth's own doctoral thesis, *By Rocket to Interplanetary Space*, was published in 1923. Washington patent attorney Henry C. Parker also discovered that Goddard had documented many developments in rocket propulsion long before the early experiments at

Kummersdorf. Referring to a U.S. patent awarded November 23, 1934, Parker noted Goddard's obvious prior rights in a letter written March 1, 1945: "[I am], to say the least, rather astounded to see that the Nazis had apparently copied the ideas in your No. 1,980,266 in their [V-1] rocket bomb."

Not only the V-1. The V-2 as well. Further digging revealed that more Goddard patents described features later incorporated in that deadly product of Peenemünde East. This claim was easy to substantiate because Goddard had access to a cache of V-2 parts captured in France and sent to Annapolis for study by the Navy Bureau of Aeronautics. Two patents, issued in July 1914, anticipated the V-2's use of pumps for supplying fuel to the rocket chamber; a power plant for driving the pumps; separate tanks for liquid fuel and an oxidizer; and nozzles to ensure the even distribution of propellant within the rocket chamber. Patents granted in September 1932 describing other features later found in the V-2 included a jacket for cooling combustion chambers; a pilot gyro; and chamber-wall perforations to help position the hottest flame in its center. Although Goddard was restrained from speaking out about these "firsts" on his own behalf, he found a dedicated champion in the person of G. Edward Pendray.

Ten years earlier, when helping to engineer Willy Ley's emigration from Germany, Pendray had been science editor of the prestigious *Literary Digest*. In the fall of 1936, however, that widely circulated national weekly's credibility was destroyed by a colossal blunder. Its publisher and editorial board heavily promoted their sponsorship of a poll predicting a landslide victory by Republican candidate Alfred M. Landon over incumbent President Franklin D. Roosevelt. In the subsequent election, Landon was swept into the forgotton ranks of also-rans by a ten-million-vote Roosevelt plurality. Watching circulation dwindle and advertising revenues plunge in the wake of that debacle, Pendray read the handwriting on the wall and, before the *Digest* eventually folded, moved on. Following the lead of Ivy Ledbetter Lee, the prosperous adviser of the great and near great, Pendray turned his back on journalism to be a public-relations aide to the president of Westinghouse Electric Corporation. In his eight years of service there, he masterminded many publicity successes, including sponsorship of the time capsule at the 1939 New York World's Fair and organization of the annual national Westinghouse Talent Search.

Pendray had earned Goddard's heartfelt gratitude for a vigorous response to a humiliating putdown in the pages of *Time*. On July 31, 1944, the newsmagazine's science section reported: "Astronauts, people who dream of traveling through instellar space, have been sleeping dreamlessly since the war began. . . . But by last week many enthusiasts were stirring in their sleep and dreaming again of the interplanetary take-off." Backing up this premise was a statement by Harry Harper of the combined British Aeronautical Societies boasting that members of his group—competent chemists, physicists, and aeronautical engineers—were well along in their plans to launch experimental rockets sixty miles into space. The next expert to be quoted was Willy Ley, whose new book, *Rockets*, contained much to boggle a reader's mind. A few titillating tidbits were reported. Speed required to escape Earth's gravity: seven miles per second. Best fuel: liquid oxygen and alcohol. Minimum length of craft for round-trip to moon: one third the height of New York City's Empire State Building. And so on. Impressed by seers who talked "in fairly low voices without breathing hard," *Time* then offered a startling conclusion: "With the impregnable calm common to astronauts, [Ley] observed: 'The idea of space travel has by now reached a rather high state of perfection.' "

For Goddard, however, there was only faint praise: "No astronaut, Professor Goddard has restricted his aim to rather low altitudes." Bridling at the implication that Goddard was "no astronaut," Pendray fired off a protest to the editor: "Your reporter evidently has not read Goddard's classical report on rockets published in 1919 by the Smithsonian Institution. This is the monograph that reopened rocket experimentation and really started the modern era of rocket research." Pendray then claimed that Goddard's brilliant theoretical analyses clearly qualified him for better treatment: "Goddard was not only an 'astronaut,' as you call them, but actually started the whole modern cycle of astronautics. He is the spiritual father [of all rocket experiments] in the 20s and 30s, though Ley gives him scant treatment in his book."

Goddard later confided to Pendray that "the Ley book tried my patience." Yet Goddard failed to recognize that his displeasure was largely the consequence of his own secretiveness. Journalists such as Ley, who was then a science writer for *PM*, an ultraliberal New York evening newspaper, were kept at arm's length. To Ley, the man was an enigma. *Time* echoed that assessment: "Because Goddard has published little on his findings and has experimented mostly in the privacy of a New Mexican desert, fellow rocketeers consider him a 'mystery man.' "

Gazing through the windows of the house at Tydings-on-the-Bay, Goddard brooded over his present circumstances. The world was passing him by. During his four years with the navy, he believed that he had accomplished much, but no word of those accomplishments was permitted to pierce the veil of secrecy. True, his imminent move into the commercial sector would soon offer opportunities for public and professional recognition. Others, however, were ahead of him. He was just another face in the crowd, no longer a pioneer in unexplored territory. Then there was his health. For much of his life he had managed to cope with periodic lung problems, but the irritation in his throat was another matter.

While refusing to yield to the pain, a severe choking spell later in the evening persuaded him that another trip to Baltimore was inevitable. The next day, June 15, he sat in an examining room while Dr. Slack, standing next to a bright light, peered into his throat. Seeing that the condition had passed beyond the realm of passive treatment, the specialist immediately arranged for his patient to visit Dr. Edwin Looper, a surgeon on the staff of the University of Maryland Hospital. Looper confirmed the presence of a growth, and four days later, it was removed. Acting on the assumption that the procedure would not seriously delay his plans to join Curtiss-Wright, Goddard went ahead with arrangements to move machinery in his Annapolis workshop to the company's New Jersey plant. Writing to one of the executives there two days before the operation, Goddard estimated that he "shall be hospitalized for a week, and out of the running for three or four weeks more." The anticipated one-week hospital stay stretched into two, three, then four. In late July, his condition worsened, and on the morning of August 10, he died.

Goddard's legacy to rocketry, barely acknowledged at the time of his death, blossomed in the ensuing years. His work on liquid-propellant-assisted takeoff devices, though important, was later eclipsed by descendents of his successful variable-thrust motors, also developed during his navy research. Using those designs as a model, Curtiss-Wright built the celebrated XLR25-CW-1 15,000-pound-thrust throttleable rocket engine that subsequently powered the record-setting Bell X-2 research aircraft. Patents issued in his name uncannily mirror the increased esteem accorded his work in later years. Less than one quarter of the Goddard patents were validated in his lifetime. Those original forty-eight were supplemented by thirty-five more awarded after his death. However, an additional 131 applications were submitted to the Patent Office by Esther C. Goddard, his widow and executrix, which she based on notes, sketches, and photos left in his papers. All were granted, raising the number of patents in his name to a total of 214.

PART THREE

The Adversaries

30

Just a Few Good Men

August 1945
Frankfurt am Main, Germany

AFTER SALUTING SMARTLY, the corporal swung the duffel bag over his shoulder and asked the American officer to follow him. Colonel Holger N. Toftoy kept his eyes fixed on the back of the young soldier as he weaved through the crowd in the air base terminal building, carrying all the gear that Toftoy had brought with him. Exuberant men in uniform were everywhere. Yet Toftoy felt strangely apart. While the shooting war in Europe was over and soon to end in the Pacific, he knew that his own most worrisome challenges still lay ahead.

Nothing in his military experience had equipped him for this assignment. Orders in his breast pocket directed him to proceed immediately to the European Theater of Operations "to select and recruit approximately one hundred German scientists and engineers to conduct rocket experiments in the United States." As the corporal stowed the duffel in the trunk of a staff car parked at the curb, Toftoy climbed in the rear door. Settling back on the seat, he recalled that in the past, thinking through a problem and carefully evaluating each option usually had produced a successful plan of action. But this situation was different. There were too many loose ends, too many forces over which he exercised no control. Was he to be checkmated before making his first move? Were the most important prospects hopelessly out of reach? A news story in the August 1 issue of *Stars and Stripes*, the army newspaper, seemed to confirm that gloomy possibility: "Consistent reports coming from Peenemünde (scene of Hitler's buzz and rocket bomb experiments, captured by the Russians) indicated that just before the Red Army moved in, a German submarine evacuated key scientists."

While Toftoy knew little about his mission, one man who should have known more knew nothing. Brigadier General T. J. Betts, U.S. Army Director of Intelligence in Germany, was in a foul mood. A request by his chief, General Lucius D. Clay, the military governor, to explain a reference to "Project Overcoat" in a message from Washington caught Betts far off base. Urgent calls to officials in the U.S. Control Group Council and staff members at headquarters of United States forces in the European Theater elicited no clues. Betts was furious. How was he to monitor what was going on in Germany if kept in the dark about sensitive American operations within his jurisdiction?

Toftoy's arrival cleared the air. The first thing he set straight was the project's identity. It was not "Overcoat." The correct code name was "Overcast." Betts, in turn, was able to ease Toftoy's anxiety. "Forget that nonsense about the German submarine," Betts said reassuringly. "We have the key people, including the kingpin of them all, Wernher von Braun." Toftoy's spirits soared as Betts told him that von Braun had been cooperative and was anxious to work for the Americans. Von Braun had even compiled a list of the most competent people involved in rocket development. Toftoy could hardly believe his ears. What he had feared to be a maddeningly frustrating scavenger hunt had turned into a piece of cake.

Yet Betts was not candid in implying that the most important German rocketmakers were in his custody. True, he had von Braun. But the British had taken the most valuable members of the entourage with him in the flight from the advancing Soviet army. Two months earlier, on June 7, 1945, the combined Allied chiefs of staff had sanctioned an elaborate field study of German rocket development. Known as Operation Backfire, the linchpin of the exercise was to be the firing of many captured V-2s. Operational responsibility for Backfire went to the British War Office in London, which lost no time in ordering the roundup of all German rocketmakers, including eighty-five dragooned from the American zone of occupation.

By the time Toftoy landed in Frankfurt, over two hundred experienced V-2 personnel were in British hands. Overcast was in jeopardy because America's ally had most of the key players. Although lacking the clout to face down the Allied chiefs of staff, Toftoy had some powerful ammunition of his own—an agreement negotiated by U.S. General of the Army George C. Marshall. While the "Backfire" plan was being moved up the chain of command,

Marshall wrote to British Field Marshal H. Maitland Wilson asking if the British chiefs of staff "favored a U.S. proposal to bring German civilian scientists and technicians to the United States for the purpose of exploiting their knowledge . . . in the development of weapons which could be used against the Japanese." In June 1945, this was a persuasive argument. The war in Europe had ended. But until the explosion of the first atomic bomb at Alamogordo, New Mexico, in mid-July, the assault against Japan was expected to be long and to exact a high cost in dead and wounded. Wilson answered Marshall's letter on June 14, 1945, agreeing to Marshall's proposal and asking that "the knowledge so obtained . . . be made available to [the British chiefs of staff] as well as to the interested United States agencies."

Although eighty-five members of von Braun's team had been taken from the United States zone, Toftoy, endeavoring to make the Marshall–Wilson accord more palatable, submitted a request for the return of only twenty-six. The British ordnance officers controlling Backfire responded with a counterproposal. They offered the release of fourteen. Toftoy, who had pared his list down to a critical minimum, adamantly insisted that he must have all he asked for. Brigadier General Betts brought the impasse to the attention of General Clay, who angrily informed the United States chiefs of staff. With the characteristic restraint common to all controversial communications dispatched to its British ally, the American high command reported that it had been advised "that a question has arisen as to the assignment of certain German scientists and technicians desired for both Operation 'Backfire' and Project 'Overcast.' " Gently pointing out that two hundred German personnel were being held by the British for Backfire and that eighty-five of them had been obtained from the United States zone, the message went on to observe that "in the interests of cooperation only twenty-six specially qualified German scientists were requested to be returned to U.S. control for 'Overcast' [but] the British officers [overseeing] 'Backfire' have declined to return twelve of these scientists."

In an attempt to justify their call for the release of the contested twelve, the message then intimated that American objectives were considerably more advanced than those sought by the British: "These twelve men [are] essential for 'Overcast' which requires [participation] of key experts in all phases of research and development. 'Backfire,' on the other hand, is limited to the assembly and launching of V-2 rockets." With von Braun's guidance, Toftoy had provided the names of possible alternates, also in the hands of the British, who were more than qualified to perform the relatively low-level tasks required in Backfire.

Instead of Kurt Debus, the exterior ballistician, von Braun proposed that the British use a man named Graetz, the chief engineer and technical adviser of the former southern V-2 launching division, or his assistants: Kox, Knoethe, and Krueger. Replace Arthur Rudolph, the seasoned project leader who supervised assembly of V-2s, with Dr. Kuchen, who had directed operations at Peenemünde's largest static firing stand. For test engineer Heimberg, substitute Huttenberger, who had amassed as much experience in that specialty as Heimberg.

In two cases, von Braun suggested that the British release the men he wanted by replacing them with their former superiors. He told Toftoy, in asking for Wilhelm Hintze, to recommend that his duties be assumed by Professor Wiener, who had been Hintze's boss and chief electrical engineer at Peenemünde. He also asked to have Kirchstein direct "Backfire" radio and control operations and to have Nuhlner, Kirchstein's former assistant, be released. Because the special skills of two other men whom von Braun valued highly—Gerhard Heller, a research chemist, and Hans Palaoro, a rocket-motor designer—were of no use to Backfire, no substitutes were suggested for them. Alternates with identical experience, however, were put forward for the remaining five (Hans Lindenberg, Albert Zeiler, Gerhard Hoelzer, Hans Friedrich, and Heinz Millinger).

Toftoy was confident that his strategy was sound. By revealing that the British held more German scientists than they needed, he hoped to reduce their recalcitrance to the level of a dog in the manger that permits no one else to share what he himself has no use for. But in the barrage of official messages exchanged with Backfire leadership, Toftoy made a costly blunder. He based his appeal for the release of the contested twelve solely on the fact that they were urgently needed to help develop weaponry for the war in the Pacific. When the detonation of atomic bombs over Hiroshima and Nagasaki on the sixth and ninth of August nullified that argument, the British were quick to exploit their advantage. On the twenty-fourth, the War Office in London played its trump card: "The British Chiefs of Staff would like the United States Chiefs of Staff to know that when the Japanese surrender came about, they were on the point of informing the United States Chiefs of Staff that they were quite prepared to withdraw . . .

restrictions on the removal from Germany of such scientists or equipment as the United States Chiefs of Staff thought might be useful in the war against Japan. However, now that the Japanese surrender has come about, the British Chiefs of Staff assume that this [issue] is now dead. They intend, at an early date, to raise the broader issue of the post V-J Day exploitation of German scientific personnel, equipment, etc."

Toftoy stared at these words in disbelief. Cursing silently to himself, he saw an impenetrable barrier arising between him and the twelve key rocketmakers. His mission was now on indefinite hold. Von Braun would not get the needed men until the British high command agreed to set an "early date" to renegotiate the issue. It promised to be a long wait.

31

Malina and the Sounding Rocket

September 1945
White Sands, New Mexico

THOUGH POLES APART in temperament and philosophy, Frank J. Malina and Wernher von Braun shared personal attributes rarely found in men thirty-three years of age. Malina and von Braun, who was six months older, were distinguished scholars, yet neither flaunted his talents. While trained in the precise black-and-white world of science, both nevertheless acquitted themselves superbly in the amorphous gray area of human relations. Von Braun's outstanding leadership skills propelled him to the pinnacle of the Peenemünde establishment. Similarly, when Theodore von Karman's membership in high-level wartime counsels kept him away from Pasadena for months at a time, Malina became de facto head of Caltech's Jet Propulsion Laboratory. By September 1945, operations there had grown to include more than 250 professionals working in facilities spread over thirty-two acres along the Arroyo Seco.

Malina's rockets, however, became too powerful for the once barren arroyo to accommodate. Now, under his direction, work in the laboratory included basic engineering in thermal jet propulsion engines, propellants, and guided missiles as well as the building of rockets and launching frames for firing tests. While preliminary rocket research and nonhazardous experimental work were permitted within Pasadena's city limits, anything more ambitious required vast open spaces far from population centers. The first missile model tested at a remote site for the army was the PRIVATE A. Its solid-propellant power source was based on a design proposed by Malina and Hsue-shen Tsien in 1943. Firing tests of these five-hundred-pound projectiles took place in December 1944 near Barstow, California, while Malina was in Europe inspecting captured V-1 launch sites along the Strait of Dover. Twenty-four rounds were ignited. The average distance flown was slightly over ten miles from a maximum height of approximately 14,000 feet at speeds up to 1,300 feet per second.

In rapid succession, additional designs progressed from drawing board to firing range. After the four-finned PRIVATE A came the PRIVATE F with vertical fins, horizontal stabilizers, and short, stubby wings. Then liquid-propellant missiles: the CORPORAL E using gas pressure feed and the CORPORAL F with turbine-driven pump. In September 1945, Malina flew east from Los Angeles to supervise the first tests conducted on the new missile range at White Sands, New Mexico. He and several members of the Jet Propulsion Laboratory staff sat strapped in hard bench seats arranged along the cabin walls of a C-47 transport. Lashed to the deck between them was the sounding rocket conceived during Malina's conversation with Colonel Trichel ten months earlier. It used the same gas pressure feed designed for the CORPORAL E. But the diminutive shell—665 pounds when fueled compared to the five-ton mass of its predecessor—prompted the inventors to adopt the acronym for the women's army corps to identify this "little sister." Henceforth, Malina's sounding rocket was known as the WAC CORPORAL.

Because the C-47's droning engines made talking or listening difficult, Malina lapsed into a reverie. He momentarily savored a surge of pride as he recalled the stunning success of the guided-missile projects he had managed for the army during the preceding year. Yet the exhilaration was tempered by a feeling of discomfort that was aggravated by a growing realization that he was philosophically at odds with the entire concept of military rocketry. In the beginning, he had had something entirely different in mind. A decade had elapsed since he, Parsons, and Forman strode into von Karman's office seeking permission to build a high-altitude sounding rocket. Throughout the ensuing years, that goal continued to elude him. Now, at last, he was about to loft a long thin cylinder high into the stratosphere. Unlike previous ordinance tests, height was the objective, not a distant target far beyond the range of conventional artillery.

Although Goddard had failed in his quest for a high-altitude flight after years of effort, Malina's confidence in their ability to do what Goddard could not was buttressed by possession of two important assets. One was his deep appreciation of the value of teamwork.

Malina believed that "Goddard had not succeeded in constructing a successful sounding rocket because he had underestimated the difficulties involved—the day of the isolated inventor of complex devices was over." Also, the technology had matured. Goddard's primitive liquid-oxygen-gasoline propulsion engines did not deliver the massive initial acceleration essential for high flight. Nor were his on-board guidance systems sufficiently precise to accurately hew to a desired course.

Malina was certain that solutions to both of Goddard's problems were within reach. Increased power posed no difficulty because thrusts of adequate magnitude and duration were comfortably sustained by either solid-fuel or storable liquid-propellant engines previously developed in the laboratories strung along the Arroyo Seco. The other problem—course deviations caused by a vehicle's instability during flight—could be circumvented by the addition of a booster stage. Even a tiny departure from a true vertical heading in a low-speed ascent is exacerbated by the force of gravity, which causes the rocket to tilt further from the vertical. However, when a projectile is launched at very high speed, gravity, with much less time to work its mischief, is a negligible influence. Malina intended to capitalize on this peculiarity by coupling the WAC CORPORAL with a modified solid-propellant engine adapted from an ordnance rocket known as the "Tiny Tim."

The booster, also lashed to the C-47's cabin floor, was approximately eight feet long, just an inch or so less than one half the length of the WAC itself. Aside from the difference in this dimension, the rocket and its booster were remarkably similar in appearance. Maximum body diameter of the WAC was 12.2 inches; the booster, 11.75 inches. Each was equipped with three tail fins: the WAC, twenty-four inches half span; the booster, twenty-six inches half span. Three tail fins were a marked departure from tradition. Until that time, aerial bombs and earlier rockets had always been outfitted with four. When W. J. Stewart, a member of Malina's staff, proposed the reduction to save weight, army ordnance "experts" ridiculed the design, predicting that the WAC, in flight, would be radically unstable. Stewart defended the change by citing the accuracies achieved by English longbowmen who, for centuries, had used three-finned arrows. To check the novel tail configuration as well as other flight characteristics, a one-fifth scale model had been constructed and tested two months earlier at Camp Irwin, California. The Baby WAC, as it was called, performed admirably.

Nearing the end of the four-hour flight, the C-47 began the descent toward a shimmering sea of gypsum crystals stretching as far as the eye could see. "White Sands," of course, is a misnomer. At first glance, it may appear that the earth's surface there is blanketed with the familiar opaque granular particles of disintegrated rock. But closer inspection reveals tiny crystals, the product of thousands of years of erosion from an exposed strata in the nearby San Andres Mountains. A crewman inched his way aft, testing tension of the lines securing the rocket, booster, and other cargo. Malina and his companions rechecked the tightness of their seat belts and policed the area around them, stowing books, magazines, and playing cards in the army duffel bags issued to them before leaving Pasadena. A few craned their necks to get a better view of the glistening dunes below. Rising as high as two hundred feet, they resembled undulating huge waves of foam frozen in time. Suddenly the dunes were obscured by clouds of dust swirling up around the windows as the plane jolted along the landing strip serving the new missile range.

The next few days seemed to fly by as Malina and his crew, immersing themselves in a thousand and one details, prepared for their moment of truth. Before firing the fully fueled WAC, four practice shots of the booster stage alone were attempted. These initial rounds not only verified performance expectations of the booster but also enabled the team to become familiar with launcher, fire controls, radar, and tracking cameras. The launcher was a triangular steel structure, seventy-seven feet high, which rested on a steel tripod about one third the height of the tower. The ample work area afforded by the tripod simplified mounting the booster and WAC on the three guide rails inside the tower that provided vertical course alignment. The booster's work was done quickly. It consumed its entire charge of 150 pounds of solid propellant in six-tenths of a second. But during that brief instant, it would give the WAC a massive 50,000-pound push.

Following the four solo tests of the booster, another four were conducted with a payload. The first two lofted dummy replicas of the WAC, constructed of steel tubing weighted with concrete, nearly a thousand feet into the air. The final two were made with a partially fueled WAC in order to check out operation of the liquid-propellant engine, separation of the booster from the main rocket, and the release of a parachute to return the spent shell and motor safely to earth. During the last test, the partially fueled WAC reached an altitude of 28,000 feet.

Twelve days after their arrival from California, Malina and his crew were finally ready to attempt a high flight. Early on the morning of October 11, Malina made a final inspection of booster and rocket suspended in the launcher, climbed into an army jeep, and drove four hundred yards to a concrete control shelter. Before entering, he glanced up at an open window in a nearby weather observation tower. An army meteorologist leaned out, giving a thumbs-up sign. Visibility was excellent. Winds were minimal and the sky was a glorious blue dome. Malina went inside and waited for the controllers to run through their checklists. When that bit of housekeeping was out of the way and he received confirmation that the surrounding area was clear of all personnel, he turned to an assistant, took a deep breath, and nodded. Two seconds later, they saw a bright flash of light and then the launch tower was obscured in a cloud of dust. Peering through viewing ports, everyone craned their necks as they followed a thin white vapor trail shooting up into the blue sky. A record shot? It was hard to tell. In five minutes, the data started coming in. Engine shutdown was at 80,000 feet. Maximum altitude exceeded forty-three miles, more than twice as high as any balloon ascent. Velocity at burnout, approximately 3,100 feet per second. Total time of flight, about seven and a half minutes. The impact point—the spot where the rocket, slowed by a small parachute, returned to earth—was only 3,500 feet from the launch tower. Obviously a near-perfect vertical flight path had been maintained.

In the euphoria of the moment, there were cheers of victory, laughter, vigorous handshaking, and backslapping. For Malina, however, it was more a finale than a glorious beginning. A few days earlier, during an aerial reconnaissance of the vast missile range, Malina had asked his pilot to make a small detour and fly over the site of the world's first nuclear explosion near Alamogordo, New Mexico. Viewing the evidence of the devastating power of that blast physically sickened him. He vowed then and there never to be a party to the mating of rocketry and nuclear weapons.

32

Odyssey to White Sands

October 1945
Fort Strong
Boston Harbor, Massachusetts

STANDING ALONE ON the beach, his back to the sea, Wernher von
Braun admired a stand of glistening green pines. Beyond were apple
trees, sumac, and sapling poplars. Off to his right, a freshwater marsh
stretched into the distance, where bullfrogs croaked in the gathering
dusk. The peaceful scene helped to mask the turmoil within him as
doubts, long suppressed, resurfaced.

Five months earlier, von Braun and several companions had encountered a detachment of the U.S. Army's 44th Division in the small
Alpine village of Reutte, Austria. The euphoria of that moment—
successfully eluding the Russians to fall happily into the arms of the
Americans—was short-lived. Their captors failed to rise quickly to
the bait dangled by von Braun, an offer to commit the considerable
expertise of his rocket cadre to the exclusive service of the United
States. In return, he asked only for guaranteed employment by his
sponsors for a reasonable period of time. Weeks later, after much
dickering, authorization was granted to sign up some Germans for six
months, with options to renew for an additional half year.
Responsibility to recruit about a hundred of the best prospects fell on
the shoulders of Colonel Holger N. Toftoy, whose efforts to hire
them, as we have seen, were thwarted by Britain's Operation Backfire. Alarmed that von Braun and the few V-2 men still at large might
also be impressed into service for Backfire, Toftoy hastily signed them
up and spirited them out of Germany. The vanguard of the rescued
rocketmakers, comprising von Braun and six associates, arrived at an
island army outpost in Boston Harbor on September 20, 1945.

Resuming his stroll along the beach, von Braun was unable to quell
a suspicion that he faced a dead end. The Americans were bluffing.
Held incommunicado for fourteen days in a decaying, obsolete fort,

he was to be squeezed dry and soon cast aside. The interrogations helped to break up the monotony, but the questions were disorganized, repetitious, and frequently inane. One particular question usually put forth by eager young men striving to make an impression sought to smoke out a hidden motive behind von Braun's surrender to the Americans. Weary of responding that he believed only the United States possessed the resources to support an ambitious space exploration program, he finally waved off such probing with the comment: "Germany lost two wars during my life and the next time I want to be on the winning side."

Fort Strong, despite a dominant-sounding name memorializing a fallen Civil War hero, did not evoke a feeling of confidence. Established on the harbor's largest island in 1867, the installation's last major renovation had been in 1899 and included twelve-inch gun emplacements to repel naval attackers. In time, the defenses crumbled in pace with the fort's eroding mission. Now deserted, the old garrison's officers' quarters seemed a convenient temporary hideaway for seven German rocketmakers who had been secretly smuggled into the country.

Nor did Boston's Long Island itself conjure up a positive image for any first-time visitor to the United States. The army, however, was not solely responsible for the blight. In 1882, Boston's mayor had ordered the conversion of a decaying resort hotel there into an almshouse and promptly installed about 650 paupers. Forty years later, the derelict population was moved elsewhere, and the city fathers, wishing to banish wayward females to the remote reaches of their jurisdiction, turned the structure into a home and hospital for unwed mothers. That move so effectively kept an unpleasant problem out of sight that a dormitory for homeless men was built there in 1928 and a treatment center for three hundred alcoholics was added in 1941.

Turning and retracing his steps along the beach, von Braun wondered how he might have managed things differently. In the final months of the war, when Germany's armies were reeling back into the fatherland, he had been confronted by two conflicting demands. The Armaments Ministry directed him to abandon Peenemünde and move west. At the same time, the field marshal commanding the Pomeranian sector pressured him to remain and release the thousands of rocket workers under his jurisdiction to serve in the defense against the advancing Red Army. Sensing that a stronger bargaining chip was to be gained by surrender to the Allies, particularly the Americans, von Braun had exercised the high priority that the military transport system gave the V-2. After hundreds of freight cars were loaded with machinery and rocket parts, orders were cut that triggered movement of these long rolling caravans in a westerly direction. Meanwhile, members of his staff commandeered a fleet of vehicles, enabling them to flee south toward the Alps and hide in a dozen isolated villages, where they waited out the final weeks of the war. This certainly was no hardship—von Braun later acknowledged that for more than a month he lived "royally in a ski hotel high on a mountain plateau."

The high life had ended, however, when von Braun and a few companions drove into Reutte and surrendered to the Americans. Within days, scores of other Peenemünde veterans turned themselves in and all were interned in a prison camp at Garmisch-Partenkirchen. A distinguished cadre of American civilian experts had been assembled there. Physicists, chemists, and engineers from leading industrial corporations and educational institutions had been summoned to Garmisch-Partenkirchen to help debrief hundreds of captured German scientists. The interrogations were structured to achieve three objectives. The first and most immediate need was the collection of information pertinent to current military research and development goals. In conjunction with that task was the identification of those with outstanding talent who might be recruited to work in the United States. The third objective, though controversial, but in accord with American strategic military interests, was the implementing of a policy of "denial." Many of those detained who were not to be offered employment were nonetheless accomplished researchers, working on the leading edge of their chosen professions. Their skills, while seemingly redundant in terms of American needs, were considered too advanced to risk forfeiting to an adversary. By preventing emigration of these "rejects" to Russia or the eastern bloc countries, the United States denied the Soviets the advantage of exploiting their expertise.

The blatantly undemocratic thrust of this policy troubled many Americans conducting the interrogations. Among those facing the possibility that they might be impeding, rather than advancing, legitimate scientific inquiry were Dr. Fritz Zwicky and Dr. Carl Millikan of the California Institute of Technology and Dr. Richard Porter of the General Electric Company. In addition to the distasteful task of perhaps abetting the termination of promising scientific careers, these three were also handed the difficult assignment of determining von

Braun's future. Was he to be milked dry, recruited for work in the United States, or kept on ice indefinitely in Germany? Shortly after meeting them, von Braun concluded that his three interviewers knew considerably more about rocketry than most American scientists. Indeed, they did. Through their familiarity with von Karman's sponsorship of Malina's experiments, Zwicky and Millikan, senior members of the Caltech faculty, were well equipped to ask cogent and penetrating questions. Porter was the pragmatist of the trio. His industrial background provided the practical counterpoint to the theoretical orientation of Zwicky and Millikan. Porter, in fact, had already been named to direct "Project Hermes," code name for an army contract awarded to General Electric to plan and conduct V-2 test firings at the White Sands Proving Ground.

Zwicky, Millikan, and Porter were as impressed by von Braun as he was by them. Yes, the trio agreed, sign up von Braun and all the former Peenemünders he requests. Another recommendation urged the provision of enough latitude for him to work effectively. Minimize restrictions and, above all, give him sufficient decision-making authority to truly manage technical research. The only negative observation was that his enthusiasm had a tendency to blur lines between the past and the future. Among the notes taken at Garmisch-Partenkirchen was the comment that von Braun "confuses what he hopes to do with those things which [already] have been reduced to practice."

Following the few stimulating sessions with Zwicky, Millikan, and Porter, von Braun was the object of a series of interrogations by considerably smaller fry. After weeks spent answering the same questions for rotating teams of junior officers, he and six companions were bundled into the rear of a small army truck to begin the first leg of their tortuous journey to America. For enduring several hundred backbreaking miles seated on bruising wooden benches, they were rewarded with a respite at Le Grand Chesnay, a palatial hideaway in a suburb of Paris. Then, after dinner on the fifth night, they boarded a military transport plane at Orly Field. The transatlantic flight, interrupted twice for refueling in the Azores and Newfoundland, ended eighteen hours later at New Castle Air Base, Delaware. There they boarded a chartered DC-3 that flew them to Boston's Logan Field. On the ground once more, they were hustled into army staff cars and driven to a remote pier on the city's waterfront. After stepping warily on the deck of a waiting launch, they huddled in a cabin below during five miles of bobbing through choppy waters to Fort Strong on Long Island.

Two weeks later, tiring of his stroll on the deserted beach, von Braun headed back toward his quarters. Nearing the entrance, he heard exultant shouts heralding a major financial coup in another marathon game of Monopoly, which helped to fill the hours between interrogations. Entering the dayroom, von Braun found Erich Neubert and Theodor Poppel negotiating a deal making them uncontested masters of most of the valuable real estate on the board. Back at Peenemünde, Neubert had been a production manager in the eletronics and guidance laboratory. Poppel had worked on ground support equipment. The four others completing the circle of players included Wilhelm Jungert, an expert technician; Eberhard Rees, von Braun's right-hand man and deputy at Peenemünde; August Schulze, a systems engineer; and Walter Schwidetzky, an instrumentation designer.

Lacking interest in the future course of the game, von Braun was about to go to his room for some quiet reading. Suddenly his path was blocked and everyone jumped to their feet as an American army officer strode through the door. Major James Hamill, followed by a young blond private first class, introduced himself and told the startled group that they were to be packed and ready to leave at dawn the following day. Hamill, who had been selected to shepherd the group to their next destination, was well fitted for the task. In his midtwenties and therefore likely to develop a closer empathy with the youthful von Braun than a more senior officer, he was trained as a physicist and, though not needed to communicate with von Braun, was also fluent in German.

Private First Class Eric M. Wormser, the enlisted man accompanying Hamill, spoke the language, too. Born in Germany, Wormser had emigrated while in his early teens, completing his education (a graduate degree in mechanical engineering) in the United States. Three months earlier, Wormser had been handed a staggering assignment. Over ten tons of documents and drawings, hidden in an abandoned mine in Dornten, Germany, by von Braun's orders, and later recovered after he revealed their whereabouts, had arrived at the Army Ordnance Proving Ground near Aberdeen, Maryland. Wormser's job was to translate and abstract the most important sections. But the complexity of the engineering coupled with unfamiliar German technical terminology were too much for him. He needed help. Consequently, after the interrogation teams completed their final interviews at Fort Strong, Wormser was dispatched to Boston to escort von Braun's six companions back to Aberdeen.

Early the next morning, Hamill, Wormser, von Braun, and the others boarded a launch waiting at the fort's small pier for the return to the mainland. Because the military brass in Washington had different plans for their prized weapons expert, von Braun bid farewell to his colleagues at the railroad station in Boston before they departed for Aberdeen in the custody of Private Wormser. Von Braun was too valuable an asset to waste on mundane translations of technical documents. The possibility of using his considerable management skills in an as yet undefined rocket development program prompted Major General Gladeon L. Barnes, chief of the army ordnance technical division, to summon this young weapons prodigy to the Pentagon in order to personally size him up. Hamill, who was under orders to escort von Braun to the White Sands Proving Ground, where a huge inventory of V-2 parts had been amassed, was therefore instructed to go by way of Washington, D.C. Although an easier choice would have been to take von Braun on the same Washington-bound streamliner selected for Wormser and his charges, Hamill opted to drive by car in order to better take the measure of the man.

As Hamill negotiated his way through traffic to the Boston Post Road, Major General Gladeon Barnes, four hundred miles southwest, sat down at his desk in the Pentagon. Scanning his calendar for the coming week, he saw that Colonel Leslie Simon, director of the Ballistic Research Laboratory, had appended a request for an appointment. Thorny problems generally percolated to the top and Simon's bid for an audience was no exception. Barnes correctly surmised that Simon was maneuvering him into a commitment to give the technical leader of Germany's V-2 offensive a powerful voice in army rocket development. Unprecedented? Of course. But Simon was no stranger to controversial ideas. Three years earlier Barnes had approved a Simon proposal to build a huge electronic computer at the University of Pennsylvania. The jury was still out on that one. But Simon's enthusiastic optimism was keeping the nay sayers at bay. Swiveling his chair to gain a view of the Washington Monument near the opposite shore of the Potomac, Barnes silently agreed with Simon. Yes, he wanted very much to meet this von Braun.

33

Operation Backfire

October 1945
Cuxhaven, Germany

ARTHUR RUDOLPH KNEW the goal was hopelessly beyond reach. He had even known it three months earlier when British Army Colonel C. W. Raby, sitting in a sparsely furnished office in the Krupp Gun Proving Ground, had directed him to oversee rehabilitation of thirty rockets. Raby, technical chief of Operation Backfire, did not view this as an unrealistic request. He was aware that Rudolph had first planned and later managed the pilot production plant at Peenemünde. Moreover, when the British air raid in August 1943 had forced the transfer of assembly operations to Mittelwerke, a vast underground factory near Nordhausen, Rudolph had further distinguished himself by boosting output of V-2s from an average of approximately one hundred per month in early 1944 to more than six hundred per month throughout the final winter of the war.

Yet the Krupp range at Cuxhaven was no Mittelwerke. Rudolph's former domain had been equipped with all the modern tools of mass production: cranes, gravity rollers, power conveyors, rolling jigs to move components as well as completed rockets. None of these was available at the gun proving ground. Nor was there even a small fraction of the sheltered work space afforded by Mittelwerke's two parallel main tunnels, each more than a mile long and connected by forty-seven shorter cross chambers like rungs on a ladder. Raby tried to dispel Rudolph's doubts by stressing the Krupp assets, emphasizing the proving ground's workshops, good road system, and convenient railroad sidings.

Raby's goal of thirty V-2s was based on a conservative assumption that only one third of the reconditioned inventory would be successfully launched to soar over Heligoland and plunge into the North Sea target area forty miles west of the Danish coastline. He was confident that those ten would provide sufficient data to fulfill Back-fire's two main objectives. First, Raby's cadre was to compose a detailed description of rocket manufacturing procedures while also preserving for posterity "all technical lessons which gradually come to light in doing so." Second, a brother officer, Colonel W.S.J. Carter, was to direct the writing of a field manual covering the "handling of the completed rocket, setting it up on its firing site, and recording so far as possible, its behaviour in flight."

A few weeks after Raby had revealed the plan to recover thirty rockets, Rudolph was not surprised to learn that British search parties dispatched to scour storage depots and railroad sidings for ready-to-launch V-2s had returned empty-handed. No immediately usable rockets were found because, as Rudolph could have told them, V-2s did not age gracefully. At Peenemünde, he and his colleagues had found that storing rockets for months, or even a few weeks, signifi-cantly increased corrosion-induced failures of electrical circuits and valves. In order to minimize these malfunctions, General Dornberger had secured the highest transport priority for assembled V-2s, ensur-ing that most arrived at launch sites within days after rolling off production lines.

The consequent scarcity resulting from Dornberger's efficiency effectively squelched the original plan to prepare thirty rockets for Colonel Carter's field operations. Lacking V-2s to fire, and therefore having nothing to show for time served in his present assignment, Carter grew anxious. While parrying gibes from this brother officer of equal rank, Raby was less able to cope with concerns voiced by Backfire's commander, Major General A. M. Cameron. With no battle reports or strategy conferences to monopolize the attention of the War Office in London, a minor operation such as Backfire assumed a high profile. Cameron was in the spotlight and he could ill afford to stub his toe, much less fall flat on his face. Reacting to growing pressure to deliver usable rockets, Raby leaned on his V-2 production chief, Arthur Rudolph. Under the circumstances, Rudolph may have been inclined to thrust his hands in his pockets and do nothing. Yet he knew that such a posture was against his own best interests. Alienating the British might jeopardize his chances of ul-timately joining von Braun in America. Therefore, when presented with a hastily devised backup plan to build eight rockets using V-2 components and subassemblies rounded up in the British dragnet, he meekly went along.

Throughout these weeks of preparation, Raby had to walk a fine line. While pressing his charges to produce launch-ready vehicles by mid-September, he dared not push too hard. To meet the target date, full cooperation was essential. But continuously cracking the whip snuffed out initiative. Then passive obedience set in or, worse yet, temptations to commit sabotage. Further complicating the situation was the question of how much the Germans could be trusted. To detect and counter subtle attempts to impede progress, an elaborate cross-checking system was devised. Soldiers and civilians assigned to workshops and the launching unit were organized under the command of a senior Wehrmacht officer. The man selected for this post, Lieutenant Colonel Wolfgang Weber, was no neophyte. Early in 1944, he had been in charge of an experimental V-2 battery at Peenemünde that staged drills for the training of field units. Later, when the V-2 became operational, he headed one of the newly formed tactical groups.

To keep Weber's people honest, General Cameron ordered the establishment of a separate contingent of civilian rocket specialists, who were isolated in a camp near the village of Brockeswalde. This second group did not participate in the assembly work. Their only function was to answer questions posed by British interrogators, who then compared notes with colleagues looking over the shoulders of Arthur Rudolph's production team. Cameron also gained custody of Lieutenant General Dornberger, who was brought from detention in England and temporarily billeted with Lieutenant Colonel Wilhelm Zippelius, a former V-2 fuel logistics officer. Other than brief contact with Zippelius, Dornberger was kept incommunicado from others because, as explained in Cameron's subsequent report to the under secretary of state in the War Office, "it was feared that his considerable influence [over former subordinates] might be embarassing [sic]." After a few interviews, Dornberger's usefulness was outweighed by the rigorous security required for his solitary confinement and he was returned to Britain.

While Colonel Raby rode herd on Arthur Rudolph and the 186 members of his assembly crew, Colonel W.S.J. Carter, who was to direct the firing of the rockets, tried to make the best use of his time. It was not easy. Because many of the specialists in his launch detachment were otherwise engaged in rebuilding necessary support equipment, Carter was unable to include them in the elaborate rehearsals he wished to stage in preparation for the mid-September countdowns.

Carter reluctantly concluded that fulfilling his primary mission—
reenacting and documenting every step from delivery of a V-2 at a
railhead to ignition of its main stage—was impossible with the personnel and resources under his control. True, over a hundred German
soldiers at Cuxhaven were competent V-2 veterans. Yet their skills
did not match every technical specialty needed to man a troop in the
field. Nor was there enough support equipment to adequately illustrate a document describing these procedures. The *Preufwagen* was an
example; because none had been found intact, there would only be
cursory illustrations of this important mobile test center. It housed
instruments for analyzing virtually every critical function performed
in the V-2. Arrayed along its walls were devices that measured the
response of servo motors controlling the steering vanes, pitch gyros,
and roll detectors. Other instruments regulated the entry of compressed air into the complex pneumatic system, simulated gyroscopic
signals, and monitored operation of all valves supplying liquid oxygen
and alcohol.

The failure to recover a *Preufwagen* in suitable condition to be
photographed forced Colonel Carter to settle for drawings of the
three-ton truck and its contents. There were other compromises, too.
He also canceled the original plan to reenact the duties of a V-2
technical troop. This sequence was to begin with the unloading of a
rocket at a railhead, then transfer to a *Vidalwagen* (a special trailer for
carting assembled rockets over short distances), installation of a warhead, tests in a field service shelter, and repairs of any damage
suffered by sensitive circuitry en route. While Arthur Rudolph's
production crew supplied a shiny dummy rocket for practice drills,
this empty shell was a poor substitute for the real thing. Although the
most basic tasks—unloading from a rail car or simulating a fueling
operation—were easily staged and photographed, the lack of functioning interior components thwarted more ambitious reenactments.

When not supervising various drills with the dummy V-2, Colonel
Carter regularly inspected his five radar sites along the coast east and
north of the proposed line of fire. One, on the outskirts of Cuxhaven,
was easy to visit. Three others, however, nearer Denmark, were as
much as a day's drive from his headquarters in the Krupp Proving
Ground. The fifth outpost, furthest north and adjacent to the target
zone, was located close to the Danish city of Ringkobing, almost two
hundred miles by truck from Cuxhaven. The radar detachment there
saw less of Carter than he wished because unusual circumstances

prevented any prolonged absence from the nerve center of the British Special Projectile Operations Group.

First, documenting the lengthy procedures required to ready a rocket for launch demanded Carter's constant attention. Progress was slow because the recovery teams sent out to scour the countryside for parts and equipment returned with dismally few source materials. The scarcity of V-2 printed matter at Cuxhaven was neither the product of slipshod searches by the British nor efficient record destruction by the Germans. Little was found because little was ever produced. To enhance security, General Dornberger had prohibited publication of a comprehensive manual on the design and operation of any of the rockets produced at Peenemünde. Soldiers in a V-2 firing regiment gained most of their know-how by observing experienced trainers demonstrate procedures in numerous practice drills. With vital information locked deep in the brains of his charges, Carter, daring not to browbeat or bully, was forced to handle them with kid gloves.

Second, the delicacy of this task, coupled with the potentially disastrous consequences if botched, threatened to give Carter's superior, Major General A. M. Cameron, a severe case of the jitters. Some serious handholding was obviously in order. To allay the general's uneasiness, Carter demonstrated, through constant vigilance, that everything was under control. His top priority, he assured the general, was to keep the rocket specialists in a "co-operative frame of mind." Instilling that utopian ideal in the hearts of this disillusioned band of de facto prisoners would tax even the wisdom of Solomon without the help of incentives. Seeing the need for more sweeteners to make their lot more palatable, Cameron secured the War Office's authority to grant a few. The pay scale was raised. Better rations were served. Elaborate precautions were taken to assure safety on the job. And, though no formal commitment was offered, Cameron allowed his subordinates to pass the word that compensation would be made for any work-related injury. Then, when the novelty of these extra benefits began to wear off, a bonus plan was announced. At the successful conclusion of Backfire, extra remuneration was to be distributed "*pro rata* according to responsibility and technical efficiency."

By mid-September, as Arthur Rudolph foretold earlier, Colonel Raby's ambitious plans to see at least ten V-2s rise off the recently completed concrete firing pad in the Krupp Proving Ground had been severely curtailed. Working against the calendar (for the War Office in

London was badgering General Cameron to get on with it), Rudolph had tried but failed to meet Raby's quota. Only three, possibly four rockets would be ready in October. When reporting this disappointing news to Cameron, Raby softened the shock with an assurance that the rockets would be launched early in the month, possibly as soon as the first day.

True to his word, Raby delivered a thoroughly rebuilt rocket to Colonel Carter's operations team during the last week in September. At midmorning on the first day of October, Carter proudly announced to General Cameron that he was ready. A V-2 was on the firing pad ready for fueling. This was no news to Cameron, who, having arrived at the launch site shortly after dawn, was anticipating that his report of a successful firing would be flashed to London before the day was over. Told to proceed without delay, Carter saluted smartly, turned to his second in command, and instructed him to begin the fueling operation.

Carter issued that order at 9:45 A.M. An hour passed before two loaded tankers left the fuel dump of the Krupp Works and headed for the launch site, a short two-and-a-half-mile drive. Not until three in the afternoon, however, were the last liters of alcohol and liquid oxygen sealed in the V-2's tanks. Then the fuel tankers left the area and an all clear sounded. Fifty-four minutes later—after final orientation of the vehicle on its base, recording sites alerted, igniter inserted, and steering tested—a red flare warned that the launch was imminent. But nothing happened. The Stotz plugs (ground connection cables) were not ejected from the rocket. Carter's German charges shrugged their shoulders, and after appropriate safety measures were taken in the control bunker, they went back for another look. At 6:15 P.M., after two and a half hours, another red flare arched over the clearing. Again nothing happened. Carter reluctantly ordered his crew to "stand down" and reported to a frustrated General Cameron that another attempt before dark was impossible.

The next day, October 2, ended on a high note. At 1:47 P.M., preceded by six hours of preparation, a V-2 rose high above the Krupp Proving Ground and headed north toward the sea. A second shot on October 4 and a final launch on October 15 also provided considerable data for subsequent study. Although the grandiose plan had been drastically curtailed, Operation Backfire was hailed as a resounding success.

34

V-2 Debut at White Sands

May 10, 1946
White Sands, New Mexico

M AJOR GENERAL CURTIS E. LEMAY impatiently chewed on a cigar while staring at a garishly adorned V-2, poised for lift-off. Its shiny aluminum skin was painted brilliant yellow and black. On one side, a Teutonic rendering of the traditional scantily clad pinup girl added a carnival atmosphere to this second attempt to launch a captured German rocket from American soil. The first try, a month earlier, had failed to achieve its objective. Today, however, Major General Everett S. Hughes, the new chief of army ordnance and official host of this demonstration, was convinced that his neophyte rocket team had everything under control. Flaunting his confidence, Hughes audaciously invited a contingent of distinguished guests, including American General Joseph Stilwell, British Field Marshal Sir Henry Maitland Wilson, United States Navy Admiral Dewitt S. Ramsey, and Major General Curtis E. LeMay, representing the army's air branch, a potentially serious rival of the ordnance department in rocket matters.

LeMay, who was then deputy chief of the air staff for research and development, was not intimidated by this obvious move to nail down the ordnance department's claim on military rocketry. On the contrary, LeMay was having difficulty keeping his anger in check. He viewed the hoopla touting this alleged head start in a new branch of weaponry with undisguised disdain. Already on record for deploring the lack of "an integrated program for missile development" and the wasteful duplication of effort by the army, navy, and air service, LeMay urged establishment of a single military rocket development group. And the organization best equipped to assume this responsibility? LeMay's answer: the air force, of course. Ordnance chief Everett Hughes had other ideas. With von Braun and his proven team of rocket professionals, Hughes argued that his command was uniquely endowed with the expertise to do the job. Hughes was determined to carry forward, with honor and distinction, the standard passed to him by Major General Gladeon E. Barnes, the recently retired chief of ordnance.

Barnes was a tough act to follow. In addition to numerous other wartime duties, Barnes had headed the vast maintenance and support operations that kept tanks rolling and artillery blazing on all the fighting fronts. To buttress his proven administrative skills, Barnes had been adept at getting his way when rules and regulations might have stymied less resourceful officers. For one thing, he had worked behind the scenes and pulled the strings to assure the secret entry into the United States of von Braun and his associates. Colonel Leslie Simon and some members of the general's staff who helped recruit the German rocketmakers hailed their chief's participation in that operation as inspired leadership. But others called the scheme a recklessly dangerous gamble. A reasonable reaction, perhaps, for those desk-bound career officers who studiously avoided taking chances. Barnes, however, was a high roller. In his job, he had to be. Calculated risks were the catalysts that—once in a great while—miraculously transformed baffling problems into stunning breakthroughs.

Just before his retirement in March 1946, Barnes had been privileged to bask in the brilliant payoff of one of those gambles. Four years earlier, as America's war industries had shifted into high gear, delivery of many new weapons to the troops in combat threatened to be slowed by a technological bottleneck. During an engagement with the enemy, a change in wind direction, a drop in temperature, or a switch to another type of ammunition might draw well-sighted guns off target. When this happened, precalculated firing tables quickly guided a change to the new correct angle of elevation. But with more guns rolling off production lines, computing the firing tables for them required a staggering number of calculations. Mathematicians in the army's main ballistics research center near Aberdeen, Maryland, and a substation at the University of Pennsylvania in Philadelphia were hard-pressed to keep pace with the diversity of weaponry. Faced with the specter of huge guns stored and silent in depots because no one had compiled the data needed to aim and fire them, an ordnance officer in Philadelphia took the time to listen to a bizarre idea conceived by two members of the university faculty. John Mauchly, a thirty-six-year-old physicist, and his associate, J. Presper Eckert, an electrical engineering instructor ten years his junior, proposed building a giant calculator with thousands of electronic vacuum tubes replacing the customary moving gears and ratchets. Word about their brainstorm percolated up the chain of command to General Barnes. Gambling that such a radical proposal might be the key to a major leap forward, Barnes authorized a series of grants during the next four years that culminated in the assembly of the world's first electronic digital computer, the ENIAC (*Electronic Numerical Integrator and Computer*). On February 15, 1946, a front-page news report in the *New York Times* announced: "One of the war's top secrets, an amazing machine which applies electronic speeds for the first time to mathematical tasks hitherto too difficult and cumbersome for solution [now] computes a problem 1,000 times faster than it has ever been done before."

Major General Hughes hoped to crown his career with a comparable coup. By securely positioning his command at the pinnacle of all military rocket development, he sought to assure himself a place of honor in the annals of army ordnance. He might have succeeded had he not been destined to cope with the "can do" personality of Curtis E. LeMay.

In less than eighteen years in uniform, LeMay had climbed far and fast. When promoted to major general in March 1944, four months after his thirty-seventh birthday, he was the youngest officer of that rank then serving in the United States Army. Even during the relatively quiet decades of the twenties and thirties, when isolationist policies had severely curtailed growth of the country's armed forces, he far outpaced his peers. Joining the army immediately after graduation from Ohio State University in June 1928, he was appointed a second lieutenant in the reserve and posted to a field artillery brigade at Camp Knox, Kentucky. Three months later, convinced that shepherding cannons and caissons over hill and dale was not the life for him, he transferred to the army air corps. Following a year of flight training, and another six months as a reserve officer in a pursuit squadron, he was awarded a second-lieutenancy in the regular army. Next was a series of assignments in Columbus, Ohio; Selfridge Field, Michigan; Schofield Barracks, Hawaii; and Langley Field, Virginia. At Langley, in January 1937, he was assigned to a bombardment group equipped with the new B-17s, the legendary heavy aircraft in which he would win fame and glory over Europe a few years later. With America's entry into World War II, LeMay, though a junior

officer, was poised for high command. Personal fortitude, outstanding
leadership skills, and his innovative tactical ability propelled him to
the top ranks of the air service in the campaigns against Germany with
B-17s and later against Japan with B-29s.

LeMay's world then turned upside down. For a man who had
experienced the intoxicating power of wartime command, the onset of
peace was as sobering as a cold shower after a riotous night on the
town. Instead of issuing orders that each day dispatched hundreds of
bombers to wreak vengeance on the Japanese aggressors, LeMay sat in
his Pentagon office fending off probes by ambitious bureaucratic
jackals eager to trim fat and cancel redundancies in his research and
development budget. It was a vastly different kind of combat—but for
LeMay, a necessary learning experience. His position was not unlike
that of a hotshot regional manager in a large industrial enterprise who
is brought into corporate headquarters for seasoning. In the field,
where he was king of his own turf, his word was law. But in the
backbiting jungle of executive staff politics, where there is no law, he
had to fight hard merely to survive. LeMay, however, was a fast
learner. An advocate of the legendary military axiom that holds that
the best defense is an aggressive offense, he kept opponents off balance by forcing them to play the game according to his rules.

On this visit to White Sands, LeMay chose to apply that strategy
with unmitigated zeal. Although a guest of the ordnance command,
and obviously not a participant in the day's program, he nevertheless
intended to exploit the occasion as a platform for his air force propaganda. As he and other important observers waited and watched
from their vantage point about a half mile from the launch site,
LeMay seized the opportunity to make news. Correctly sensing that
the celebrated Pacific Theater B-29 leader might brighten up their
dispatches with a colorful quotation, reporters hovering around him
tried to stoke the fires with leading questions. When LeMay, rising to
the bait, branded American rocket development as "fragmented" and
brashly labeled direction by the joint chiefs of staff in this matter as
"inadequate," Hanson W. Baldwin, military correspondent for the
New York Times, scribbled furiously.

What LeMay called fragmented was viewed as sound development
policy and the correct response to current circumstances by the navy
and most of the army's other nonflying services. Lack of a unified
rocket development organization was not the problem, countered
LeMay's critics. According to them, the scarcity of trained personnel

was the main deterrent to progress. They saw a diversified multi-faceted effort as the best way to indoctrinate the most people in the shortest time.

The ordnance command was then the unchallenged leader in the race to launch a long-range missile, and Major General Hughes, counting heavily on the support of the well-seasoned von Braun team, was determined to maintain his advantage. LeMay was equally committed to his crusade for air force dominance in rocketry. To ensure achievement of this goal, he had strongly endorsed the award of a top-secret research contract to Consolidated Vultee Aircraft Corporation in Downey, California. Let Hughes and his Germans monkey around with their two-hundred-mile-range V-2, LeMay had gloatingly told his staff a few weeks earlier. Within three years, maybe two, the air force would have the MX-774, a vehicle that would far outdistance any missile that von Braun could put up against it.

Yet no war of words could wither the laurels justly won by von Braun's team and the army ordnance men. This was their day. Hanson W. Baldwin captured the immense feeling of pride and accomplishment in the first paragraph of the story he filed for the *Times:* "WHITE SANDS PROVING GROUND, Las Cruces, N.M., May 10—A fourteen-ton German V-2 rocket, launched by the United States Army, roared into the ionosphere here this afternoon and officially started a United States long-range missile program which in time will revolutionize the art of war and may solve the mysteries of the sky."

35

The Rockefeller Rescue

September 1947
New York City

LAURANCE SPELMAN ROCKEFELLER picked up a pen to sign the check. After months of haggling with numerous advisers, Rockefeller Brothers, Inc., was about to commit a half-million dollars in venture capital to stave off the imminent bankruptcy of a small, cash-starved rocket-engine company in Pompton Plains, New Jersey.

Though a bright young star in the United States Navy's galaxy of high-tech suppliers, Reaction Motors, Inc., was merely a fizzle under the penetrating scrutiny of Wall Street's money moguls. Before concerned navy brass came to the Rockefellers, several potential rescuers had responded to the floundering company's S.O.S., taken one look at the balance sheet, and promptly shoved off. One could hardly blame them. Since December 1941, when four part-time rocket builders, who were RMI's founders, won a modest development contract from the navy, their tiny company had grown steadily. Revenues climbed but deficits mounted faster. Then, on the horizon, came the prospect of a turnaround. The year 1946 had begun on a high note. A flood of new business prompted expansion of RMI's work force from 55 to 120. At year end, however, instead of reaping a profit, the four owners found themselves presiding over a disaster. Total assets increased from $333,000 to $924,000. But losses for the year exceeded $117,000. As a result, net worth plummeted to minus $92,970, and the working-capital account registered a deficit of nearly $200,000. The company's financial image was besmirched further by a stack of unpaid bills. RMI owed more than $550,000 to creditors.

Laurance Rockefeller, however, was not blinded by the red ink. Seeing beyond the obvious fiscal ineptitude of the company's management, he shrewdly recognized potential arbitrarily discounted by other less-perceptive venture capitalists. Apart from an alarming tendency to gobble up cash, RMI's record was impressively positive. Working long hours for little pay, the four founders, in the first nine months of operation, had successfully designed, built, and delivered ten different types of engines ranging in propulsive power from a hundred to a thousand pounds. In their first year, they enlarged their modest initial capital equipment inventory of one lathe and a few secondhand machine tools by an additional $11,200 of spanking-new electronic gear. During the next three years, they broadened their customer base, developed several new products, and moved from the company's original work site—a former tailor shop and two-car garage—into a three-story building providing 11,600 square feet of floor space.

Ironically, two of the founders, John Shesta and Lovell Lawrence, came to demonstrate a three-thousand-pound-thrust liquid-oxygen-gasoline jet-assisted takeoff system where bad luck and the arbitrary disablement of a thermal cutoff switch had thwarted Robert H. Goddard sixteen months earlier. In January 1944, as bitterly icy blasts buffeted the shores of Chesapeake Bay, Shesta and Lawrence stood on a precarious perch at the end of a narrow dock in the estuary of the Severn River. Hovering above them was the tail of a navy PBY flying boat. Underfoot was an improvised scaffold supported by several wobbling soapboxes. Their task was the same after every one of a series of test flights. Sixteen bolts, each stubbornly refusing to turn in threaded orifices drilled in the fuselage, were ultimately wrenched free and the rocket motor removed. Shesta subsequently recalled: "When we finally got it off, we took it into the hangar to make an inspection. After satisfying ourselves that the rocket would not explode in mid-air the next day, we began the gruelling job of replacing the motor." The navy had ensured that these inspections were thorough and the installations flawless by inserting a clause in the contract requiring "an official of the company" to be aboard every test flight. Neither Shesta nor Lawrence coveted an exclusive right to this duty, so they agreed to be RMI's airborne representative on alternate days. Shesta later revealed the cause of their reticence: "I had seen too many motors blow up on the test stand because of hard starts or other idiosyncrasies that rocket engines are subject to. Hard starts are [hazardous] even when viewed from behind a massive concrete bulkhead. . . . What a hard start would do to a plane, I shudder to think."

Fortunately, they were spared the ordeal of a hard start. Shesta never forgot the wave of relief that swept over him after each test as the PBY finally came in for a landing. His exhilaration was highest "on Fridays, when I knew the next flight would not be until Tuesday, and we had a three-day reprieve." The four weeks of tests were completed without a serious mishap, prompting Shesta and Lawrence to succumb to a temptation to show off. A contract for a production order of their JATOs had been approved and signed. They had received an advance payment for the first delivery. Yet instead of being content to take the money and run, they stayed on to stage a needless demonstration for some admirals and other high officials in the Navy Department.

On the appointed day, a bright sun shown in a clear sky. Lashed to a platform, the PBY was rigged for a static firing of the JATO system to enable the distinguished guests to witness a close-up of the entire burn from start to finish. After the motor and fuel-supply lines had been carefully checked and rechecked, word was passed to throw the ignition switch. The anticipated blue-white stream of burning gases failed to spew from the combustion chamber. Instead, billowing yellow flames nearly engulfed the PBY's huge tail section. An emergency cutoff was activated and before sailors who were standing by could bring extinguishers within range, the fire was out. It was obvious that the oxygen flow was deficient. Although the diagnosis was easy, a cure was not. Shesta and Lawrence frantically inspected valves and feed lines. No blockages or other cause was found. Baffled and embarrassed, they reluctantly informed their guests that there would be no show after all. Not until days later was the reason for the failure uncovered. One oxygen valve, hidden deep in the hull, had never been purged throughout the four weeks of trials. Sloshed frequently by salt water in the bilge, the valve eventually blocked the adjacent line with a sticky residue, finally terminating the flow at the critical moment.

Laurance Rockefeller, surrounded by lawyers and accountants, sat at a conference table on the fifty-sixth floor of Rockefeller Center's RCA Building, closing a deal that his late grandfather, John D. Rockefeller, Sr., would have scornfully rejected. Laurance agreed to pump $500,000 into Reaction Motors' coffers in return for 21-percent ownership. In his heyday, "Senior" had demanded much more. Known for his ruthless drive to gain complete control of any company he got his hands on, the elder Rockefeller would have scarcely been content with 21 percent of anything. Of course, times and the family had changed. Influenced perhaps by the tranquilizing guidance of Ivy

Ledbetter Lee before his death in 1935, the third generation of brothers had abandoned the public-be-damned posture of turn-of-the-century tycoons. Public service was now the watchword. Foundations, grants, charities—these were the means through which the Rockefellers sought to win respect and approval. Even the sordid business of making money was tempered by a nonexploitive policy of nurturing pioneering companies opening up new fields.

Reaction Motors was a near-perfect match for this profile: small, undercapitalized, and a proven performer in a discipline so young that the documentation necessary to support growth was not yet written. The hidden strengths that attracted Laurance Rockefeller as an investor also caught the eye of an aeronautical engineering manager facing the most awesome challenge of his career. In March 1946, Karel J. Bossart, chief of structures at Consolidated Vultee Aircraft's plant in Downey, California, learned that his company had won a top-secret government contract to design a long-range ballistic missile. Project MX-774 was initiated to test the feasibility of firing an unmanned rocket-powered projectile high into the stratosphere and hitting a target over five thousand miles away. There was no scarcity of scoffers in Consolidated's management hierarchy. Although harboring doubts, they were not reluctant to take the government's money if some wild-eyed air force generals insisted that they do so. Others, conceding that the goal was attainable, nevertheless thought the price was too high. They preferred the proven capabilities of a well-trained crew in a heavy bomber that would deliver more explosive power to the target with greater certainty and far less cost. Bossart, however, headed a small group of associates who saw MX-774 as attainable *and* practical. They got the job.

Bossart faced a host of unknowns, including a troubling technical question: How is a missile's heading corrected when veering off course in the initial powered phase of flight? Von Braun's response was installation of movable vanes in the exhaust stream. If the onboard guidance system sensed a deviation from the programmed trajectory, corrective signals adjusted the vanes, which presumably steered the V-2 back on course. This solution, though straightforward and uncomplicated, exacted a high penalty. In deflecting the propulsion flow, the vanes reduced thrust as much as 17 percent. Unwilling to forfeit so much power, Bossart devised a way to alter a missile's heading without impeding the jet stream. By mounting engines on swivels that responded to commands from the guidance system, course corrections could be executed continuously by appropriate positioning of the entire engine.

Although Theodore von Karman's Aerojet Engineering Corporation was operating practically in his backyard, Bossart reached across the continent to find a qualified engine supplier for the MX-774. Intrigued by the power plant Reaction Motors had designed for Bell Aircraft Company's supersonic rocket-propelled plane, the X-1, Bossart asked Lovell Lawrence and his partners to produce some modifed versions for the missile project. On May 20, 1946, Bossart formally presented his requirements to RMI. He believed that four upgraded X-1 engines could do the job. The original X-1 engine delivered 1,500 pounds of thrust. To fulfill Bossart's total requirement of eight thousand pounds, the four new engines had to be souped up to generate two thousand pounds each. Lawrence's team met that goal by adding turbopumps that forced fuel into the combustion chambers much faster than the X-1's slower pressure-feed system. They also implemented Bossart's flight-course-correction scheme by adding rods that tilted each engine at the precise angle commanded by the missile's inertial guidance system.

The inspired response by Reaction Motors to the MX-774 challenge was a tribute to Karel J. Bossart's shrewd judgment. At first glance, groping down into the bottom of the barrel for a tiny unknown company, operating on a shoestring, and entrusting one of the most daring engineering feats of the decade to its skeleton staff seemed sheer madness. There's little doubt that, if Lovell Lawrence and his partners had fallen on their collective faces, most of Consolidated Vultee's management would have questioned Bossart's sanity, whereas a failure resulting from a more rational choice—General Electric, Curtiss-Wright, or one of the other big names in the industry—would have been seen only as rotten bad luck. Bossart, however, had gambled and won. Now Laurence Spelman Rockefeller was taking a flier on the little company in Pompton Plains, New Jersey. A half-million dollars was on the line. He and his brothers could easily afford to lose the money. But it was the stigma of bad judgment that failure might cast on the family name that was the more troubling risk to contemplate. Yet the die was cast. The check was signed. The deal was made. Laurance Rockefeller stood up and prepared to congratulate the company's four founders, who had come to New York to witness this little ceremony.

The first to step forward and grasp Rockefeller's outstretched hand was the company's chief engineer. John Shesta had basked in the high esteem of his colleagues ever since joining the roving band of gadgeteers who, more than a decade earlier, had gathered regularly in the open fields of northern New Jersey to try out their odd assortment of experimental motors. The urgent need to set up and tear down quickly, particularly when complaints of strange howling noises and intermittent explosions brought the local constabulary to the scene, prompted Shesta to devise a portable test stand that neatly camouflaged their activity. Dismantled at a moment's notice, the rugged framework appeared to be an innocuous stack of metal pipes when stowed in the trunk of the nearest car.

Next, was James Wyld, director of research. Wyld had staked out an unchallenged claim to that title late in the summer of 1938. One September Sunday afternoon in a cow pasture near Stockton, New Jersey, his tiny rocket motor had astonished the assembled membership of the American Rocket Society. In those days, thrust-to-weight ratio was the most critical performance yardstick. Wyld's motor, small enough to hold in one hand, tipped the scales at only five pounds. Yet when mounted on Shesta's test frame and ignited, the tiny combustion chamber spewed out gases with a thrust of nearly one hundred pounds. The power was twenty times greater than weight committed. A very respectable ratio indeed.

Rockefeller moved on to congratulate Franklin Pierce, the third RMI partner. Pierce's expertise in setting up equipment and monitoring pressure gauges and manometers at various field tryouts had earned him the title of chief test engineer. Before rocketry progressed from part-time hobby to his full-time occupation, Pierce had earned his living as a conductor on New York's BMT subway system.

Finally, Rockefeller shook hands with the man he knew best, Lovell Lawrence. As business manager, dedicating the most time to raising capital, beating the bushes for prospects, and negotiating contracts, Lawrence appeared to be the appropriate choice for president when the company's incorporation papers were filed. He also merited the lion's share of the praise for managing to keep RMI afloat, and creditors at bay, during the company's darkest hours. Now, beaming broadly and thanking Rockefeller profusely, he accepted the check and slipped it into his breast pocket.

36

The Departures

A FROZEN CRUST on the snow crackled underfoot as Fritz Zwicky made his way along a narrow path. His destination this evening was the observatory. The domed structure, glistening in the fading rays of sunset, was perched on the crest some two hundred yards ahead. Impatient to begin the night's work, Zwicky quickened his pace. At the entrance, he stamped his feet, dislodging the snow from his boots, and opened the door. Inside he encountered an assistant, who, after acknowledging Zwicky's greeting, moved quickly to his accustomed place at the control console. The assistant had already opened the dome's huge shuttered roof, exposing the interior to the crisp evening air. Suspended in a mammoth horseshoe bearing, the girders and frame of the telescope towered above them. Zwicky went to the observatory's darkroom, retrieved a few photographic plates, and returned to board a small elevator, which took him up the side of the dome to a cage at the top of the telescope. There he sat down and slid one of the plates into a camera affixed to the prime focus. Then, while consulting a chart on his lap, he lifted a telephone handset from its cradle and dictated instructions to the assistant seated at the console fifty feet below him. Responding to commands punched in by the assistant, the dome slowly revolved on a wheeled track and the telescope rotated within its horseshoe bearing until aligned with the sector of the sky Zwicky planned to explore.

Astronomy was Zwicky's true calling, not teaching or the fascinating research at Aerojet Engineering Corporation, the company founded by Theodore von Karman to produce JATO boosters for army and navy aircraft during World War II. Nor were his speculations about space travel the response to an urge to venture beyond our earthly environment. What fueled his significant contributions to rocketry was a desire to learn more secrets of the stars. As an associate professor of physics at Caltech, Zwicky had been obligated to address all aspects of that broad discipline since joining the faculty in 1927. By 1942, however, he had earned the opportunity to limit his teaching to his own chosen field of study. Eligible then for elevation to senior rank, he was named professor of astrophysics.

While Zwicky's career path is simple to plot, his national roots are not as easily identified. He was born in Varna, Bulgaria, on February 14, 1898, the son of an accountant engaged in international trade who, at the time, was also the Norwegian consul for that southeast European nation. Shortly after the turn of the century, the family moved to Switzerland, where young Zwicky and his two sisters were educated. In 1916, he entered Zurich's Federal Institute of Technology, majoring in mathematics and physics. Following graduation, he was drawn to the mathematical study of gases, solids, liquids, crystals, and the behavior of slow electrons and ions in gases. In 1925, he won a Rockefeller International Education Board fellowship at Caltech, which, in 1927, led to his appointment as an assistant professor of physics. During his first meeting with Caltech president Robert A. Millikan immediately after his arrival in Pasadena, young Zwicky, who was an ardent climber and skier, inquired about the proximity of good mountains in the area. Slightly perplexed, Millikan turned to his window and pointed to Mount Wilson, which is approximately 5,700 feet above sea level. Zwicky, who was accustomed to a virtually unlimited supply of Alpine peaks well above ten thousand feet, gazed at the modest blip on the horizon and said: "Ja, I see the foothills."

When faced with the difficult task of recruiting suitable talent in 1943 for his fledgling Aerojet Engineering Corporation, von Karman was fortunate to find a willing and able candidate for the important post of director of research. Zwicky guided the development work of the new company throughout World War II but later reduced his involvement by shedding management responsibilities and assuming the less onerous duties of a consultant. About the same time, Frank Malina and Jack Parsons, two other Aerojet veterans, also contracted cases of itchy feet.

Malina's disenchantment with his situation had been developing for a long time. A major irritant was the circumstances that forced him to be an administrator rather than a researcher. In the beginning, he was free to dirty his hands along with Parsons, Forman, and Tsien, working on primitive, yet exciting, experiments in the deserted Arroyo Seco. But those days, long past, were replaced by the need to sit in an office overseeing the comings and goings of nearly four hundred chemists, engineers, and technicians. The burdens of management were also harder to bear without ready access to his mentor and father figure, Theodore von Karman. America had discovered this elder statesman of science and claimed him for much bigger things. Drawn more frequently into serving on special commissions and dispensing advice to numerous high councils of government, von Karman finally sold his home in California and took up permanent residence in Washington, D.C.

The void in Malina's professional life that resulted from von Karman's move to the East Coast was made less tolerable by the alarmingly militaristic orientation of rocket research. With the exception of Malina's pet project—the sounding rocket launched at White Sands in November 1945—development goals were consistently expressed in terms of warhead weight and target range. As acting director of the Jet Propulsion Laboratory, Malina was a participant in all critical contract negotiations and found himself on a dizzying fast track, shuttling constantly from Pasadena to Wright Field, Ohio, the air force research center, or completely across the country to Washington, D.C. Some mornings, bleary-eyed and bone weary, he alighted from an all-night flight to be rushed to a prebreakfast conference at the Pentagon, then raced to catch a California-bound airliner in order to preside at a staff meeting in Pasadena later the same day. The pace was suicidal and the work, in Malina's view, was a form of "national insanity" that was applying advanced technology to build a capability for mass murder. Trapped on an endless and seemingly senseless treadmill, he was mentally and physically exhausted. In a revealing self-appraisal decades later, Malina cited some causes of his burnout at the age of thirty-four: "I had dealt [with problems] requiring the use of explosives and toxic chemicals, the safety of our staff and of aircraft test pilots . . . [coped with] frustrations resulting from [working for] administrators who had no grasp of the nature of research, and traveled by air and train to many meetings that frequently were not really necessary."

The time had come to pass the torch to others more attuned to the political and military thinking of the country's leadership. Under the circumstances, Malina saw his abandonment of rocketry as no great loss to its future. When he and his companions had first trucked their equipment to the Arroyo Seco, the number of engineers throughout the world then seriously interested in astronautics was, in Malina's opinion, "less than fifty." By 1948, however, those few-score enthusiasts had grown to many hundreds, perhaps as much as a thousand.

Severing old ties is rarely easy. For Malina, it was made more difficult because members of his staff were also close friends with whom he "had shared many good and many trying times." Yet his new passion, "international cooperation," was far removed from the interests or ken of his colleagues. He was not ready, however, to make an irrevocable break with the past. Instead of submitting a resignation, he negotiated for and obtained a two-year leave of absence.

The United Nations, the new consortium of sovereign states dedicated to the preservation of international peace, represented the kind of world movement to which Malina wanted to hitch his wagon. One of its agencies in particular—the United Nations Educational, Scientific and Cultural Organization—promised to be a logical vehicle for promoting his hopes for the future. Julian Huxley, an Oxford-educated botanist and grandson of the celebrated English naturalist, Thomas Henry Huxley, was also a behind-the-scenes promoter of UNESCO and was ultimately named the organization's first director-general. After setting up his headquarters in Paris, Huxley began to recruit a secretariat. One of the applicants who came knocking on his door was a bright young American scientist voicing a remarkable affinity to Huxley's way of thinking. Frank Malina shared the new director-general's vision of implementing programs that fostered cooperation and understanding among people everywhere. Their common interests even extended to a mutual admiration of the state of Texas. It was Malina's birthplace and Huxley remembered a happy three years in Houston, 1913 through 1916, when he had taught at Rice Institute. Malina was hired, and then he returned to Pasadena to prepare for the relocation to Paris.

Malina's military contacts at Wright Field and the Pentagon were understandably dismayed by this high-ranking defection from a valued developer of a potentially powerful new strategic weapons family. Pressure urging Malina to reconsider came from several sources, including an army general, calling from Washington, who said the country needed Malina's expertise in rocketry. Wavering, Malina sought advice from von Karman, who responded that if younger, he, too, would vigorously pursue a similar goal. Strengthened by von Karman's approval, Malina knew that no one else could dissuade him from joining Huxley. Prior to assuming his post in the UNESCO secretariat, he sought to arm himself with ideas offered by prominent educators, scientists, and politicians. Before returning to Paris, he made a tour of the northeast, interviewing many intellectual and political leaders including Vannevar Bush in Boston, Albert Einstein in Princeton, and Congressman Lyndon Baines Johnson at the nation's capital.

Einstein told Malina that he agreed with UNESCO's stated goal of promoting economic and social progress in disadvantaged third-world countries. Yet he warned that the new organization must also demonstrate the courage to fight for "real" issues, lest it become impotent like its predecessor, the Commission for International Intellectual Cooperation of the defunct League of Nations. Most others, however, pleaded that they did not know enough about UNESCO to contribute any useful comments. Vannevar Bush, for example, uttered nothing more substantive than a wish that all scientists should work together to stop any future wars from starting. Lyndon B. Johnson, the congressman representing Malina's home district in Texas, was comparably uninformed. Johnson admitted that he was "not acquainted with UNESCO's intentions" but excused his ignorance by noting that the United Nations was just a "baby" anyway.

While Frank Malina was conducting his unfruitful canvass of East Coast intellectuals, Jack W. Parsons, another Aerojet veteran, was severing his ties to rocketry in order to apply all of his energy to the making of explosives, a far more lucrative pursuit. Besides, Aerojet was becoming too big and too regimented for his free spirit. He was definitely not in step with a corporate psyche that nurtured management by objective and policymaking by committee. Yet it must be acknowledged that Parsons, possibly more than anyone else, had helped to shape the products that enabled Aerojet to become a viable business entity. Although his early experiments in the Arroyo Seco had frequently ended in explosions that frazzled von Karman's nerves, the eminent professor excused these failures because no one else could do the job better. Von Karman also tolerated the eccentricities. He considered Parsons "an excellent chemist and a delightful screwball [who] loved to recite pagan poetry to the sky while stamping his feet."

Parsons, at times, acted strangely, but when on his good behavior, he might be mistaken for one of the male hopefuls who haunted nearby film studios, waiting to be tapped as Hollywood's next romantic matinee idol. He was tall, debonair, and sported a shock of wavy black hair and a dashing mustache, prompting heads to turn when he walked by.

Although he never appeared on the silver screen, Parsons was a leading character in a show von Karman staged on the deck of the aircraft carrier U.S.S. *Charger*, moored in Norfolk Harbor in August 1943. Navy officers in the Bureau of Aeronautics were urging approval of a large order of JATOs from Aerojet. Yet higher-ups would not let the deal go through until the secretary of the navy and his admirals witnessed a demonstration. Parsons was called upon to oversee the installation of two units under the wings of a new Grumman torpedo-bomber. On the appointed day, the secretary and navy brass assembled on the flight deck. After Parsons completed a last-minute inspection, a pilot in the Grumman revved the engine and then released his brakes. The plane began to move across the flight deck. Then the pilot threw a switch firing the JATOs, and the Grumman zoomed upward, billowing a cloud of smoke that enveloped the secretary and his party. When it cleared, the uniforms of all the onlookers were covered with a dusty yellow residue. The test was a success but the contract was not approved until Parsons worked more magic in his laboratory and eliminated the unwanted by-product.

In the years following his departure from Aerojet, Parsons drifted in and out of a series of jobs. When things were tight, he curbed his bias against big companies and sullenly endured the hypocrisies of corporate culture. If they were offered, he vigorously pursued new opportunities while laughing at risks. Late in the 1940s, his spirit of adventure carried him into the clandestine channels of the international arms business. Contacts developed in these ventures subsequently led to an invitation from the Mexican government to organize and operate an explosives manufacturing plant in Baja California. One of many amenities that his Mexican hosts lavished on Parsons was exclusive use of a fully staffed seventeenth-century castle. The good life ended, however, on a trip to Los Angeles for supplies. As he helped to load chemicals into a trailer, a bottle containing fulminate of mercury slipped from his hands and exploded. Critically burned, he died a few hours later.

Malina abandoned rocketry for an ideal. Parsons sought more excitement. Zwicky, after his years of quiet, steady leadership in propulsion research, returned to his first intellectual love. High on his perch in the Mount Wilson Observatory, he continued his quest to uncover the secrets of cosmic rays, novas, and supernovas. Malina, Parsons, and Zwicky, each in a unique and personal way, had left his mark on rocketry, and moved on.

37

The Tsien Affair

August 1950
Washington, D.C.

LOYALTY OR FRIENDSHIP? Faced with a choice that might confound any man of honor, Dan A. Kimball struggled with his conscience. Knowing that to uphold one he must sacrifice the other, the under secretary of the navy wondered whether to act quickly or do nothing. The cause of his dilemma was a plan revealed to him in confidence by Hsue-shen Tsien.

Tsien had come a long way since he accompanied Frank Malina and Jack Parsons on those Saturday excursions to the Arroyo Seco. At that time, Tsien was a relative newcomer to America. Born in Shanghai in 1909, he was the son of middle-class parents who were able to give him what was, in Chinese society of the 1930s, an advanced university education. But in 1935, having progressed as far as the limited curriculum would allow, he sought a scholarship from the Boxer Rebellion indemnity fund, the modest reparation paid by China (and subsequently returned by the United States to aid worthy students) for attacks on American citizens and property there in 1900. He began by undertaking graduate studies in mechanical engineering at the Massachusetts Institute of Technology. Shortly thereafter, he switched to aeronautical engineering and, upon earning his master's degree, opted to continue under the tutelage of the renowned Theodore von Karman at the California Institute of Technology.

A love of classical music and an attraction to rocketry moved Tsien to become friendly with other similarly disposed Caltech students, including Frank Malina, Apollo M. O. Smith, and Martin Summerfield. Smith had collaborated with Malina on his initial mathematical analyses of their proposed sounding rocket and Summerfield's inspired contributions to liquid-fuel development influenced von Karman to name him vice-president of the newly formed Aerojet Engineering Corporation a few years later.

As von Karman's protégés immersed themselves in government-sponsored research in 1939 and early 1940, Tsien found himself on the outside looking in. Malina, for example, was forbidden to discuss his work with Tsien, who, as an alien, was disqualified for clearance necessary to gain access to classified data. This ban was lifted in 1943, however, when Tsien's obvious value was finally acknowledged, at von Karman's urging, by the government. Tsien then became a frequent associate on many von Karman projects, working with Malina on early military missile experiments and later branching out into jet-propelled aircraft studies. He accompanied von Karman to Europe in 1945 to participate in an evaluation of comparable work in Germany during the war. After Aerojet Engineering was formed, he also served as a consultant on special projects undertaken by the company. For outstanding technical support rendered during the final months of the war, he received a commendation from the air corps citing his "invaluable contribution" to victory. Those in a position to know the scope of his involvement hailed his work as very important to the current need but potentially even more significant to the future.

Tsien, however, was like a fish out of water. His true professional home was a university environment. When offered a full professorship by the Massachusetts Institute of Technology in 1946, he readily accepted to become the youngest holder of that senior rank on its prestigious faculty. Three years later, the goodwill generated by earlier grants to Caltech impelled the Guggenheim Foundation to enhance its commitment by funding the establishment of a new chair: the Goddard Professorship of Jet Propulsion. Tsien was lured away to become its first occupant as well as resident director of research. Settled comfortably and now the beneficiary of a substantial salary plus many other amenities, Tsien and his wife, Yin, whom he had married on a prewar visit to China, decided to establish their home in America. During the summer of 1949, they made a brief trip to Canada, secured permanent residence visas at an American consular office there, and shortly after returning to Pasadena submitted applications for United States citizenship. It was a joyful, carefree time for Tsien, Yin, and their two young children.

Tsien, therefore, was understandably not prepared for the blow in June 1950 that blasted his idyllic future into oblivion. Several events in the preceding months had led many Americans to believe that an enormous international conspiracy was brewing that threatened to engulf them all. Alger Hiss, a former high State Department official, was brought to trial on charges alleging he was a communist spy. Detonation of an atomic bomb by Russia suddenly broke the exclusive hold the United States had on that awesome weapon. Mao Tse-Tung's marauding communist armies overran mainland China, forcing Chiang Kai-shek's forces to flee to sanctuary on the island of Formosa. In Britain, authorities revealed that some of the western alliance's vital atomic secrets had been passed to the Russians by one of the alliance's own top scientists, Dr. Klaus Fuchs. And Joseph McCarthy, the junior senator from Wisconsin, waved a sheaf of papers as he informed startled members of the Women's Republican Club of Wheeling, West Virginia, that in his hand he held the names of more than two hundred communists then at work in the State Department. Amid the furor stirred up by these perceived menaces to America's national security, William F. Hynes, a retired Los Angeles police officer who had headed the department's "red squad," dutifully notified the Federal Bureau of Investigation that Hsue-shen Tsien, an alien cleared for classified government work, had been a member of Professional Unit 122, the Pasadena section of the American Communist party.

The response to this charge was predictable and inevitable. Tsien was summarily stripped of his security clearance and bluntly told that his services were no longer needed by the government of the United States. Reeling from this assault on his integrity, he vigorously denied that he had ever been a Communist. Although Hynes and William Ward Kimple, another former "red squad" investigator, subsequently identified copies of a Communist party registration card with Tsien's name on it, no other evidence was brought forth to support their claim. It is true, however, that Tsien had engaged in numerous late-night bull sessions with fellow students throughout the 1930s. Politics was usually the main discussion topic. But these gabfests were never claimed to be anything more subversive than some harmless jawboning about the country's ills. The first amendment to the United States Constitution notwithstanding, talk, colored by the temper of the times, was enough to bring Tsien's world crashing down around him.

Commendably, his superiors and friends rallied to his side. Caltech's president, Dr. Lee DuBridge, led a phalanx of scientists and educators who failed to right what they all viewed as a disgraceful miscarriage of justice. Although treated no more harshly than other alleged members of Professional Unit 122, Tsien bitterly complained to a colleague, "I am an apparently unwelcome guest in this country." Depriving him of the opportunity to work on classified government projects was more a swipe at his pride than his pocketbook. Because he was highly regarded by DuBridge and other top scientists, there was little danger that his career would suffer even though he was cut off from the flow of government grants.

The humiliation he endured during the ensuing weeks seemed to amplify a responsibility largely ignored before his fall from public favor. For several months he had received appeals, with escalating frequency, from his father in China, who was in failing health. The aging parent, a widower, was told he must undergo an operation. He needed the comfort and support of his son, and Tsien's much younger sister, who was at an extremely impressionable age, required guidance, which the father was poorly equipped to provide. Growing more sensitive to the developing crisis within his family, Tsien gave serious thought to an option he had decisively rejected earlier. The prospect of a prolonged visit to China now appeared attractive. It would give him time to think through plans for the future while succoring his parent and counseling his sister. Although agreeing with friends who suggested that the new communist regime might be applying pressure through his father to orchestrate the return of a prized and talented scientist to the homeland, Tsien nevertheless now believed that his filial responsibilities must be acknowledged. He therefore purchased airline tickets to Hong Kong for himself, his wife, and children. Alarmed by the imminent loss of one of Caltech's brightest stars, Lee DuBridge was tempted to persuade him to postpone his departure in order to give the matter more thought, but he said nothing. Instead he urged Tsien to make one last appeal for exoneration by going to Washington and seeing their mutual friend, Dan A. Kimball.

Kimball seemed ideally positioned to set things right. His high office endowed him with considerable clout within the Truman administration, and in addition to knowing Tsien well, the genial navy under secretary admired the brilliant young rocket scientist. However, when Tsien walked into Kimball's office in the Pentagon, neither was aware that the difficult situation, which both wished to resolve, would, as a result of this meeting, grow intolerably worse.

Kimball, a supercharged former industrial marketing executive, and Tsien, now an uncharacteristically outspoken Oriental, had been drawn together by their mutual affiliation with von Karman's Aerojet Engineering Corporation. Kimball, who was a dozen years older than Tsien, had been a pursuit pilot in the army's air branch during World War I. When mustered out in 1919, he was hired by General Tire and Rubber Company and went to work in the firm's Los Angeles sales office. Progressing upward through the organization, he eventually headed the company's operations in eleven western states. When von Karman and his partners exchanged their ownership of Aerojet Engineering for shares of General Tire and Rubber in 1947, Kimball became executive vice-president and general manager of the new subsidiary. Politically well connected, Kimball was appointed assistant secretary of the navy for air in February 1949, becoming the first former army pilot to set aviation policy for the navy. Three months later, caught up in a Defense Department budget turmoil involving the B-36 bomber and navy supercarriers, he survived the imbroglio, emerging as the under secretary, the second highest civilian in the Navy Department.

Kimball tried to suppress his alarm when Tsien stood up and they shook hands. It had been a highly emotional meeting. In recounting details of his ordeal during the previous weeks, Tsien lost his composure at one point and burst into tears. Certain that Tsien was not a Communist, Kimball had tried several times, unsuccessfully, to have his security clearance reinstated, and he promised to try again. But Kimball's faith in his troubled friend faltered when he learned that Tsien was privately making plans to return to China. When the door closed behind his visitor, Kimball sat silently, drumming his desktop with his fingertips. A minute later, he called the Justice Department, informing his opposite number there that Hsue-shen Tsien must not be permitted to leave the United States.

PART FOUR

The Achievers

38

Project Bumper

July 24, 1950
Cocoa Beach, Florida

I T WAS MARTIN Summerfield's idea: a brilliant scheme to trigger a quantum leap forward—quickly, with known and proven components. Nearly five years earlier, soon after the first sounding rocket experiment at White Sands, Summerfield had come to Frank Malina to show him some calculations. The zenith of the WAC CORPOR-AL's vertical climb on that memorable day had been forty-three miles. Summerfield's data, however, suggested that much loftier altitudes were within reach. With luck, a rocket might be fired higher than 350 miles into extraterrestrial space.

The proposal he presented was audacious, yet simple in concept. No wild theories. Just a logical analysis of current capabilities, which formed a basis for a startling recommendation. Combine the power of two seasoned rockets, he urged, to surpass a goal that neither could accomplish alone. The plan he offered required mounting a WAC CORPORAL on the nose of a V-2. The sounding rocket then becomes a second stage, which is fired after the mother vehicle, the V-2, has exhausted her fuel. Malina showcased this proposal in a technical essay that was subsequently published in the July/August 1946 issue of *Army Ordnance Journal*.

Within three months, work on "Project Bumper," as Summerfield's brainstorm came to be known, was under way. First, lengthy wind-tunnel and static tests were conducted, which led to the development of an efficient decoupling system to separate the WAC from its booster at precisely the right moment. Despite this auspicious beginning, subsequent progress was slow. It was not until February 24, 1949, almost two and a half years later, that Summerfield's projections were corroborated. On that date, an initial boost by a modified version of Hitler's vengeance weapon enabled an instrument-laden WAC to rocket nearly 250 miles above the glistening crystal surface of White Sands Proving Ground.

For Summerfield and his JPL colleagues, "Bumper" was indeed a distinguished achievement. For the army brass, however, it was more of a teaser, a tantalizing invitation to test another dimension—the horizontal distance that a warhead can be rocketed from one point on earth to another. Although the army's forty-by-sixty-mile plot of open space centered around White Sands was adequate for the range of conventional artillery, aiming a Bumper-WAC in any direction except straight up was courting disaster. A heading into the north quadrant might carry a fully powered second stage into the city of Albuquerque. To the east, there was the Mescalero Indian Reservation and the towns of Roswell, Artesia, and Carlsbad; to the west, Hot Springs; to the south, El Paso, and beyond that most western city in Texas, the Mexican state of Chihuahua. Obviously, the army's wide-open spaces were not wide enough.

But the Atlantic Ocean was. Facing east from deserted Cocoa Beach on a thin strip of the sand and dunes that line much of Florida's shoreline, Colonel Harold R. Turner found the thousands of square miles of open sea needed to test Bumper safely. Turner, former commandant of the White Sands Proving Ground, was now stationed at Redstone Arsenal in Huntsville, Alabama. He and Wernher von Braun's cadre of German rocket scientists had been moved there from Fort Bliss, Texas, in December 1949. The relocation was ordered because the expanding rocket program required more and better facilities than were available at the aging cavalry outpost near the Mexican border. Rehabilitating old structures and adding new ones would have depleted the army's meager construction budget by a whopping $4.5 million, a tidy sum in the eyes of a vote-seeking cost-cutting Eightieth United States Congress. Redstone Arsenal, however, offered many thousands of square feet of vacant warehouses, toolshops, and office space. Filling that void with an important ordnance development activity, while also not spending funds for comparable quarters elsewhere, was efficient and prudent management.

Almost five months to the day after Colonel Turner first stepped onto the sandy spit that was Cocoa Beach, he and a crew, summoned from White Sands, were ready to launch a Bumper-WAC on a long horizontal trajectory above the waters of the Atlantic. Offshore, two destroyers, aided by six navy aircraft, patrolled the sector surrounding the rocket's planned flight path and ultimate splash into the sea. Ships had been warned to remain clear of the potentially hazardous longitudes and latitudes when an "alert" was called. For Turner, the policy of issuing this advance notice had been the source of a humiliating embarrassment five days earlier. Before dawn on the previous Wednesday, July 19, word had gone out to all ships plying the north-south sea lanes adjacent to Florida to remain outside of the proscribed sector for an early-morning launch. Scores of vessels slowed speed or altered courses, awaiting an expected all clear after a short interval. It never came. Hour after hour the anticipated firing was postponed. Most delays were caused by last-minute recording-equipment glitches or communications breakdowns. Also, once, just before noon, the countdown was halted when a blockade plane was forced to abandon its patrol and return to base for fuel. Finally, at 5:45 P.M., with apparently all snags untangled, the countdown progressed into the final ninety seconds. When "zero" ultimately echoed over the loudspeaker system, a puff of smoke and a red glow appeared at the base of the V-2. Recording instruments displayed a slow buildup of thrust to eight tons. No higher. Too little for lift-off but enough to dangerously impair the delicate balance of the vehicle on its base. Turner immediately cut the power. He later explained to a dubious crowd of news reporters that "heat and high humidity" had undoubtedly impaired some of the rocket's components.

Five days later, Turner waited tensely in a sandbagged bunker three hundred yards from a new carefully assembled Bumper-WAC. Standing next to him was Kurt Debus, a veteran of hundreds of V-2 launches from Test Stand Number Seven at Peenemünde, carefully ticking off boxes on his clipboard checklist as he monitored progress via the control center communications channel. Beside Debus was a man whose career was to be marred or enhanced by the events of the next few minutes. Dr. Richard W. Porter's reputation was on the line. As director of General Electric Company's rocket development, he was the one to whom heads would turn if Bumper failed to perform according to plan.

General Electric was the proclaimed technical partner of army ordnance. Although von Braun and his team worked extensively behind the scenes, their contributions throughout the 1940s were soft-pedaled and rarely acknowledged publicly. Porter therefore, as head of "Project Hermes," the name assigned to the postwar V-2 research program, was one of few scientists then known to be engaged in American rocket development. At the time, he directed General Electric's highly secret rocket propulsion test center at Malta, New York. Secluded in a forest about twenty miles from the company's main operations at Schenectady, the three-thousand-acre testing ground, surrounded by barbed wire and watchtowers, was remarkably similar to Dr. Walter Thiel's engine works at Peenemünde: thick-walled concrete buildings, massive steel test frames obscured by large earthen revetments, and deflectors and fire pits to cushion the destructive thrust of the flaming exhaust. Three months earlier, on April 11, 1950, General Electric had proudly opened a small section of the acreage for inspection by a busload of journalists. Porter, whom the *New York Times* described as the "youthful but gray-haired" host of the event, was circumspect and closemouthed. According to the *Times*, "The only indication [Porter] gave of progress was that the rocket power plants developed by General Electric were 10 percent more efficient than the German V-2 which, he said, meant they could do about twice the job of the Nazi weapon." Despite additional prodding, he refused to give specific performance figures.

Porter was similarly constrained three months later at Cocoa Beach. Waiting in the bunker with Colonel Turner, Kurt Debus, and a dozen technicians, he knew that he was to say little during a meeting with the press later in the day. There to help take the heat in the wake of a failure, Porter watched Debus look up from his clipboard and nod to Turner. At that instant, a red flare arched high over the control bunker. Then, amid spewing smoke and flame, the V-2 and its hitchhiking WAC rose from the pad, accelerated rapidly, and disappeared into a cirrus cloud high overhead. Just eighty seconds later, at an altitude of 51,000 feet, the WAC decoupled from its booster and arched downrange. Within minutes, telemetered data confirmed a successful flight. General Electric and the army had captured vital data needed to move ahead. Porter, after pausing to light his pipe, savored the moment as he shook hands with Turner and Debus.

39

The High-Tech Newcomers

February 1952
Culver City, California

LEANING BACK IN his swivel chair, Dean Wooldridge read the letter again. A faint smile flickered on his lips as he savored this happy conclusion to a delicate negotiation. As director of research and development for Hughes Aircraft Company, Wooldridge bore major responsibility for recruiting managers to support the recent rapid growth of the company's airborne electronics business. The task was maddeningly difficult. Experienced engineers had long since been snapped up by hundreds of defense contractors across the country struggling to satisfy the demand for high-technology systems needed to fight the war in Korea. A further complication was the danger of being caught in the cross fire of interservice rivalries if Hughes, as a major air force contractor, enticed key people away from other companies working for the army. Yet Wooldridge had gone one step further by successfully penetrating one of the strongest bastions of military research itself—the army's missile development center at Huntsville, Alabama.

Six years before this coup, Wooldridge had terminated a promising career at Bell Telephone Laboratories in New York City to accept the co-directorship of research and development at Hughes Aircraft. His new partner at Hughes was Simon Ramo, an old friend. Both had been awarded doctorates by the California Institute of Technology in 1936, then gone their separate ways. Ramo, who was hired by General Electric in Schenectady, New York, later claimed that his musical talent, rather than his academic record, was the deciding factor in landing the job. His prospective boss, who was also a patron of the city's symphony orchestra, was on the lookout for likely candidates to strengthen the string section. With the discovery that Ramo was a skilled amateur violinist, the interview became a love feast. Ramo, however, subsequently proved that the decision to hire him was inspired, despite the motivation. Before leaving General Electric ten years later, he had served brilliantly as section head of the general engineering laboratory and chief of the physics branch of electronics research. Yet he was impatient to apply his expertise to projects that produced visible practical results. Carrying scientific discoveries to logical conclusions by actually building a usable product was the carrot on the stick that ultimately lured Ramo away to work for the eccentric industrialist, Howard Hughes.

Wooldridge's arrival in Culver City in 1946, a few months after Ramo came aboard, completed the magic combination that was to transform a third-rate aircraft company, perennially wallowing in red ink, into the paragon of modern-day business success—the high-profit, high-tech corporate enterprise. Prior to the advent of Ramo and Wooldridge, Hughes Aircraft was little more than an expensive toy manipulated by the whims of its unpredictable owner. Even as a youth, Howard Hughes had been larger than life. Before celebrating his twentieth birthday, he had been orphaned, inherited his father's majority share of the enormously profitable Hughes Tool Company, secured a court order removing his "disabilities as a minor" to thwart being overseen by a legal guardian, acquired 100 percent control of the tool company by orchestrating purchase of minority interests from his uncle and grandparents, married the beautiful Ella Rice, and hired Noah Dietrich as his "financial adviser," an association that would continue for thirty-two years. Before his thirtieth birthday, Hughes had survived his first plane crash, was divorced by his wife, produced an Academy Award–winning motion picture, set a new air speed record, and founded Hughes Aircraft Company.

When established in 1932, Hughes Aircraft was no more than a convenient vehicle for funding an expensive diversion. Money earned by the tool company was funneled into this corporate subsidiary to transform a Boeing military pursuit plane into a sleek racer, which Howard planned to fly in the All American Air Meet in Miami in January 1934. Instead of dissolving this accounting shell after the race, Hughes, enthralled by his role as president of an aircraft company, devised various stratagems to keep it going. By 1946, however, Howard's folly had become a voracious parasite, which, each succeeding year, consumed a larger share of the prodigious profits generated by its parent, the Hughes Tool Company. A prime cause of these deficits was Howard's determination to develop a medium-range two-engine bomber, constructed of plywood. For nearly three years, the ill-fated D-2 monopolized the working days of the aircraft subsidiary's five hundred employees and cut viciously into the earnings of the lucrative Hughes oil-drilling equipment business. The fact that Howard never put a model into production—nor even captured a modest share of any of the industry's numerous peripheral markets—continuously rankled Noah Dietrich, who, in 1946, was executive vice-president of the parent company.

Not even during America's frenzied drive to build thousands of warplanes after the bombing of Pearl Harbor was Hughes Aircraft able to carve out a piece of the action. Although a torrent of war contracts spewed out of the Pentagon, the army air corps only tossed Hughes a few crumbs to build wooden wings and other components for military gliders. Hughes's unorthodox methods and his proclivity for promoting his own ideas rather than adapting proposals to government specifications made him persona non grata in military procurement offices. This distaste was summed up in a memo circulated January 16, 1942, by the Air Matériel Command at Wright Field near Dayton, Ohio: The Hughes "plant is a hobby of the management . . . [its] facilities, both in engineering personnel and equipment, are not being used to the full advantage in this emergency . . . the Air Corps should discontinue any further aircraft projects with this organization."

Finally, in 1948, Howard capitulated by embracing an entirely new action plan to win some significant government business. To neutralize the venom of the "Hate Hughes Club"—a label he applied to his air force critics—a trio of managers was brought in to instill new vigor in the floundering aircraft operations. In a classic variant of the if-you-can't-beat-'em-join-'em strategy, Hughes hired two members of the club: Ira C. Eaker and Harold L. George, recently retired air force lieutenant generals. To round out this stellar management team, Hughes tapped Charles B. Thornton, a former Ford Motor Company executive. Eaker, as a vice-president and chief liaison officer of the tool company, was to be a much-needed buffer between Noah Dietrich and the notorious wastrels at Culver City. Harold George and Charles Thornton were to put the aircraft operations in order. Their job was to install controls, tighten procedures, and generally make Hughes Aircraft more palatable to the military procurement clique. When George and Thornton moved into their new offices at Culver City, the books had just been closed on another bad year. A $700,000 loss was reported on gross sales of $1.9 million.

Prospects for a quick turnaround were virtually nil. The only plus in a bleak sea of negatives was the modestly profitable research being conducted for the air force by two able young scientists, Simon Ramo and Dean Wooldridge. Their outstanding talents were enough to prompt the powers-that-be at Wright Field to temporarily overcome their distaste for the company and commission some studies leading to the design of an airborne radar detection system for locating and destroying enemy aircraft on the blackest nights and in the foulest weather. Ironically, no other company had ventured to undertake such research. Therefore, when Pentagon planners moved an all-weather interceptor capability to the top of their priority list, Hughes Aircraft enjoyed a comfortable lead over potential competitors. In fact, thanks to Ramo and Wooldridge, Hughes was so far ahead that the air force had no other choice but to award the company an $8-million contract—more than four times the previous gross annual sales—to equip two hundred Lockheed F-94s with the new weapons system.

Ramo, Wooldridge, and Hughes Aircraft were on a roll. The success of the interceptor system paved the way for more lucrative contracts. The next major project was the design and assembly of a complete weapons package for pinpointing the location of an enemy plane and automatically guiding a 110-pound air-to-air missile directly to the target. This feat was capped by submission of the winning entry in an industry-wide competition to produce the most efficient weapons and navigation controller for the F-102, the new air force interceptor that flew faster than the speed of sound. In six brief years, Ramo and Wooldridge had literally created a new hot, fast-moving, high-tech powerhouse. Hughes Aircraft had come from nowhere to emerge at the top of the heap, an industry superstar operating on the leading edge of scientific development.

Sitting in his office as the late-afternoon sun dipped closer to the horizon, Dean Wooldridge laid the letter aside, reached for a pad at his elbow, and began jotting a note to the company's vice-president of personnel. The way is now clear, Wooldridge wrote, for Hughes to make an offer to Dr. Walter Schwidetzky. The letter had authorized Wooldridge to openly recruit Schwidetzky, who was then chief of measurement at the Ordnance Guided Missile Center of Redstone

Arsenal. Schwidetzky, however, not Wooldridge, had initiated the negotiations. Upon learning that a key scientist on Wernher von Braun's team wanted to join Hughes Aircraft, Wooldridge, rigidly adhering to defense industries protocol, forbade his deputies to offer any encouragement to Schwidetzky until Redstone Arsenal had been notified. On February 15, 1952, Wooldridge dispatched a letter to von Braun explaining in the most diplomatic terms that Schwidetzky had applied for a position at Hughes Aircraft. Eleven days later, von Braun replied. If he harbored any resentment about this defection of an associate who had shared the trials and triumphs of Peenemünde, the months of internment, the interrogations, and finally the journey from Germany to America and those nerve-racking weeks at Fort Strong in Boston Harbor, von Braun kept such feelings to himself. But he was quick to advise Wooldridge that the news of Schwidetzky's imminent departure came as no surprise: "Dr. Schwidetzky has indicated his intention to leave Redstone Arsenal on 1 July, 1952. . . . The sole reason for his taking this step is the detrimental effect of the North Alabama climate on the health condition of his wife. Under these circumstances our installation will lose him anyhow, regardless of which new assignment he may decide to take. Thus, our work will not be affected if you make him an offer."

Indeed, the "North Alabama climate" was a more effective disassembler of von Braun's team than he dared to admit. After more than two years' exposure to the hot dry air of west Texas and New Mexico, the transplanted Germans proved particularly vulnerable to the cold and dampness experienced during subsequent winters in Huntsville. Schwidetzky, consequently, was only one of several who ultimately fled the debilitating environment. Dr. Helmut Schlitt, for example, was faced with a situation remarkably similar to Schwidetzky's. Schlitt's wife had contracted a chronic sciatic condition following a harrowing six months in Landshut, Germany, during the winter of 1946–1947. Before securing clearance to join Schlitt in Texas in April 1947, she had been housed in a building in such disrepair that her husband later reported that "the water running down the walls inside her room literally froze to icicles and her bed comforter froze tight to the wall." In Texas, her sciatic problem improved, but when the von Braun team was transferred to Redstone Arsenal, her condition worsened, prompting Schlitt to seek employment elsewhere.

Having assured Wooldridge that the loss of Schwidetzky would not adversely affect the work at Huntsville, von Braun generously hastened to add: "This should not be construed to mean, however, that Dr. Schwidetzky's separation from our organization will not be sorely felt. I have known him for about ten years and consider him an outstanding and extremely inventive electronic engineer with a very thorough and broad scientific background. He is familiar with inertial and radio guidance systems for guided missiles and did an outstanding job in developing and adapting a great variety of [components] for our telemetering program. I am sure that you will soon come to appreciate his work if you can secure his services. He has a pleasant personality and is a good team man." Just the kind of managers we need, Wooldridge concluded. Then he stapled his note to von Braun's letter and flipped them into his "out" box.

40

From Soldier to Businessman

March 24, 1952
Frankfurt, West Germany

SITTING ALONE IN a salon of the Parkhotel on Wiessenhüttenplatz, Walter Dornberger poured cream into his second cup of coffee. He had time to kill before his appointment with a prominent Frankfurt business executive whose office was nearby. But his mind was on other matters. Particularly the unexpected interview with an American journalist earlier that morning. Initially puzzled by the urgent call from the front desk, he finally concluded that word about his arrival must have been leaked by someone at the airport or on the hotel staff.

Jolted from a deep sleep by the ringing of his bedside telephone shortly after 8:00 A.M., he groggily had agreed to see a reporter who claimed to represent the Associated Press. Gathering his composure, Dornberger dressed quickly, went downstairs, and greeted his visitor. Because the young man was in a hurry, their meeting was brief. His questioning centered on a subject that Dornberger was eminently qualified to address: What was Herr Dornberger's assessment of current United States missiles in relation to the wartime V-2? The former Peenemünde commander's answer was included in the lead of a dispatch printed the following morning in the *New York Times:* "A German expert who advised the United States Air Force on guided missiles said today the United States had started mass production on missiles 'which are far better and much more effective than the German V-2s of 1945.' "

Dornberger was having second thoughts. Had he overstepped the line and breached security? Or worse yet, would his act of candor jeopardize his employment by Bell Aircraft Corporation? Then there was his comment about Russia. In response to another query by the AP reporter, he said that the Soviet Union had not reached the same high level in development of guided missiles as the United States. How did he know? This was a question Dornberger later asked himself. Was secret allied military intelligence his only source for this assessment? If so, he was courting disaster by blabbing about it. Unfortunately, any defense Dornberger might later put forward alleging that this was solely personal speculation was weakened by the dogmatic tone of another statement quoted in the *Times:* "Soviet research [is now about] at the place the Germans were in 1945."

Yet Dornberger had been in tighter spots in the past and had always managed to wiggle out of them. In March 1944, for example, Wernher von Braun had been arrested by the Gestapo. The charge was treason. Gestapo chief Heinrich Himmler, miffed because his attempt to seize control of the growing rocket operations had been thwarted by von Braun's refusal to go along, charged that among other disloyal acts von Braun was planning an escape to England with secret military documents. A court of inquiry was convened that was ready to declare von Braun guilty unless he could decisively prove his innocence. The rocket program and Dornberger's future were about to go down in flames. While a web of concocted evidence slowly tightened around von Braun, he was suddenly rescued. Years later he described the dramatic scene in an interview with *The New Yorker:* "One day while the inquiry was in full swing, Dornberger burst into the room and presented some papers that brought about my immediate release. . . . [He] had gone directly to Hitler's headquarters about my predicament."

Dornberger's resourcefulness was also instrumental in saving his own neck after his surrender to the Allies. When interrogated by the British, he was abruptly informed that inasmuch as they were unable to find Obergruppenführer Hans Kammler, ostensibly the commander of the V-1/V-2 assault on the English civilian populace, Dornberger was to be tried in his place as a war criminal at Nuremberg. Dornberger protested, claiming that if he were brought to trial, every military technician who worked on the atomic bombs dropped on Hiroshima and Nagasaki should also be called to account. For the next two years, he languished in a military prison at Brigend in South Wales, while the war crimes prosecutors wrestled with the problem, trying to fashion a case that would not boomerang on Allied arms makers.

Though incarcerated, Dornberger was not held incommunicado. From family and friends, he learned that von Braun and nearly a hundred other veterans of Peenemünde were billeted at Fort Bliss, Texas, while working for the United States Army at White Sands. Dornberger's extensive exposure to political gamesmanship, practiced by many top-ranking militarists, sharpened his sensitivity to the nuances of interservice rivalries then building within the American defense establishment. Aware that the American army ordnance branch enjoyed exclusive access to German rocket expertise, Dornberger, using highly placed intermediaries, got word to the United States air staff at Supreme Headquarters Allied Expeditionary Force that he could provide vital know-how that, until then, had been denied to them.

The seed, once planted, eventually blossomed. Three months later, plucked from the brink of a Nuremberg trial, he found himself on an American military transport headed for Wright-Patterson Air Force Base near Dayton, Ohio. Installed there as the top German rocket guru, Dornberger enjoyed a comfortable livelihood while scouting, at his leisure, large aircraft manufacturers and budding rocket companies for attractive employment opportunities. In 1950, the right one came along. After three years as a civilian government employee, and fed up with the red tape and shilly-shallying, he left the air force and joined Bell Aircraft Corporation in Buffalo, New York. When questioned about this career move by columnist Joseph Alsop, Dornberger responded: "Over there [in wartime Germany] you could get a decision made. It was often wrong, but at least you knew where you stood. . . . Now you have to get twenty-seven men to make any decision, all generals, all changing their jobs and minds all the time." While Dornberger's assessment of working conditions at Wright-Patterson was an obvious exaggeration, it was nevertheless time to move on. As Bell's revenues grew, Dornberger's status in the organization rose, too. In addition to his duties as an adviser to the company's chief executive officer, he eventually became Bell's international ambassador of new business, traveling frequently to Europe to hobnob with prospects.

After draining the last swallow of coffee from his near-empty cup, Dornberger dabbed his lips with a napkin. Reflecting that possibly he was unnecessarily anxious about the consequences of his unguarded comments to the AP reporter, he tried to put himself in a more positive frame of mind by directing his thinking to a project recently undertaken with a former Peenemünde subordinate whom he recruited to join him at Bell. Dornberger had lured Krafft Ehricke away

from von Braun's team at Huntsville to help draft plans for an experimental passenger-carrying rocket plane. Ehricke, though five
years younger than the youthful von Braun, could reasonably claim
that he was a twenty-year veteran of rocket development when he
came to Bell. In 1931, at the tender age of fourteen, he had been a
faithful observer, though not yet an active participant, in the
Raketenflugplatz experiments. When von Braun began hiring a staff for
the new development works at Peenemünde in 1937, Ehricke was too
young and lacked the experience to qualify for a position there. Two
years later, when Hitler's legions marched into Poland, he was drafted
into the army.

Ehricke might not have survived the war had not Field Marshal
Walther von Brauchitsch, circumventing Hitler's orders, arranged to
secure needed technical specialists for Peenemünde by culling them
from combat units. Injured at Dunkirk, Ehricke was subsequently
thrown into the fierce fighting on the Russian front. Luck seemed to
be running out for the young tank commander until he was ordered to
report to a new battalion then forming in a tiny village on the Baltic
coast. Arriving there in June 1942, Ehricke was assigned to a rocket-
engine development section headed by Walter Thiel. To his army
superiors, Thiel was a hardworking and innovative engineering manager. Privately, he was also a visionary. Ehricke, a kindred spirit,
listened enthralled to his chief's plans for the future. Late at night,
when others were asleep, Ehricke watched while Thiel drew sketches
of test and launch emplacements for rockets large enough to carry men
to the moon and the planets beyond. With eyes blazing through thick
glasses, Thiel excitedly explained that the deep natural gorges in
isolated regions of Bavaria would be ideal sites for developing and
firing the huge rocket engines. At the same time, he inspired the
creative talents of his young assistant by encouraging him to explore
the potential of yet undeveloped sources of propulsion, such as liquid
hydrogen and nuclear energy.

As Hitler's empire crumbled outside his Berlin bunker, and von
Braun and his companions wended their way south to their Alpine
hideout, Ehricke also abandoned Peenemünde. He set out on foot for
Berlin, where he located his wife, who was staying in a damaged,
though inhabitable, apartment on the city's outskirts. Determined to
work only for the Americans, he hid whenever there was a knock on
the door. If the caller was Russian, French, or British, his wife
routinely said, "I don't know where he is." One day she answered

with the usual denial of his whereabouts and then belatedly recognized the United States insignia on the officer's uniform. As he turned away, she excitedly called after him, "He's here. He's here."

Ehricke was in the second contingent of Peenemünde expatriates to arrive in Fort Bliss, Texas. While there, he worked on several V-2 launches at White Sands, and when the team was transferred to Huntsville, Alabama, he went with them. But he was restless. Philosophically at odds with von Braun's ultraconservative approach to rocket design, Ehricke preferred to work closer to the edge. He was more of a risk taker than von Braun, who religiously added redundant strength to his designs as "insurance." Ehricke deplored this "Brooklyn Bridge" construction and argued vehemently that gains in thrust and payload capacity more than made up for the increased risk. Von Braun, however, was not swayed. Consequently, Ehricke was ready and anxious to move when Walter Dornberger dangled the invitation to work on Bell's proposed rocket plane.

As Dornberger walked out of the Parkhotel onto Wiessenhüttenplatz, the earlier uneasiness about the Associated Press interview disappeared. Bracing his shoulders in the manner of a proper aristocratic Prussian general, he waited aloofly while the doorman summoned a taxicab from the line waiting at a nearby corner. Once seated inside, he perfunctorily gave the driver his destination and settled back on the cushions, preparing to enjoy the ride. He smiled as he thought about the many who had fallen by the wayside. But not Walter Dornberger—he was a survivor.

41

A Think Tank for Rocketry

September 1954
Inglewood, California

A TALL MAN, wearing a blue seersucker suit, approached the entrance of a former public school at 409 East Manchester Boulevard. Tanned, fit, and sporting a Panama hat, Brigadier General Bernard A. Schriever, clothed in the natty attire of a successful businessman, sprinted up the steps and into the building. Yet, at forty-four years of age, his only exposure to the world of commerce had occurred sixteen years earlier when he had been briefly employed as a co-pilot for Northwest Airlines.

That abandonment of a military career had by no means been Schriever's choice. After serving five years as a pilot in the army reserve, he was transferred to inactive status because of budget curtailments. In October 1938, however, he was back on track with a commission in the regular army. Given a second chance to carve out a prominent niche in the air service, Schriever methodically executed the right career moves. His starting point was the Seventh Bomb Group at Hamilton Field, California. From there, wearing the silver bars of a first lieutenant, he went to Wright Field, Ohio, assuming the duties of test pilot. Next, graduation from the Air Corps Engineering School qualified him for promotion to captain. In June 1942, after earning a master's degree in aeronautical engineering, he began his World War II overseas service as a major in the 19th Bomb Group in the southwest Pacific. He flew most of his sixty-three combat missions as a B-17 pilot for which he was awarded the Distinguished Service and Air Medals, the Legion of Merit, a Purple Heart, and two unit citations.

Beginning in December 1942, he was appointed to a succession of ground-based posts, ranging from head of the Fifth Air Force mainte-

218

nance division to the engineering chief of staff and then to commanding officer of the advanced headquarters of the air force's Far East Service Group. After the war, he was assigned to the Pentagon in Washington, D.C., in charge of scientific liaison for deputy chief of staff, matériel. He continued in this work when the air force became independent of the army the next year.

Schriever was moving up, but unlike his former heavy-bomber colleagues, he did not subscribe to the maxim that bigger is better. As the most vocal of a small minority, he excoriated the alleged assets of that much-praised linchpin of the Strategic Air Command, the B-52. Although just a colonel at the time, he brazenly stood nose to nose against SAC's leader, General Curtis E. LeMay, railing that the B-52 was too big and too slow. Arguing that its huge fuselage—enlarged specifically to accommodate the cumbersome hydrogen bomb—was unnecessary with the smaller, improved thermonuclear weapons then in the development pipeline, he lobbied vigorously for a lighter, faster bomber, one that would deliver just as much punch when launching air-to-ground missiles equipped with atomic warheads. LeMay, while grudgingly admiring the young colonel's brashness, remained unconvinced. Yet LeMay's intransigence failed to discourage Schriever, who continued to warn against the day when manned bombers would be rendered obsolete by globe-girdling, less vulnerable ballistic missiles. Wherever he could find a receptive ear in the Department of Defense, he preached a doctrine extolling their superiority. This proselytizing was undertaken with a single-minded, almost fanatical fervor, prompting one of his friends to observe that "they thought Ben was insane."

Schriever's military career probably would have come to an abrupt end without the clarion call of alarm voiced by John von Neumann of the Institute for Advanced Study in Princeton, New Jersey. The world-renowned mathematician had recently served as chairman of a select group of scientists and industrialists convened to assess the competitive caliber of America's national defense establishment. Initially known as "Teapot" but later renamed the Strategic Missiles Evaluation Committee, it set out to postulate the progress of international weapons technology eight years into the future. Using the committee's projections as a base, von Neumann called for a crash program to build an inventory of operational intercontinental missiles before the end of the 1950s. To direct this gargantuan effort, air force assistant secretary Trevor Gardner campaigned for the selection of a "brigadier general of unusual competence to work directly with the contractors [providing] top-level support and technical supervision."

Pentagon insiders raised their eyebrows in surprise when Bernard Schriever was plucked from the pool of available brigadiers and handed full responsibility for this crucial undertaking. The few who welcomed the appointment decided that Schriever's unorthodox style seemed oddly appropriate for the emergency. But to some of Schriever's less enthusiastic fans, the advancement was seen as a Machiavellian maneuver to assure the swift departure of an opinionated malcontent by saddling him with an impossible mission. Others, however, considered him a brilliant choice. "We created Bennie Schriever in 1953," crowed Trevor Gardner, alluding to the young colonel's promotion to brigadier general in June of that year, conveniently qualifying him for the important new post created nine months later.

Schriever, in his early years, had been the modern prototype of the boy hero popularized in Horatio Alger's dime novels: athletic, hardworking, and a scholar. Growing up in the suburbs of San Antonio, Texas, he was a teenage whiz on the golf course, playing eighteen holes under par while also earning high academic scores and membership in the National Honor Society. He went on to Texas A&M, where he joined the Reserve Officer Training Corps. That experience, coupled with an engineering degree, won him an appointment as a second lieutenant in the army reserve. In the summer of 1932, however, he might have been launching rockets from Rudolf Nebel's *Raketenflugplatz* in Germany, not practicing landings at an army-pilot training field in Texas.

Bernard A. Schriever was born September 14, 1910, in the Baltic seaport city of Bremen. His father, Adolf Schriever, was a maritime officer employed by the Norddeutscher Lloyd line. Not long before Bernard's fourth birthday, Adolf's ship was docked at Corpus Christi, Texas, taking on cargo, when World War I broke out in Europe. Under the terms of a proclamation of neutrality signed by President Woodrow Wilson, the vessel was declared a "wartime belligerent" and the crew was promptly interned. Two and a half years later, only weeks before the United States declared war on Germany, Adolf was finally reunited with his wife, Elizabeth, and two sons, when they joined him in Texas. Their time together was brief, for a year later Adolf was killed in an industrial accident. Deciding to remain in America, Elizabeth applied for United States citizenship. She was naturalized in 1923, and her two sons, Bernard, then thirteen years of age, and Gerhard, eleven, gained citizenship, too.

Thirty-one years later, Brigadier General Schriever paced down a corridor of the former school on Manchester Boulevard in Inglewood, California. Passing the open doors of converted classrooms, he approvingly noted several shirt-sleeved young men diligently working at their desks. Like Schriever, no one was in uniform. Their presence in mufti was to avoid attracting attention to the fact that this building was the temporary headquarters of the western development division of the Air Research and Development Command. At the end of the corridor, he entered an office previously used by the school's principal, hung his hat on a coatrack, and sat down behind a large steel desk.

Immediately, as if in response to a spoken order, a master sergeant, wearing gray slacks, white shirt, and blue polka-dot tie, came through the door carrying a clipboard and top-secret file folder that he placed on the desk. Schriever initialed a log sheet on the clipboard and returned it to the noncom, who exited as quietly as he had entered. Opening the file, Schriever noted a recent addition. It was a report by Dr. Simon Ramo. Schriever had great respect for Ramo and his partner, Dean Wooldridge. Their transformation of the electronics division of Hughes Aircraft from a small components supplier into a major systems contractor was, in Schriever's view, phenomenal. Now their expertise was to be applied to a much larger theater of operations.

A year before they were offered exalted authority crafted by Schriever, Ramo and Wooldridge first had to deal with the erratic meddling of Howard Hughes. Their problems with the unpredictable owner of the company began in 1950. Before that time, when the electronics business was small in comparison to the immensely profitable petroleum equipment operations, Hughes paid little attention to the high-tech magic coming out of Culver City. But the rapid series of successes engineered by Ramo and Wooldridge called for a major expansion of facilities and staff in order to honor the gigantic commitments dictated by the flood of military contracts. Hughes, however, demurred. Rankled by confiscatory policies formulated by the state tax bureau in Sacramento, he adamantly refused to sanction any new investment in California. Instead he decreed that the entire electronics business was to be uprooted and transferred to a site he selected near Las Vegas, Nevada. This news met with outright revolt at Culver City. Unwilling to cope with the inevitable personal and professional trauma that relocation would impose upon the entire organization, Ramo and Wooldridge argued that the move would wreak havoc on production schedules and violate contract commitments. This was a costly penalty to pay in supporting Hughes's vendetta against the revenuers. But the greater and more serious danger was that many key people would simply refuse to go.

Faced with a choice of backing down or triggering a mass exodus of personnel, Hughes grudgingly canceled the Nevada plan. Then, in stark contrast to his earlier lack of interest, he abruptly interjected himself into the most mundane aspects of the operations at Culver City. No detail was too small to escape his scrutiny: wall colors, window placements, corridor widths. All must be approved by him before a brush was dipped in a paint can or a nail driven through a wall. Even the location and number of vending machines were subject to his veto. In order to compile necessary data for addressing this matter, he commissioned a survey of all confectionary and beverage sales throughout the company.

Not surprisingly, morale plunged. Putting up with Hughes sticking his nose into practically everything was a heavy cross to bear. But for Ramo and Wooldridge, there were additional irritants. Unlike most companies, which reward successful managers with generous stock options, Hughes refused to share his 100-percent ownership with anyone. Then there was Noah Dietrich. Although a shrewd, feared, and ruthless prime minister of the Hughes empire, Dietrich never understood the intricacies of the defense electronics business. He slowed the whole process by his uninformed questioning of urgently needed working capital, arbitrarily delayed authorized payments to suppliers, and maintained a police-state environment in which his network of informers routinely conducted secret internal investigations throughout the company.

By April 1953, the situation at Hughes was intolerable and growing worse each day. Ramo and Wooldridge, unwilling and unable to take any more, finally cried, "Enough!" With the relieved blessing of the United States Department of Defense and financial backing by Thompson Products Company, a parts maker for the automobile and aircraft industries, they and several executives and scientists departed to set up their own company. The new Ramo-Wooldridge Corporation had barely settled into hastily organized office space when a fat government contract blew in through the transom. Trevor Gardner, air force assistant secretary for research and development, arranged to get the fledgling enterprise off to a running start with a grant authorizing "Long-Range Analytical Studies of Weapons Systems."

If Trevor Gardner and the Department of Defense "created Bernie Schriever" in 1953, they also virtually created the unique new organization through which Schriever was to manage America's entry into the missile age. The advent of the Ramo-Wooldridge Corporation proved to be a lucky solution to a thorny problem. Consolidated Vultee Aircraft, now known as Convair, was, at the time, the largest and most experienced manufacturer in the business. Convair's work on the MX-774, as well as thousands of man hours already invested in a follow-up vehicle known as "Atlas," put it comfortably ahead of competitors.

As acknowledged front-runners, Convair's management adopted a hard line in dealings with the government. Anxious to protect their substantial expenditures for engineering development, they resisted moves by the air force to update Atlas specifications in order to capitalize on rapidly advancing technology. Instead, they doggedly stuck to their old design. This was a serious point of contention. Even more troubling was the growing suspicion that Convair, or any other airframe manufacturer for that matter, was poorly equipped to cope with the complexities of modern systems management. Building a huge intercontinental ballistic missile was a formidable undertaking. But directing scientific specialists, sufficiently knowledgeable to integrate the numerous electronic and electromechanical components, was clearly beyond the ken of most aircraft makers.

Convair's management, of course, denied that they were not up to the task. Schriever and his superiors, however, were wary about relinquishing complete authority for a vital new weapon to a single supplier. Putting the systems management responsibility into the hands of professionals who had already demonstrated similar competence seemed a prudent course to follow. Consequently, for a brief time, Pentagon planners toyed with the idea of setting up a large scientific laboratory at a prestigious university. Attracting top talent to such a center appeared to offer a much better chance of success than relying upon recruitment appeals by the employment department of a defense contractor. Closer inspection, however, uncovered fatal flaws in that scheme. Any university deemed eligible for consideration was simply not interested. Some trustees claimed their institutions already were involved in too many outside pursuits. Others feared academic

freedom might be compromised by any liaison with the Department
of Defense. As this feedback filtered into the Pentagon, doubts also
surfaced about pitting scientists in a university-sponsored systems
management team against savvy industrial production veterans in a
large aircraft company. Nearly everyone agreed, on second thought,
that such an arrangement would not work.

No matter; Brigadier General Schriever had devised a solution that
satisfied every objection except, perhaps, those raised by a few die-
hards at Convair. Sitting in his temporary headquarters in the school
on Manchester Boulevard, the commander of the western development division read the latest report from Simon Ramo. Schriever's
plan assigned tasks to those best fitted to perform them. Ramo-
Wooldridge, with a small and extremely competent technical staff,
conducted studies and dispensed advice. Convair, the prime-systems
contractor ultimately selected to build America's first operational
intercontinental ballistic missile, was to fabricate and assemble the
hardware. Ramo-Wooldridge also devised solutions for interface
problems involving the mating of various components and subsystems. In short, the small company's one and only product was
brainpower. This asset skillfully guided Convair through the intricacies of a new technology. At the same time, it provided incisive
evaluations of contractor performance, enabling the air force's western
development division to keep tabs on progress. As he finished reading
Ramo's report, Schriever concluded that his scheme for dividing
authority and responsibility was working out very well indeed.

42

An Emigré Returns

September 17, 1955
Los Angeles, California

THE DOLEFUL BLAST of a steam whistle filled the air as tugboats slowly inched the S.S. *President Cleveland* away from a Los Angeles pier. A minute earlier, longshoremen had freed the last hawser binding the huge ship to its berth. Now the gap between hull and wharf grew wider, inspiring passengers on the promenade deck to wave excitedly to well-wishers in the crowd below. Paper streamers arched down toward upturned faces as the ship's small band struck up a lively John Philip Sousa march. Gaiety and laughter prevailed nearly everywhere. Yet, for some, tears also marked the beginning of this long Pacific voyage to Hawaii and Hong Kong. Among the few one-way passengers booked to the final port of call were Hsue-shen Tsien, his wife, Yin, and their two young children.

Standing at the rail, Tsien relived the humiliating events that had followed his visit to navy under secretary Dan Kimball's office five years earlier. Tsien's return flight from Washington had ended in Los Angeles near midnight on August 23, 1950. Waiting at the concourse gate was an agent of the United States Immigration and Naturalization Service. The business that he was there to conduct was over with quickly. After handing Tsien an official document, the agent walked away. Dazed and weary, Tsien waited until he was inside the terminal to read the words prohibiting him from traveling beyond the borders of the United States. At the baggage claim counter, Tsien handed his suitcase to a waiting cabdriver, who drove the twenty-odd miles to Tsien's home in Pasadena. Despite his fatigue, Tsien sat talking with Yin until nearly dawn. Unable to foresee if or when the restraining order might be lifted, Yin decided that she and the children would remain with Tsien, even though only he was barred from leaving the country.

Kimball's telephone call to the Justice Department had been motivated by his fear that Tsien's considerable rocket expertise might
eventually be applied in the service of the Chinese Communist government. When customs inspectors began their examination of packing crates that Tsien had delivered to the shipping company earlier,
Kimball's suspicion seemed startlingly prophetic. Inside them was
almost a ton of papers. Concluding that they had uncovered a cache of
secret documents, the officials summoned news reporters and announced that Tsien was attempting to export "code books, signal
books, sketches, photographs, negatives, blueprints, plans, notes and
other forms of technical information."

Two weeks after he was handed the restraining order, Tsien was
arrested by agents of the Federal Bureau of Investigation and jailed.
The charge was perjury. Upon his return to the United States after a
brief visit to China in 1947, Tsien had signed an affidavit that the
immigration service claimed illegally concealed his alleged membership in the Communist party. Tsien had emphatically stated that he
was not, and never had been, a communist. Albert Del Guercio, the
immigration officer in charge of the case, believed otherwise. His
remedy, however, was incongruously out of step with Kimball and
the Justice Department's original intent. Amazingly, Del Guercio
called for Tsien's immediate deportation from the United States.
Determined to redeem his honor and reputation, Tsien found himself
in the curious position of now resisting Del Guercio's efforts to send
him back to China by fighting for the right to remain in America.

Stunned by the Pandora's box opened by his call to the Justice
Department, Kimball sought to control the damage. While Tsien
languished behind bars, he and Caltech president Lee DuBridge
besieged the attorney general with petitions seeking his release. Both
presented letters from Tsien pledging that he would not run away if
let out of jail. The authorities ultimately relented and a federal judge
set bail of $15,000, an unusually high figure for a deportation case.
Kimball and DuBridge found a wealthy anonymous admirer of Tsien
to put up the money, and after two weeks in custody, Tsien was
freed. Apparently wary of permitting Tsien to roam about at will, the
judge also imposed a modified form of house arrest by prohibiting any
travel beyond the boundaries of Los Angeles County. Docilely adhering to the restriction of his movements, Tsien quietly went back to
work at Caltech.

Meanwhile, the evidence in the confiscated boxes supporting the allegation that Tsien had tried to smuggle defense secrets out of the country began to fall apart. Closer examination of the contents revealed a harmless collection of class notes, article reprints, and reams of technical reports authored by Tsien himself. Not contraband but merely the stuff that any dedicated teacher might need to organize courses in his specialty. It was also belatedly discovered that weeks earlier Tsien had combed his files diligently, removing all classified documents and surrendering them to the security officer at Caltech. The thoroughness of that search was beyond question, for not one unauthorized paper was found in any of the packing crates that Tsien intended to ship to China.

Del Guercio nevertheless charged ahead and ordered a hearing, which convened about two months after Kimball and DuBridge succeeded in securing Tsien's release on bail. The first witnesses to testify for the government were participants in the student discussion meetings that Tsien had attended twelve years earlier. Most readily admitted that they knew the gatherings were sponsored by the American Communist party and that Tsien was frequently present. All, however, confirmed that guests were sometimes invited, particularly foreign nationals, who were not informed about the group's political orientation. Tsien, it appeared, fitted this category because no one could say with certainty that he was acknowledged as a member. Nor did a previous treasurer of the chapter recall collecting dues from him. The most damning testimony that Del Guercio elicited came from a witness who had serious problems of his own. Under indictment for perjury, this defendant had been told by an FBI operative that things would go easier for him if he talked. He did. But the only information he offered was his own undocumented belief that Tsien was a communist.

Two former officers in the undercover "red squad," organized by the Los Angeles Police Department to infiltrate subversive groups during the 1930s, then came forward. William Ward Kimple identified Immigration Service exhibits that he claimed were membership rosters of Professional Unit 122, the Pasadena chapter of the Communist party. Tsien's name appeared prominently on one of them. However, cross-examination by Grant Cooper, Tsien's attorney, revealed that they were in the handwriting of Kimple and his former superior on the squad, William F. Hynes. Forced to admit that these were copies of other lists, purportedly missing and therefore not introduced into evidence, Kimple could not refute Cooper's proposition that they were merely names of prospective members, compiled for possible recruitment in the future.

On the witness stand, Tsien continued his vigorous denials of any involvement with communism. He also claimed that he was not guilty of perjury for saying so in the statement he signed when returning from the visit to his homeland in 1947. Despite repeated objections by defense counsel, Del Guercio succeeded in interjecting a series of hypothetical political opinions into the record. At one point, he asked Tsien if the United States should open up diplomatic relations with the communist regime then controlling mainland China. Tsien replied that he lacked an opinion on the matter because he was not privy to sufficient relevant information to develop an argument for or against such a move. Del Guercio continued to attack: "Do you owe allegiance to the Nationalist Government of China?" While admitting his limited enthusiasm for Chiang Kai-shek's Nationalists in Taiwan, Tsien replied that his allegiance was to the people of China. However, when asked if that allegiance extended to Communist China, Tsien emphatically said that it did not. Hoping to smoke out the object of the defendant's basic loyalties, Del Guercio conjured up a bizarre international scenario: If Red China and the United States were at war with each other, would Tsien fight for Red China? Weighing his words carefully, Tsien replied: "My essential allegiance is to the people of China and if the war between the United States and Communist China is for the good of the people of China, which I think it is very likely to be, then I will fight on the side of the United States."

Tsien's forthright testimony failed to vindicate him. Functioning as prosecutor and jury, the Immigration Service sustained the original charges and declared Del Guercio's deportation order valid and legally binding. However, the restraining order instigated by Kimball, prohibiting Tsien's departure from the United States, had been issued by a federal judge with higher jurisdiction. The deportation decision, therefore, could not be carried out without the attorney general's approval. During the next five years, Tsien lived in a legal limbo, simultaneously threatened by deportation and prevented from venturing beyond the Los Angeles County line.

To his credit, he made the best of a difficult situation. Withdrawn from the world around him, he worked hard, immersing himself completely in study and research. Life, for the most part, was grim and bitter. However, there were compensations. To a few true friends who stuck by him, putting their reputations on the line and helping to pay his burdensome legal fees, Tsien was warm and eternally grateful. There were also the particularly joyous times when Theodore von Karman came to town for consultations at Aerojet General or the Jet Propulsion Laboratory. Because most of the elderly professor's advice and counsel was now rendered in the service of the North Atlantic Treaty Organization, he had sold his house in Washington and established residence in Paris. Tsien and Yin welcomed von Karman's rare visits with gusto, throwing elaborate parties for him at their home or taking over a restaurant in Chinatown and laying on a sumptuous Oriental banquet.

Not friends, but unknown faces in government ultimately ended the suspense of Tsien's unhappy state. Neither Dan Kimball, who rose to become secretary of the navy during the final years of the Truman administration, nor Lee DuBridge, who was named science adviser to succeeding President Dwight D. Eisenhower, materially influenced the policy that was to determine Tsien's destiny. Early in 1955, a discreet dialogue began between officials in the State Department's Bureau of Far Eastern Affairs and emissaries of the Chinese Communist government concerning the plight of interned American airmen, missionaries, educators, and businessmen. A deal was struck and Tsien was included in a list of detained Chinese scholars to be released in exchange for the imprisoned Americans.

Later, on the deck of the S.S. *President Cleveland*, with tears welling in his eyes, Tsien savored a last look at America as he gathered his family around him.

43

The Air Force Entries

April 20, 1957
Southern California

"BLACK SATURDAY" WAS bleaker than usual. The day set aside at the end of each week to diagnose problems and prescribe remedies was beset with the customary score or more of technological hang-ups. Yet the gloom pervading the large conference room in the head-quarters of the western development division was difficult to dispel. Major General Bernard A. Schriever sat at the head of a huge table, dourly surveying the faces turned toward him. Seated around the periphery were a dozen men; half were clad in air force blue, the remainder were civilians who had shucked jackets and loosened ties. Behind each place at the table were at least two assistants, perched on the edge of folding chairs and balancing stacks of technical reports and data sheets on their laps. The walls were covered with bar graphs and charts and the little remaining floor space was crowded with three-legged easels loaded with the overflow.

The event causing the prolonged tension in the room was too recent to ignore. One day earlier—Friday, April 19—a Thor intermediate-range ballistic missile had been poised on a launching pad near an isolated stretch of beach on the east coast of Florida. Thor was the keystone of America's evolving military strategy at the dawn of the missile age. At the low end were the short-range tactical weapons, descendants of the United States Army's Nike and the air force's Matador. At the high end was the Atlas intercontinental ballistic missile and ultimately the more advanced follow-ups, the Titan and the solid-propellant Minuteman. Bridging the gap between the two classes was the vitally important Thor. The first operational squadron equipped with these intermediate-range rockets was to be on station in England early in 1959. Additional squadrons were to be handed over to the British in rapid sequence until, a year later, a formidable line of missile launch teams extended from Scotland's northern shore to the white cliffs of Dover.

As attention focused on one man seated at the conference table, his companions secretly rejoiced that none of them was director of Thor development. "We have a top priority problem here," General Schriever announced, alluding to the second successive failure of the air force's only entry in the intermediate-range missile class. Thor's program manager, who had presided over the debacle twenty-four hours earlier, had just arrived after an all-night flight. He was tired, despondent, and without answers. It was too soon to make sense out of the voluminous printouts that were spewing out of computers in Florida. Days, possibly weeks, of study would be necessary before his staff might spot the telltale clues explaining the failure. Schriever understood the process, but time was short and he was impatient. Until the start of the ballistic missile program, development cycles for a major new weapons system had stretched as long as eight years, sometimes ten.

Schriever was determined to cut the time between gestation and ultimate deployment by half, or better. Four years from award of the prime contract in December 1955 to operational status in mid-1959 was his sworn commitment for Thor. The strategy was untried and audacious. Assuming that the creation of a new weapons family for the armed services involved several separate phases, each to be completed in sequence before proceeding to the next, the fastest possible delivery was not less than the sum of the most optimistic schedules for all phases. Yet Schriever, Ramo, and Wooldridge were to turn the conventional wisdom topsy-turvy by undertaking all phases simultaneously. Rocket engines, inertial guidance, testing, crew training curriculums, missile site plans, and a host of additional elements were to be developed at once and without the benefit of knowing precise specifications for other components with which they were to interact.

A radical departure from a norm is risky even under favorable circumstances. But with a scant prior history in rocketry, embarking on an untried program of parallel development seemed foolhardy and potentially disastrous to conservative weapons makers. They had a point. The know-how available was woefully skimpy. When he headed air force research in 1946, General Curtis E. LeMay had envisioned the MX-774 as the answer to von Braun's V-2. Only three were built, however, before government support ended in 1947 under the pressure of a tight defense budget. A revival of the air force's commitment to ballistic missiles came in 1951 with the award of a contract to Convair for Project MX-1593. Karel J. Bossart, leader of the company's earlier venture with the MX-774, took over again. Anxious to replace the program's prosaic numerical designation with an identity more fitting for the largest and fastest missile yet planned by the Western democracies, Bossart turned to Greek mythology. He borrowed the name "Atlas" from the rebellious giant who was condemned to carry the heavens on his shoulders.

A memorable name is a good start. Bossart knew, however, that awesome problems lay ahead. In the forefront was an immediate and pressing need to augment his small crew of MX-774 veterans. Experienced rocketmakers, at that time, were an extremely rare breed and in short supply. Relief for Bossart's plight came from an improbable source: northern Alabama. Huntsville in January was no match for the sunny clime of southern California. The first of several V-2 scientists to succumb to Bossart's blandishments was Dr. Hans R. Friedrich. The adverse reaction of Friedrich's wife and young children to the transfer from the warm dry air of Fort Bliss impelled him to leave von Braun's team at the Redstone Arsenal and seek a more healthful environment for his family. His departure ended a twelve-year association with von Braun. It had begun in the summer of 1939 when a young Friedrich, single and ambitious, saw a newspaper advertisement announcing a staff opening for an experienced physicist and mathematician. No company or employer was identified and the aura of mystery surrounding the unusual opportunity persuaded him to send a résumé to the post office box cited in the small classified listing. Friedrich, who was then engaged in a molecular physics project sponsored by a prestigious technical institute in Berlin, was contacted a few days later by an anonymous caller. A meeting was arranged during which he was questioned intensively about his knowledge of physics. Satisfied with the responses, the interviewer then offered Friedrich a challenging assignment in a research center on the Baltic coast where important secret work was being conducted. He accepted and was quickly whisked away on a train bound for Peenemünde. When he arrived, Wernher von Braun informed him that he had been selected to help develop inertial guidance systems for a series of experimental rockets. Friedrich went to work and ultimately headed the group that produced the automatic control system used in the V-2.

Another Bossart conquest was Dr. Walter Schwidetzky, one of the six who had accompanied von Braun to Fort Strong in Boston Harbor in September 1945. When Dean Wooldridge won written permission from von Braun in February 1952 to offer Schwidetzky a job at Hughes Aircraft Company, he was outmaneuvered by Bossart. Convair was staffing up for Project Atlas at the time, and the prospect of actually working on a new rocket—a plum job that Wooldridge was then unable to duplicate—wooed Schwidetzky away from Hughes. The asset that had created the opportunity for Schwidetzky to come to America and work for the army at Fort Bliss was his outstanding ability to design innovative electronic instruments for the V-2. This skill had matured considerably during the years in Texas and Alabama, inducing Bossart to put him in a senior position at Convair overseeing performance analyses and computing.

Heeding Horace Greeley's advice to American youth a century earlier, Krafft Ehricke, growing disillusioned with his work at Redstone Arsenal, also yearned to go west in the footsteps of Friedrich and Schwidetzky. At odds with von Braun's conservative approach to rocket design, he impatiently waited for his turn to climb on the Project Atlas bandwagon. A chance to see Bossart finally came during a trip to southern California for an industry technical conference. Bossart, warming immediately to Ehricke's adventuresome philosophy, wanted to hire him. But the spot he intended to create for Ehricke was much closer to the core of the project than those occupied by other former V-2 veterans. It required a higher level of security clearance, which proved to be an impenetrable roadblock. Bossart was forced to withdraw the offer and Ehricke remained at Huntsville until Walter Dornberger eventually opened another escape hatch by persuading him to work on Bell Aircraft's proposed experimental rocket plane.

A behind-the-scenes rivalry inevitably grew between Karel Bossart and Wernher von Braun. Bossart's association with the MX-774 and later the Atlas put him solidly in the air force camp. Von Braun, through an accident of history, owed his allegiance to the army. Bossart, like Krafft Ehricke, was an advocate of light structural design to increase payload. Von Braun, on the other hand, derided these proponents of "flimsy" engineering. Because von Braun's criticism of the Atlas's thin pressure-stabilized tanks was creating new skeptics in high places, Bossart, late in 1955, invited a contingent of engineers from the Army Ballistic Missile Agency to witness a test of their toughness. A huge Atlas tank, using no internal struts for stability, was pressurized as it would be prior to launch. Bossart handed one of the engineers a heavy sledgehammer and suggested that he smash a hole in it. Swinging the tool high over his head, the burly volunteer brought the head down hard on a section of the tank's skin. Because the high pressure within rendered the surface virtually impervious to any external force, the hammer rebounded violently, nearly clobbering the wielder. The tank, however, remained undamaged.

Presiding over this Saturday staff review almost two years later, Major General Bernard Schriever recalled the doubts about Bossart's thin-walled tanks. But Atlas had weathered the storm raised by critics—and Thor would, too. Maintaining his equanimity, he directed that a notation be included in the minutes requiring a full report on the previous day's failure within a week. Then, turning to his deputy, he said, "Let's move ahead." Amid a rustle of paper and turning pages around the table, attention was directed to the next item on the agenda.

44

The Whistle-blower

June 1957
Redstone Arsenal, Alabama

FACING TEN MEMBERS of an army court-martial, Colonel John C. Nickerson, Jr., raised his right hand and swore the testimony he was about to give was the whole truth. On trial for leaking secret documents to the news media, the forty-one-year-old ordnance officer then seated himself in the witness chair to the right of the tribunal.

Nickerson's crime had been motivated by his refusal to obey a directive issued by Secretary of Defense Charles E. Wilson on November 26, 1956. In a redefinition of roles and missions that must have warmed the heart of the Strategic Air Command's General Curtis E. LeMay, Wilson, at the stroke of his pen, officially quashed a long-smoldering feud between the army and the air force. Henceforth the ground forces were limited to use of rockets with ranges of two hundred miles or less. All more powerful land-based missiles were to be the exclusive responsibility of the air service. LeMay's propaganda campaign, launched back in 1946 when ordnance chief Major General Everett S. Hughes sought to bag rocketry for the army, had finally succeeded.

Nickerson was not alone in his misery. Wilson's decree hit Huntsville like a bombshell. Morale plunged in its wake. The von Braun team's inspired work on the test vehicle Redstone and its successor, Jupiter, seemed destined for the scrap heap. Major General John Bruce Medaris, the head of the army's ballistic missile program, desperately struggled to salvage his command's tenuous hold on rocketmaking. His first response to the air force coup was to gather his staff together and prohibit any challenge of the defense secretary's decision. Then, in an attempt to bolster the spirits of his subordinates, Medaris downplayed the perceived negative aspects of their new narrowly restricted mission. Wilson's order, Medaris counseled,

235

only gave ultimate operational use of Jupiter to the air force. Development, he emphasized, still remained in the hands of his talented technical team.

Earlier, despite his determination to obey Wilson's decree, the Redstone Arsemal's commanding officer had vociferously denounced a reduced role for the army in rocketry. Reading the handwriting on the wall as the air force edged ahead in a compaign to win complete control of ballistic missiles, Medaris, in desperation, launched a blistering attack on the air service's limited expertise before a Pentagon meeting of top Defense Department officials. When asked to document his charges, he went back to Huntsville and ordered his staff to compose a "no holds barred" analysis of air force weaknesses and compensating army strengths.

Nickerson retrieved copies of this damaging document from the classified files and circulated them along with other secret papers to selected journalists and congressmen on committees with power to influence defense-related matters. One of the journalists was the nationally circulated columnist Drew Pearson. Another was Erick Bergaust, editor of *Missiles and Rockets*, a widely read technical newsmagazine renowned for uncovering facts not mentioned in sanitized press releases pouring out of Pentagon public affairs offices. Included in evidence already introduced at the trial was a letter from Nickerson to Bergaust requesting the prompt return of papers sent to him because "They are all secret documents."

Newspapers reported that some sympathetic observers saw Nickerson as rocketry's modern-day Billy Mitchell, whose outspoken pleas for an increased role for air power in warfare thirty-two years earlier had led to his court-martial and suspension from the army. The *New York Times*, however, revealed that others saw him as "a stubborn and insubordinate officer carrying the army feud with the air force over missile control to an absurd conclusion."

Sitting rigidly at attention in the witness chair, Nickerson waited expectantly as Roy H. Jenkins, his civilian counsel, arose from his place at the defense table and walked toward him with a friendly smile. Jenkins stopped, then, leaning foward, asked, "Colonel Nickerson, what were your motives in taking the action you took?" Well primed for this question, Nickerson replied: "[My] basic motive was to obtain permission for the army to deploy operationally the Jupiter. . . . The very fine team we have here can develop a 1,500-mile missile quicker, cheaper and better than any other group in the free world."

Then, in a blatant move to win the sympathy of American taxpayers, Nickerson argued that by keeping intermediate-range missiles under army control "the money saved could exceed $100,000,000."

Jenkins then sought to dispel any suspicion that his client had deliberately encouraged prosecution: "Is it true, as some people think, that you purposely invited a court-martial to attract the attention of the country to these issues?" A tone of barely controlled outrage surfaced in Nickerson's reply: "There is no foundation whatever for that. My intention was simply to ask influential people to explain our case to those who could reverse the decision by showing them that the army was the unqualified leader in the ballistic missile field." But Nickerson stopped short of implying that the end justifies the means. He freely acknowledged distributing secret documents to un- authorized persons but defended his action on the grounds that it did not jeopardize national security. His rationale for this bizarre claim was his belief that the army unnecessarily overclassified tons of innoc- uous documents. To support his viewpoint, he introduced into evi- dence statements by several witnesses who had recently testified before congressional committees investigating the problem.

More corroboration came from a key member of Wernher von Braun's staff. Dr. Ernest Stuhlinger, ballistic missiles research direct- or, told the court that most of the information released by the colonel had already been developed independently by Russian scientists. In response to further questioning by Jenkins, Stuhlinger, a former V-2 architect and now an American citizen, praised Nickerson's zeal and devotion to duty. He extolled the defendant as one of three men most responsible for the success of Redstone Arsenal's most recent rocket development, the Jupiter-C. Then, in an attempt to persuade the court that an acquittal would benefit the national interest, Stuhlinger strayed into a position that was blatantly self-serving by pointing out that in working together over two decades he and other members of von Braun's team had amassed more experience than any other missile-making group in the world. Permitting the Wilson decision to stand unchallenged, Stuhlinger concluded, would not only bring current important work to a stop but would also seriously harm America's future military potential.

Stuhlinger's testimony was vigorously seconded by Wernher von Braun himself. Von Braun did some politicking of his own by assert- ing that the Jupiter-C was then the best longer-range missile available to the Western democracies and was far superior to the air force's

Thor. Yet there was no unbiased arbiter to support or reject von Braun's claim. Defense Secretary Wilson's roles and missions directive ordered the air force to select one missile, the army's Jupiter or its own Thor, and proceed posthaste to achieve operational status. The leveraged advantage thus conferred on one service was apparent to many observers, including Nickerson, who declared, "It is obvious the Air Force will favor the Thor unless it is a complete flop." If Wilson perceived the flaw in this arrangement, he ignored it. For the ten years preceding his nomination as defense secretary by incoming President Dwight D. Eisenhower, Wilson had been the chief executive of General Motors, one of the largest corporations in the United States. As a pragmatic businessman determined to maximize profits, Wilson viewed research as a necessary evil, a reluctantly tolerated investment in the future. Make the move now and reap the benefits was his preference. This penchant for demanding quick payoffs dominated his management style throughout his tenure in the Eisenhower cabinet.

While agreeing with Stuhlinger and von Braun that Wilson's decision to scale back the army's role in rocketry was premature and wrongheaded, Medaris was infuriated by Nickerson's insurbordination. When called to the witness stand, he testified that Nickerson had "absolutely and diametrically" ignored his clearly expressed order banning any lobbying against the Wilson directive. It required no prompting by the chief prosecutor for Medaris to come down hard on the accused: "Colonel Nickerson has violated the fundamental military code. He does not have any further potential value to the military service." Asked if he would accept Nickerson back in his command, Medaris emphatically declared, "I would not!" Nor would the army's ballistic missiles chief speculate about the defendant's possible value in less sensitive assignments. That, Medaris continued, would depend on the colonel's ability to exercise self-control and personal discipline. But Medaris expressed little hope that any improvement should be expected in Nickerson's attitude: "I tried to temper his impulsiveness but failed. I question today whether his judgment can be tempered. I have no idea [whether] he has learned that the end does not justify the means."

The damaging testimony by Medaris, however, was no match for the wily negotiating skills of Roy Jenkins, Nickerson's civilian defense counsel. If upheld, the major charges—one count of espionage and two of perjury—would strip Nickerson of all rank and privileges and jail him for a dozen years or more. Working behind the scenes, Jenkins persuaded the Third Army top brass to agree that a harsh sentence would not advance, and indeed night harm, the prestige of the military service. On the third day of the trial, Lieutenant Colonel William G. Barr, the chief prosecutor, rose to his feet and announced withdrawal of all major charges against Nickerson. Barr's hands were tied. Lieutenant General Thomas F. Hickey, the Third Army's commander, who originally had ordered the convening of a court-martial, now saw things differently. He decreed that the allegations accusing Nickerson of leaking secret documents to unauthorized persons and subsequently lying about those acts were to be dropped immediately.

In the deal engineered by Jenkins, Nickerson only endured a slap on the wrist. Pleading guilty to a lesser charge of misuse of classified information, he received an official reprimand, forefeited $100 of his monthly pay for a total of $1,500, and for one year was disqualified from command, sitting as a judge in a court-martial, or exercising the priority due his rank in selection of living quarters.

45

America Enters the Space Race

March 26, 1958
Washington, D.C.

IT WAS LATE afternoon before Dr. Richard W. Porter finally stepped in front of a battery of microphones in the National Academy of Sciences. The appearance of Porter and his supporting technical panel had been delayed and their audience was getting edgy. To news reporters and television crews assembled for this press conference, the white-haired and ruddy-complexioned Porter, presiding as chairman of the United States Earth Satellite Program for the International Geophysical Year, was a bearer of good and bad tidings. Boiled down to essentials, his message was disconcerting: the second attempt to place a third American satellite in orbit had been neither a dismal failure nor a brilliant success.

A few hours earlier in Cape Canaveral, Florida, Major General John B. Medaris apprehensively had watched a four-stage Jupiter-C rise from a launchpad carrying a spinning tub, resembling a huge inverted toy top, on its nose. The tub, devised by engineers at the Jet Propulsion Laboratory in Pasadena, California, was a temporary housing for the mission's three upper stages. Around the interior wall of the barrellike enclosure were eleven solid-propellant rockets. These comprised the second stage. The third stage, made up of three similar rockets, nestled inside the second. Protruding from the center of this triangle was the fourth-stage orbiter, a single solid-propellant rocket, six inches in diameter, which was affixed to an instrument capsule extending above the tub. The rapid spinning, initiated during the final phase of the countdown and programmed to continue until the second stage was free, was a precautionary measure to minimize veering forces should one of the small rockets fire prematurely.

Medaris craned his neck as the rocket roared upward toward a layer of clouds six thousand feet overhead. Now climbing rapidly, the long, thin Jupiter-C seemed eclipsed by the larger, thicker flame spewing from its tail. Medaris quietly savored this moment. If he were a man with less gumption and drive, today's attempt might have been the army's swan song in big rockets. Although invited to Cape Canaveral in deference to his earlier planning for this launch, Medaris was no longer calling the shots. Former Defense Secretary Wilson's controversial redefinition of roles and missions seemed destined to eventually cut off all government funds for Redstone Arsenal's once-flourishing large-missile development operations. Indeed, Huntsville's last tie to an intermediate-range operational vehicle had been severed on February 12, 1958, when "executive management responsibility" for the army Jupiter was transferred to the air force.

Yet Medaris was resourceful and tenacious. Those qualities had been precociously evident in his youth when he had yearned to see action in France before World War I came to an end. Although only sixteen at the time, he persuaded his mother to sign papers enabling him to enlist in the United States Marine Corps. At training camp, on the rifle range, he displayed his excellent marksmanship, honed hunting squirrels and rabbits in the backwoods of Ohio, by scoring eight bull's-eyes in a row. Impressed, the gunnery sergeant hinted that kind of shooting surely entitled him to "spend the war in the states" as an instructor. Dismayed by the prospect of not going to the battle zone, Medaris recalled that "I kicked four shots over the hill [missing the target] and was sent to France."

After his discharge from the marines in 1919, Medaris enrolled as an engineering student at Ohio State University. In the ROTC, he quickly advanced to become cadet captain and soon after earned, through competitive examinations, a commission in the Regular Army. Following six years in infantry regiments, he resigned in 1927 and for the next dozen years immersed himself in a merchandising management career in Cincinnati, Ohio. Back in uniform in July 1939, he quickly rose from junior officer ranks and commanded an artillery battalion in Tunisia during the North African campaign. He was then sent to England, where he planned and executed ordnance support operations for the First Army's invasion of Normandy, and subsequently served in General Omar Bradley's forces in France and Germany. From 1945 through the early 1950s, he progressed to assignments of increasing responsibility until, in February 1956, he was named chief of the ballistic missile command at Redstone Arsenal.

The freshly minted major general arrived in Huntsville determined to lead his new command to the forefront of rocketry. Wernher von Braun at last had drawn a superior who was sufficiently aggressive to make things happen. Total commitment, no compromises—Medaris decreed that nothing less would be tolerated. The road ahead was steep, he warned, and the competition had never been tougher. Fully aware that his first responsibility was to stay far ahead of Russia's missile builders, Medaris nevertheless also cast a wary eye on the behind-the-scenes machinations of the air force's rocket proponents in Congress and the Pentagon. The difficulty of his mission, however, left little time for him to worry about being outflanked by the followers of Curtis E. LeMay. By accelerating the development of intermediate-range vehicles, he was to establish "stepping stones" to the perfection of an intercontinental ballistic missile.

The enormity of that task was obvious considering the modest gains achieved during the previous twelve years. From April 16, 1946, through June 28, 1951, Wernher von Braun and his Peenemünde veterans reconditioned and then launched sixty-six V-2s from White Sands and the Florida Missile Test Range. Seven were used in the Bumper program and seven in Operation Blossom, an upper-air research project. Highest altitude achieved by any of those V-2s was 116 miles and maximum range (launch point to impact) was 111 miles. From mid-1951 until Medaris arrived on the scene, the most urgent matter on von Braun's agenda was development of the Redstone, a ground-fired bombardment missile. Less than a month after Medaris took over in Huntsville, a Redstone was successfully launched in Florida, prompting him to proudly announce completion of the "first test mission to gather data" for an intermediate-range vehicle. However, the Redstone's range of 200 miles was far short of a 1,500-mile stepping-stone to the ultimate objective—a 5,000-mile intercontinental ballistic missile.

Yet Medaris controlled sterling assets. In von Braun and his cadre, Redstone Arsenal possessed an extraordinary lode of skills and experience. Surrounding this nucleus were hundreds of eager young military and civilian engineers who were endowed with the motivation to move mountains. And they did. On September 20, 1956, an army Jupiter-C intermediate-range missile was fired from Cape Canaveral. At first-stage burnout, the second-stage cluster took over and imparted its accelerative thrust to a third stage, which then rocketed high over the Atlantic before plunging into the sea, 3,300 miles downrange. More Jupiter-C launches followed in quick succession, inspiring Army Secretary Wilber M. Brucker to proudly declare on October 30, 1957, that the Jupiter was "the most advanced guided missile yet produced in the free world."

Ironically, the flourishing supply of know-how in Huntsville was barred from helping America seize a grand opportunity to bolster its international prestige. Scientists in more than sixty countries were working together during the International Geophysical Year (July 1, 1957, through December 31, 1958) to amass data and discover hidden secrets of the earth and atmosphere. A widely publicized objective of the United States was the orbiting of a man-made satellite. Official government policy, however, seemed designed to render a difficult, though noteworthy, goal virtually impossible to achieve. On July 29, 1955, White House press secretary James Hagerty revealed that a rich source of expertise—America's military missile arsenals—would not be tapped. In keeping with President Dwight D. Eisenhower's wishes that the satellite be launched into orbit by an "entirely peaceful" rocket, there was to be no military involvement. This ruled out participation by the army's von Braun and the air force's Ramo and Wooldridge. Curiously, however, Project Vanguard, as the United States effort came to be known, was placed under the supervision of the United States Navy. Von Braun, who since early 1954 had been seeking approval for a satellite launch attempt by floating proposals up through channels, was outraged by the arbitrary exclusion of him and his team from a project to which they had so much to offer. Regrettably, Project Vanguard was plagued by problems from its inception. Neither time nor technology was on its side. Beset by the dual handicaps of a tight schedule and the decision to seal off military inputs, Vanguard's designers were hobbled with two strikes before stepping up to bat. Early phases of the program degenerated into a cacophony of internal backbiting and public ridicule. Despite a successful test shot carrying dummy second and third stages on October 23, 1957, the next Vanguard rocket, equipped with fueled upper stages and a functioning satellite instrument package, collapsed in flames on the launchpad six weeks later.

Nineteen days before Project Vanguard's October test launch, General Medaris had been the host of a cocktail party honoring a distinguished visitor to Huntsville. Neil H. McElroy, former board chairman of Proctor & Gamble and designated successor to departing Defense Secretary Charles E. Wilson, was in town on a get-acquainted tour of stateside military bases. While circulating and introducing McElroy to the guests, Medaris was drawn aside by a public affairs officer who passed a handwritten note. Medaris read it, then raised his hands to quiet the crowd. The Soviet Union, he announced, had just launched a satellite, which was now orbiting the earth. No longer able to contain his frustration, von Braun rushed over to McElroy and poured his heart out to the guest of honor. Give us a chance, he pleaded. We have the hardware. We're ready to go. We can put an American satellite in orbit in sixty days, Mr. Secretary. Just sixty days! While fully endorsing von Braun's impassioned pitch, Medaris, desperate as a benched running back begging to be sent into the game, nevertheless counseled prudence by interjecting, "*Ninety* days, Mr. Secretary."

Several weeks of anxious waiting ensued during which every jangle of a telephone at Huntsville triggered a nervous alert. The word all had been waiting for finally came through on November 8, 1957. On that bright Friday morning, Medaris grinned happily upon learning that McElroy had issued a directive ordering him to immediately begin "preparations for launching a scientific satellite [using] a Jupiter-C test vehicle." A carefully selected Jupiter was retrieved from "protective storage" and readied for a thorough final inspection and then transport to a Cape Canaveral launchpad.

News coverage of Redstone Arsenal's belated jump into the "space race" was restrained and low-key. Project Vanguard, after all, was still America's sanctioned entry. The official contender had not acquired immunity from occasional mishaps, but generally conditions had improved. With the successful test shot on October 23 endowing Vanguard's spokesmen with renewed credibility, nationwide attention focused on the next attempt during the first week in December. After a countdown that was measured in days, not merely hours, Vanguard's TV-3 stood poised for launch on the morning of the sixth. At 11:44:35, flame spewed from the tail and the rocket started to rise slowly. Seconds later, however, a sliver of white light knifed through the surface of its shell in the area shielding the upper portion of the combustion chamber. Thrust immediately deteriorated and the rocket fell back, tail down, then toppled on the concrete apron, bursting loaded fuel tanks and vanishing in a huge fireball.

The prospect of an "entirely peaceful" rocket soon putting a satellite into orbit faded in the flickering flames of TV-3. The spotlight now turned on Jupiter-C. Among the few experts around for journalists to corner and question about the army's chances was Willy Ley. An established science writer and lecturer himself, Ley now incongruously answered more questions about rocketry than he asked. A few days after the TV-3 debacle, Ley was in a studio of the ABC television network in New York City facing commentator Quincy Howe. Why did Vanguard fail? Because it was new and untried, Ley replied. Will Jupiter-C do any better? Yes, of course, Ley said, knowing that the seasoned Jupiter, unlike Vanguard, was a thoroughly tested vehicle that might have lofted a satellite into space months earlier if von Braun had won permission to try. Very well then, Howe asked, *when* will Jupiter fly? This was a question Ley had not anticipated but that nevertheless deserved an answer. Assuming that it was neither convenient nor likely that the army would attempt a launch before the first of the year, Ley forecasted, "In January." That prediction by a respected authority on a national TV network took on a life of its own. Repeated frequently in print and broadcast news, Ley's educated guess was based on nothing more than intuition. Consequently, by mid-January, his apprehension increased a notch each day as another number was crossed off the calendar. Nearing month's end, his anxiety soared when a Jupiter countdown was halted on January 28 because the jet stream across the North American continent had shifted too far south. Ley was destined to eat crow if the center of the high-altitude west-to-east airflow did not quickly shift back to more northerly latitudes. It did, just in time. At twelve minutes before eleven on the night of January 31, 1958, Jupiter-C lifted off a pad at Cape Canaveral carrying Explorer I into orbit. Jubilant and grateful, Ley wired Wernher von Braun: "Congratulations! And thank you for having kept me an honest man by one hour and twelve minutes."

Seven weeks later, Dr. Richard W. Porter finished reading his prepared statement and braced himself to field questions from an impatient crowd of reporters assembled in the National Academy of Sciences. One query he expected would certainly demand comparisons with the failed attempts to launch another American satellite earlier in the month. On March 5, a second Jupiter-C shot had risen above the sands of Cape Canaveral carrying Explorer II. After a perfect lift-off and subsequent successful booster firings, the last stage, inexplicably, did not accelerate sufficiently to orbit. On March 17, however, Project Vanguard finally restored some luster to its tarnished image. On that date, a tiny six-inch sphere weighing under four pounds joined the thirty-pound Explorer I and Russia's Sputniks I and II, with combined orbiting payloads of 1,304 pounds, in their unique elliptical paths around the earth.

In response to a query by a newsman in the first row, Dr. Porter patiently tried to clarify the ambiguous tone of his prepared statement. It is true, he repeated, that the fourth stage did not achieve the planned orbit needed for a long life. By missing the intended course (a maximum altitude of 1,217 miles and a low point of 218 miles), life expectancy of Explorer III would be measured in weeks instead of years. With a much lower perigee of 110 miles, each pass through the earth's upper atmosphere forced the satellite closer to the earth. Finally, Porter predicted, increased friction in denser air would generate the heat to destroy it. But, he continued, there were compensations. The orbit's high point of 1,700 miles provided the opportunity for probing a different unexplored belt of space.

46

A Compromise with ARPA

March 1959
Huntsville, Alabama

Major General J. B. Medaris refused to admit that his mission to check the erosion of army rocketry was a lost cause. Embracing the hoary military dictum that the best defense is a bold offense, Medaris and Secretary of the Army Wilber M. Brucker continued to hold a formidable array of opponents at bay.

Roy W. Johnson, head of the Defense Department's Advanced Research Projects Agency, was their most troublesome adversary at the moment. Created a year earlier by an act of Congress, ARPA allocated funds and assigned responsibility for future military satellites and antimissile systems. Medaris and Brucker's first skirmish with the agency occurred in the summer of 1958. At that time, ARPA's staff was leaning toward adopting clusters of existing rocket engines, such as those used in the air force's Atlas and Thor, to power vehicles launching men, life-support systems, and auxiliary equipment into space.

Wernher von Braun, however, was convinced that the most ambitious objectives would only be achieved through development of entirely *new* engines. (Despite the decree by former Secretary of Defense Charles E. Wilson awarding exclusive control of long-range rockets to the air force, the unquestioned technical excellence of the von Braun team enabled Medaris and Brucker to lobby successfully for retention of the Army Ballistic Missile Agency as a research and development organization.) More troubling were the signals emanating from Johnson's office indicating that ARPA's decision to cluster Atlas and Thor engines was allowing the air force to have a lock on the design of future large rockets. Alarmed that the complex at Huntsville might become a colossal white elephant, the secretary of the army, determined to fight back, maneuvered for a showdown.

Brucker was ideally suited for the contest. When nominated to become general counsel of the Department of Defense in April 1954, he was a scrappy trial lawyer in Detroit, Michigan. Ten months later, after winning the admiration of Defense Secretary Charles E. Wilson for deftly rebutting Senator Joseph R. McCarthy's charges that the army pandered to communists within its ranks, Brucker was named to succeed departing Secretary of the Army Robert T. Stevens. Just as his sharply honed courtroom skills propelled him to the pinnacle of the Michigan legal establishment, his extraordinary political savvy enabled him to win high office at an early age. At twenty-nine, he was the public prosecutor of Saginaw County. At thirty-four, he became attorney general of Michigan, and at thirty-seven was elected governor. When his term began in 1931, the country was in the depths of the Great Depression. Later, when asked about the stress of serving during that difficult time, he replied that he felt like a vagabond king: "I handled millions in the office all day and then went home at night and questioned my wife about how she spent the last five dollars I gave to her."

Unlike Brucker, Roy W. Johnson was neither an attorney nor a politician. But having gained considerable experience as a senior corporate executive well versed in the management of industrial research programs, he was far better prepared to assess the relative merits of competing technical proposals. Johnson was a fifty-three-year-old executive vice president of the General Electric Company when Defense Secretary Neil McElroy appointed him director of ARPA in February 1958. A commentary in the *New York Times* implied that in all military rocket matters, the new appointee would have the last word: "While the individual services have possibly grandiose plans for the conquest of outer space, Johnson [will] decide which [are] to be adopted."

Brucker realized that Johnson had sufficient clout to deliver a knockout blow to the army's hopes for a major role in future American space exploration. Anxious to throw Johnson off balance before his new agency had a chance to flex its muscles, Brucker summoned him to a meeting in the army secretary's Pentagon suite early in July 1958. This was a shrewd, though obvious, ploy. By scheduling a conference on his own turf, Brucker showcased the fact that he outranked Johnson in the Defense Department pecking order. More importantly, it also gave Brucker an edge by enabling him to seize control of the agenda. Johnson, however, was no fool. Sensing that he was being lured into a trap, he conveniently arranged to be out of town on the day of the meeting and assigned Richard Canright, a senior ARPA staff member, to represent him.

Canright was an inspired choice. Aware that Brucker might try to discredit ARPA's perceived bias for use of existing air force rocket engines, Johnson sent a deputy prepared to stand toe-to-toe against any expert the army might field against him. Canright had impeccable credentials. No Johnny-come-lately, he had experimented with a gaseous hydrogen-oxygen rocket at the Jet Propulsion Laboratory in Pasadena, California, as early as 1943. In 1947, he wrote a landmark report analyzing the relative merits of various propellant combinations, and later, as a member of the National Advisory Committee on Aeronautics' rocket study group, he was instrumental in persuading that body to realign resources "so that significant progress [could] be made at the pace keyed to the swiftly moving national defense effort in rocket propulsion."

Yet Canright was burdened by an apparent conflict of interest. He was not a career government scientist but on loan to ARPA from Douglas Aircraft Company, and he planned to return to his former employer at some undetermined time in the future. Worse yet from Brucker's standpoint, Douglas was the prime contractor for Thor, the air force's intermediate-range missile. The doubts about Canright's impartiality were somewhat mitigated by the presence of other ARPA representatives who were not similarly tainted. Seated next to Canright at Brucker's conference table was Dr. Herbert F. York, a physicist on leave from the University of California. York, chief scientist of ARPA, had previously been director of the Radiation Laboratory at Livermore, California, as well as consultant to the Los Alamos Scientific Laboratory. Another senior ARPA staffer present to support Canright's arguments was David Young. A veteran rocket-propulsion researcher, Young had worked under Fritz Zwicky at Aerojet Engineering during the early 1940s.

On Brucker's right, at the head of the table, sat Major General Medaris, accompanied by two aides. Brucker wasted no time in announcing his reason for calling the meeting. He bluntly accused ARPA of selling out to the air force. In doing so, Brucker fumed, a priceless national resource, the excellent team at Huntsville, has been shamefully sidelined. What's more, Jupiter, one of the most advanced missiles then available, had not been included in ARPA's extensive space exploration plans. Canright, struggling to maintain his composure, tried to justify the selection of the air force Thor rather than the army's Jupiter. Thor, he claimed, was the best prospect in the inventory of operational missiles to be a first-stage booster in the smaller-launch-vehicle class. For larger launchers, Canright was opposed to developing the new, more powerful engines favored by von Braun. Canright's alternative: Save time and money by using clusters of existing engines such as those designed for Atlas and Thor.

Canright was about to offer data supporting his conclusions, but Brucker would listen no longer. After punctuating his displeasure with several abusive epithets, Brucker abruptly stamped out of the room. Calmly and quietly, Medaris then spelled out the conditions necessary to quell the army secretary's wrath. Expenditures for von Braun's operation currently were about $90 million per year, he explained. If ARPA underwrote just half of that overhead, he assured them that the army would be satisfied.

Sitting in Johnson's office the next morning, Canright and York reported the previous day's encounter. Johnson listened silently as they described Brucker's blistering tirade and the subsequent subtle arm-twisting by Medaris. Canright was incensed and defiant. York was inclined to be conciliatory. Aware that Brucker might stir up a political brouhaha with the support of friends in Congress, York saw bowing to the army's wishes as a prudent course to follow. Johnson, however, was to call the shot. Stand tough? Or bend with the wind? When stripped down to basics, it was the classic eyeball-to-eyeball confrontation in which one adversary ultimately outstares the other.

Johnson blinked. Within days, Canright was on his way to Huntsville with instructions to brief von Braun and his associates on ARPA's requirements for a large launch vehicle. Johnson had reversed an earlier decision to delegate responsibility for the big booster to the air force and its contractors. What had not changed was ARPA's previously stated preference for a cluster of known and proven engines. Standing in a Redstone Arsenal conference room before General Medaris and the top echelon of von Braun's team, Canright ticked off the specifications. Von Braun was dismayed to hear Canright recite the same old story. For the first-stage propulsion system, a cluster of seven, possibly eight, North American H-1 engines. Von Braun, however, saw the first stage differently. He envisioned only four larger E-1 engines in a vehicle tentatively identified as Juno IV. The E-1, Canright countered, was only a "paper" engine, still in the blueprint stage. The H-1, he continued, though not as powerful, was further along in development and would therefore be available sooner and at less cost.

Sensing that Canright was loath to publicly offer concessions in a crowded conference room, Medaris adjourned the meeting and asked Canright and von Braun to join him in his office. When the three were alone, Medaris quickly pinpointed his perception of a weakness in the ARPA plan. Precisely coordinating the operation of eight complex engines in a single stage, Medaris argued, was a totally impractical engineering goal. Canright thought differently. To defend his position, he cited a favorable endorsement of it by a scientific panel assembled by the National Security Council. In no mood to bend any further, Canright, in effect, told Medaris and von Braun to accept ARPA's specifications or withdraw. If they were unwilling to build an eight-engine stage, another contractor would be found who would. Von Braun reluctantly agreed, deciding that the pursuit of a flawed concept was better than no work at all.

Eight months after that crucial concession to Canright, Medaris readied himself for another confrontation with ARPA. On March 17, 1959, Roy W. Johnson scanned a new large-vehicle systems study sent up from Huntsville and promptly challenged it. Anxious to rein in a runaway army rocket team, Johnson convened an ad hoc committee to go over every page with a fine-tooth comb. Medaris and von Braun, barreling ahead on a fast track, were applying pressure for adoption of a program far more ambitious than ARPA's wildest dreams. Their plan, virtually double the size of previous proposals, called for construction and launching of sixteen multistage vehicles in the ensuing thirty-six months. Cost was to escalate from $63.5 million in the first year to $120.4 million in the second and $128 million in the third. This far exceeded the $45 million Medaris had requested after the bullying of Canright and York a year earlier. Medaris, however, was now betting all his chips in an effort to win big.

47

The Hydrogen Flap

December 1959
Washington, D.C.

Wᴇʀɴʜᴇʀ ᴠᴏɴ Bʀᴀᴜɴ was about to best the bureaucracy again. At least he thought so. Earlier, control of a big booster had been wrested from the air force by persuading ARPA's Roy Johnson to reverse his earlier decision. Now von Braun believed he was on the verge of getting his way once more, by dictating upper-stage configurations of the massive new launcher known as Saturn.

The core of the controversy was the selection of the optimum propellant. After finally embracing ARPA's concept of clustering eight engines powered by a conventional kerosene-oxygen fuel mixture, von Braun was also pressing for use of the same propellant in the second stage. Arrayed against him were Colonel Norman C. Appold of the air force and Abe Silverstein, Abraham Hyatt, and Eldon Hall of the National Aeronautics and Space Administration.

NASA was well positioned to disrupt the carefully crafted plans of Army Secretary Wilber Brucker. This new agency, which officially began operations on October 1, 1958, was chartered to instill a decidedly nonmilitary flavor into the American space effort. Unless convincing arguments were raised proving that a project was essential to the national defense, it was arbitrarily assigned to NASA. Through application of this criterion, the air force was divested of meteorological studies, orbiting communication satellites, all space science missions, and Centaur, a new experimental upper stage fueled by liquid hydrogen. Ironically, the army fared much better. Recognizing that von Braun's development operations division, now comprising some four thousand skilled specialists, was indisputably the most qualified to develop large launch vehicles, NASA administrator T. Keith Glennan wisely opted to leave things as they were for the time being.

Glennan, a neophyte in rocketry and political gamesmanship, was just getting his feet wet. He had come to NASA fresh from the presidency of Case Institute of Technology, where, in less than a decade, he had elevated a regional school of applied science to national prominence. Not long after his agency opened for business, he mounted a campaign to remedy a deficiency that plagues many new organizations—a scarcity of experienced people. His proposed cure, a wholesale raid on von Braun's development operations division, was tantamount to killing the goose that laid the golden eggs. Glennan's scheme, which would never fly without the blessing of the Department of Defense, called for peeling off the entire upper layer of scientific and engineering talent as well as a hundred or so technicians.

The highly placed ally needed to sanction this coup was found in the person of Deputy Secretary of Defense Donald A. Quarles. From Quarles's perspective, von Braun's ambitious plans were exerting increasing pressures on an overburdened defense budget. Also harboring doubts that the army's basic mission justified this expensive dabbling in rocketry, Quarles was ready to strike a deal. The Space Act, signed into law by President Dwight D. Eisenhower in July 1958, specified that until January 1, 1959, needed resources might be transferred to NASA jurisdiction merely by executive order, a unilateral decision by the president. For Quarles to set the wheels in motion, he need only accompany Glennan to the White House and assure the president that his department approved the reassignment of personnel.

Army Secretary Brucker reacted to the imminent decimation of the Army Ordnance Missile Command with characteristic fury. His vigorous protests, nonetheless, were ignored. Nor could he carry his case to the president himself. As a service secretary, below cabinet level, he was barred from access to the executive office. Medaris was incensed that a clause in the law enabled Quarles to act without bringing his intentions out into the open, even though a comparable move, sixty or more days later, required review, debate, and approval by Congress. In Washington, the day prior to Quarles and Glennan's scheduled appointment with the president, Medaris joined a few high-ranking staff officers in a vigil at the Pentagon. As the hours ticked by, he and the others grew more depressed. Finally, unable to stand by and do nothing, Medaris made a move. Although denouncing Colonel John C. Nickerson in June 1957 for fighting an unpopular decision by leaking information to the press, Medaris himself now marched down the same road. Slipping away from the others, he surreptitiously called an old newspaper friend, Mark Watson of the *Baltimore Sun.* He related his sad tale to Watson, who promptly put a dispatch on the wire, attributing the scoop to an unidentified reliable source. Within hours, the White House was inundated with telephone calls and telegrams. Reporters sought clarification and comment. Congressmen and their influential constituents angrily denounced the impending split-up of von Braun's team. With the uproar too strong to ignore, the president canceled his appointment with Quarles and Glennan.

A reprieve, yes. But by no means a lasting settlement of the dispute. Clearly, a strategy had to be crafted to justify Redstone Arsenal's presence in the big-booster business. In the absence of any better plan, one put forward by Lieutenant General Arthur G. Trudeau would have to do. In January 1958, when relinquishing command of troops stationed in South Korea to become chief of army research and development, he had promised to inject a "vigorous attitude" into missile and weapons programs. Proof that he was not engaging in idle rhetoric came in a secret order, dispatched to Medaris on March 20, 1959, which was remarkably reminiscent of the subject of Fritz Lang's celebrated 1929 science-fiction epic. Although American rocketmakers were still launching payloads of less than a hundred pounds, Trudeau wanted to transport an army base to the moon.

Was this a hoax? Some weird practical joke? Discreet checking revealed otherwise. The message was genuine. Yes, General Trudeau had signed the order declaring a "proposal to establish a lunar outpost to be of critical importance to the U.S. Army of the future." Medaris and von Braun promptly put their heads together and organized a task force to address Trudeau's directive. One of those tapped was H. H. Koelle, who then headed von Braun's launch vehicle analysis group. Unlike other native Germans on von Braun's staff, Koelle was not a veteran of Peenemünde. Although enthralled by rockets at an early age, he never found his way to the *Raketenflugplatz.* Instead, at the outbreak of World War II, he joined the Luftwaffe, subsequently became a fighter pilot, and was later shot down by American anti-aircraft fire and captured. Reactivating his early interest in rocketry after the war, he founded the German Space Society in 1948. About that time, he began a seven-year exchange of correspondence with von

Braun, culminating in an offer of employment at the Redstone Arsenal, which he accepted, in 1955.

Koelle and his colleagues set out to compose a daringly imaginative proposal. First, there was a statement of purpose. Among several arguments put forth to justify "Project Horizon" was the obvious military benefit of acquiring a unique reconnaissance and surveillance site. In addition, the moon station was expected to improve communications on Earth and in outer space through installation of a high-power relay station. Then, throwing a bone to the scientific community, an opportunity was offered to establish an independent research laboratory there. Finally, the lunar base might also serve as a low-gravity way station for subsequent deep-space probes.

This was heady stuff. For Medaris and von Braun, it was much more than adventuresome speculation. Project Horizon gave their big booster, Saturn, a mission. The report was completed and rushed to General Trudeau on June 9, 1959. It promised that landing of cargo on the moon would begin in January 1965, with the first contingent of personnel following three months later. At that point, the moonlift was to move into high gear. By November 1966, twenty-two months after the initial landings, nearly 150 Saturn rockets were to have delivered payloads comprising over two hundred tons of useful cargo. An additional hundred tons were to be added the following year. Included in these projected deliveries were basic building blocks, cylindrical tanks—twenty feet long and ten feet in diameter—for assembling a permanent station capable of supporting a cadre of twelve men.

Despite enthusiastic backing by General Trudeau, the scant support for Project Horizon dissipated within days after the report was circulated through the Pentagon bureaucracy. The exorbitant cost of building and supplying a moon base was the albatross sealing its doom. Lacking a major mission, Saturn's future was now in jeopardy. A worse threat, however, emerged from another quarter. Dr. Herbert F. York, the chief scientist of the Advanced Research Projects Agency and subordinate of Roy Johnson, ARPA's director, was promoted to a new, much-higher-ranking post: director of defense research and engineering. In this capacity, he was principal adviser and assistant to the secretary of defense on all scientific and technical matters. Instead of taking orders from Johnson, York was now issuing them to his former boss. Having seized enormous power, York courted opportunities to take on Army Secretary Brucker and General Medaris. Although Medaris had successfully outflanked NASA administrator Glennan's plan to skim off the cream of the von Braun team some seven months earlier, York was not inclined to concede that the matter was closed. Citing his belief that "nothing yet suggested by the military, even after trying hard for several years, indicated any genuine need for a man in space," York fashioned a strategy to keep the feet of American soldiers firmly planted on the ground.

The core of York's problem with Saturn was his conviction that it was bad for the army. He saw von Braun's romance with big vehicles as a blight that was "seriously interfering with the ability of the Army to accomplish its primary mission." Diversion of funds was also a serious concern: "Whenever given another dollar, Secretary Brucker put it into space rather than supporting the Army's capability for ground warfare." During his tenure as chief scientist of ARPA, York's opinion was one of many viewpoints circulating throughout the defense establishment. His promotion to the top scientific post in the Pentagon, however, elevated him far above the crowd. Then his words were always heard, yet rarely challenged, by the secretary of defense himself.

With a new chef stirring the broth, another look at the ingredients seemed in order. The army, backed by ARPA, of course continued to tout Saturn. At the same time, the air force was promoting a first-stage booster comprised of a cluster of upgraded missile engines that some called the Super Titan and others the Titan C. Meanwhile NASA, though a relatively recent entry on the scene, was proposing a huge vehicle of its own—the Nova. It was as clear to York as to most knowledgeable observers that continuing development of three different big boosters was an extravagance American taxpayers could ill afford. York therefore ordered an evaluation of the three contenders. The panel he convened included Dr. Hugh Dryden, deputy administrator of NASA, Dr. Abe Silverstein, director of NASA's space flight development operations, and the two heads of research and development for the army and the air force. After witnessing presentations by backers of each vehicle, the panel selected Saturn. Although on record earlier as favoring the advanced Titan configuration, York went along with the majority and gave his blessing to von Braun's big launcher, too.

Aware that Defense Secretary McElroy wished to rid the army of the costly large-vehicle program, York, working behind the scenes, sought to find a home for Saturn elsewhere. The one and only haven was NASA. While the decision by York's committee proscribed development of other superboosters by the air force and navy, no constraint was imposed on NASA. York approached NASA administrator Glennan and suggested that he take Saturn under his wing. Wary about crossing swords with the army, Glennan was noncommittal. Still nursing bruises sustained when his deal with Deputy Defense Secretary Quarles was exposed, Glennan did not want to tangle with Brucker and Medaris again. York, however, was persistent. He emphasized that he was not recommending a dismemberment of the von Braun team. On behalf of the Defense Department, York was offering to transfer en masse ABMA's rocket organization of several thousand people.

On this point, Medaris and von Braun parted company. Determined to keep big boosters in the army at any cost, Medaris had foiled Glennan's earlier attempted raid by arguing that lopping off pieces of ABMA to build up NASA would seriously hamper the future of American rocketry. Although wholeheartedly supporting Medaris at the time, von Braun was less averse to a move elsewhere, provided his team remained intact. Top officials of the Defense Department and the space agency found no difficulty with that condition. Negotiators for both parties reached an agreement quickly and the only step needed to seal the deal was President Eisenhower's signature on an executive order. Yet the night before the scheduled signing in the White House Oval Office, Glennan and NASA associate administrator Richard Horner were closeted with von Braun in a Washington hotel because the celebrated leader of the ABMA rocket group was having second thoughts.

During several previous meetings, Glennan had tried to convince von Braun that NASA was capable of absorbing thousands of ABMA scientists, engineers, and technicians in one swoop. Sitting in a suite of the Mayflower Hotel on the night of October 20, 1959, von Braun shook his head doubtfully. Mustering all the persuasive powers at his command, Glennan again sought to quell his guest's suspicion that NASA was insufficiently mature to annex the entire rocket organization without trauma. Nothing less than von Braun's enthusiastic cooperation was essential to make this deal work. Von Braun nevertheless feared that Glennan might be forced to renege on his commitment to fully support Saturn. There must be no postponements, no delays, von Braun insisted. A transfer of only portions of his team in a piecemeal manner, stretched over many months, would decimate the ranks beyond recovery as the best talent found employment elsewhere. Glennan and Horner, however, ultimately prevailed. They finally succeeded in persuading von Braun that they were equipped and determined to overcome any problem. The next morning Glennan smiled as he watched the president sign the executive order authorizing the transfer.

Six weeks after ratification of that agreement, von Braun was in Washington again to help resolve a critical controversy concerning Saturn. (Glennan's determination to assure a smooth assimilation of ABMA's large-vehicle operations had been reinforced by cancellation of NASA's own big booster, Nova, in order to free needed resources.) Having been won over to ARPA's preference for clustering several engines burning kerosene and oxygen in the first stage, von Braun was also convinced that a smaller cluster of the same engines was appropriate for the second stage as well. The third stage, known as Centaur, powered by low-density liquid hydrogen, was to be developed by the Convair Division of General Dynamics Corporation. NASA's engineering management, spearheaded by Dr. Abe Silverstein, did not share von Braun's view that kerosene-oxygen was the right choice for the second stage. Silverstein was pushing liquid hydrogen and oxygen for *both* upper stages. He had a point. This high-energy propellant was found to generate up to 40 percent more thrust than conventional kerosene and oxygen. Von Braun, nevertheless, was adamantly opposed to the combination. He saw too many problems. The extremely low temperature of liquefied hydrogen makes handling and storage difficult. Also, liquid hydrogen's low density translates into increased bulk, necessitating fuel tanks larger and heavier than those used for kerosene. Added to these drawbacks was a woeful lack of experience with a fuel that he then saw as "too exotic" for use in general operations.

As he walked into a NASA executive conference room, von Braun was primed to defy the establishment. Gathered around the table were experts whom Silverstein had enlisted to help reach a consensus on an urgent unresolved issue: the configuration of Saturn's upper stages. Representing the air force was Colonel Norman C. Appold, formerly project manager of a top-secret experimental high-altitude reconnaissance aircraft fueled by liquid hydrogen. Joining Silverstein from NASA were Dr. Abraham Hyatt and Eldon Hall. The others were Thomas C. Muse, from the research and engineering division of the Department of Defense, and George P. Sutton of ARPA.

Their first meeting the previous week had been dedicated solely to briefings. NASA analysts reported on plans for the initial Saturn missions. H. H. Koelle and Frank L. Williams of von Braun's team discussed the main technical findings as well as development and funding of their ABMA Saturn systems studies. J. C. Goodwyn agreed with ARPA's evaluations of those same studies. This second meeting, however, was a closed-door session attended only by the seven working group members. Arguments for favored projects and criticisms of alternatives now had to be aired as everyone came to grips with the question of upper-stage configurations. All knew that Silverstein's proposal enjoyed the most support. Appold, Hyatt, and Hall were on the record as favoring liquid hydrogen in both upper stages. Muse and Sutton were still neutral and von Braun the only one present vehemently opposed.

After a call to order, Silverstein gently guided the discussion to a review of findings reported by a NASA systems analysis group. This special task force, headed by Eldon Hall, had discovered that the more promising of many possible combinations studied invariably included at least one stage fueled by liquid hydrogen. On the other hand, Hall reported, upper-stage combinations powered only by conventional rocket fuel resulted in vehicles with total masses nearly twice those of vehicles using hydrogen-oxygen. There was a spirited exchange about this claim between von Braun and the others, with von Braun stoutly maintaining that the disadvantage of any added mass was far outweighed by improved reliability.

In reality, von Braun's obstinacy was merely a ploy. He intended to call up his heavy artillery the next day. Frank L. Williams, a member of H. H. Koelle's system study group, had been delegated to assemble a comprehensive four-hour presentation spelling out in technical detail the risks of hydrogen and the proven advantages of RP (kerosene) engines. There was a strange inconsistency in von Braun's rejection of hydrogen; the Saturn configuration he favored (a second stage, burning RP-oxygen, topped by Centaur) called for use of liquid hydrogen in the third stage. Von Braun explained that his acceptance of hydrogen in this case was due to the fact that Centaur was Convair's responsibility. Karel Bossart and his crew would have to "work out the bugs" before he, von Braun, would be obligated to accept a hydrogen-fueled third stage. In the meantime, his team would be free to concentrate on developing the first and second stages.

Von Braun's loyal adherents in Huntsville were, to a man, prepared to confront Silverstein with not just a "no, but hell no" on the hydrogen issue. Consequently, when Frank Williams checked in at the airline desk with the charts and exhibits he planned to present at NASA headquarters the following day, he was mentally primed "to shoot Silverstein out of the saddle." But later, as Williams read his notes while flying 30,000 feet over Tennessee, Eldon Hall, holding the floor in Washington, was about to drop a bombshell. Referring to von Braun's proposed vehicle configuration, Hall claimed that eliminating the second RP-oxygen stage would enable the resulting two-stage combination (now only the Saturn main stage and Centaur) to loft almost as much payload into orbit as the original three stages.

Von Braun was incredulous. He immediately phoned Huntsville and was put in touch with Helmut Hoelzer, director of the computation laboratory there. When told about Hall's findings, Hoelzer quickly agreed to defer the jobs scheduled for that evening and run the complex computer program that analyzed vehicle performance. Von Braun instructed him to determine maximum payload mass with and without stage two. The long computer runs ended near dawn and shortly thereafter Hoelzer telephoned the results to von Braun. Hall was indeed correct. The gain in payload using RP-oxygen in the second stage was minimal. However, substitution of hydrogen-oxygen in both upper stages could increase payload 30 percent or more.

As von Braun entered the NASA executive conference room later that morning, no one knew that he had reversed his position on hydrogen. Silverstein was the first speaker on the agenda. Frank Williams, pumped up and ready to clobber the opposition, waited impatiently for his turn. But he never got a chance to state his case. After Silverstein finished a long and generally philosophical paean in support of hydrogen, von Braun walked over to the lectern, looked solemnly at his audience, and announced, "Silverstein is right. We ought to go with hydrogen-oxygen."

48

Fact and Fancy

August 19, 1960
Munich, West Germany

LINKING ARMS, A cordon of police struggled to restrain a surging crowd outside the Mathaeser Theater while nearby members of a pacifist group waved placards and chanted slogans condemning this world premiere of the new Columbia Pictures release, *I Aim at the Stars*. Several large black Mercedes sedans, with horns blaring, inched slowly toward an open space at the curb to discharge their passengers. Among the first to alight on a red carpet bordered by velvet ropes was the film's leading man, Curt Jurgens. After waving to the crowd, he turned to assist a young woman in an evening gown as she emerged from a limousine. Together, they hurried into the theater, followed closely by occupants of other vehicles in the cortege.

Jurgens, a veteran of more than fifty movies and numerous stage productions, was an international star who had long outgrown the fear of looming cameras and glaring footlights. Yet his current role had elicited an uneasiness that persisted throughout the ten weeks of shooting. The problem was that his character was not fictional. Instead of breathing life into an imaginary protagonist conjured up by screenwriters, Jurgens awkwardly coped daily with the presence of the man he was portraying. Within studio sound stages or on location, Jurgens was uncomfortably aware that Wernher von Braun lurked in the background. Ill at ease and harboring second thoughts, the celebrated rocketmaker rued the day he had succumbed to cajoling by producer Charles H. Schneer and agreed to authorize his film biography.

In his first meeting with Jurgens, von Braun sought to limit the actor's imaginative freedom: "Please do not make me too heroic. I would be embarrassed." Jurgens tried to comply but later complained to director J. Lee Thompson: "I want to be happy with my portrayal, but do not wish to underplay him so much that I do not give the role full dimension. This is making my task the most difficult yet attempted." Indeed it was. The constraints imposed upon him were virtually insurmountable, prompting *New York Times* critic Bosley Crowther to comment that the character Jurgens portrayed "is a stolid generally uncommunicative man who looks toward the sky without expression and only once or twice gets mad." A more serious travesty was the interpretation by screenwriter Jay Dratler. Although advertised as taking "no liberties with history or facts," the final script included two principal characters who were total fabrications. The first, played by Gia Scala, is the young widow of a Nazi soldier who lands a job in wartime Peenemünde and inexplicably becomes a spy for the British, keeping them fully apprised of von Braun's progress with the V-2. The other, portrayed by James Daly, is an American army officer who lost his wife and child in a V-2 attack on London. This character, Major William Taggart, vociferously opposes the decision to bring von Braun to the United States and later continues to badger him at White Sands and Huntsville.

Unfortunately for von Braun, his contract with Columbia Pictures accorded him only the right to speak his mind. After politely listening to von Braun's objections, Charles Schneer then blithely ignored them. This was by no means the first time that von Braun was unable to prevent a gross distortion of the truth. The remarkable similarity between V-weapons captured late in the war and Goddard's experimental rockets in New Mexico had prompted Washington patent attorney Henry C. Parker to observe in March 1945 that he was "astounded to see that the Nazis had apparently copied [Goddard's] ideas." Parker's theory that von Braun lifted Goddard's jealously guarded secrets was accepted as fact in February 1947. Speaking that month to a meeting of the Schenectady chapter of Kiwanis International, General Electric Company executive J. F. McAllister claimed that Goddard's rocket was clearly the prototype of the V-2 and that "his equations provided the necessary information for calculating fuel required, range, and maximum velocity."

The canard was eventually reinforced by no less an authority than the *Encyclopedia Britannica*, which stated in the 1956 edition that "Goddard proposed and had patents granted on a number of essential features which were later used by the Germans in their V-2 rockets." When Harold K. Mintz, a technical editor for the Raytheon Corporation, read that statement during research he was conducting on Goddard's work, his curiosity was aroused. Writing to von Braun on April 12, 1957, Mintz asked if the Peenemünde rockets had truly been based on Goddard's patents. Three weeks later, von Braun replied: "None of the Goddard patents were known to us in Germany for the simple reason that Goddard himself kept most of them under wraps. It was only in 1950, or thereabouts, approximately five years after my arrival in the United States, that I first had an opportunity to see [them]. There is no question that many of the essential features of the V-2 are covered by Goddard patents, but they were used unknowingly."

During the filming of *I Aim at the Stars*, von Braun acquired a new empathy for Hermann Oberth's distaste for moviemakers. Although not yet a confidant of Willy Ley when *Frau im Monde* was produced in Berlin in 1929, von Braun later heard Ley's observations about the reclusive professor's problems with Fritz Lang. Standing as an outsider on a movie set as Oberth had done thirty years earlier, von Braun experienced a stronger bond with the man many revered as the father of German rocketry.

The irony of this tribute is that, when Oberth wrote his famous thesis about space travel, he was not a German citizen. Barred from Dornberger's military rocket center at Kummersdorf during the 1930s because he was an alien, Oberth was also ineligible to work at Peenemünde. The opportunity to use resources available only in the large technical institutes in Vienna lured him away from the backwaters of Mediash in 1938. Settling down in the ancient capital of Austria to assume the duties of "investigator" of liquid-propellant rockets, Oberth had remained there before moving on, in 1940, to Dresden, Germany, to take a similar middle-level scientific post. Not until a year later, when his request to return to Mediash for a vacation was denied, did he learn that he was a virtual prisoner in Germany because he knew too much.

The discovery that he was no longer free to come and go as he pleased revealed a fork in the road. One of two options available was to renounce his Romanian citizenship and swear fealty to the German Reich. He realized that the other option—remaining an alien in wartime Germany—set him on a collision course with the authorities, who might be inclined to dispatch him to a concentration camp. Oberth chose German citizenship. That move, however, put him firmly in the grip of Nazi officials administering technical and professional manpower, who sent him to Peenemünde in 1941. After recovering from the shock of seeing how much his former apprentice had accomplished, Oberth congratulated von Braun and then added, "I would have done it differently."

At Peenemünde, Oberth was assigned to the rather inconsequential post of "consulting engineer." Remaining until 1943, he was then sent to Wittenberg and was working there as an "investigator" until the war ended in 1945. After intensive interrogations in Allied internment camps, he was eventually released, enabling him to return to his country house in Feucht, West Germany, which he had bought in 1942 with money from an inheritance. The years following the war were difficult. All his efforts to land a teaching post at a university, or even a secondary school, came to nought, prompting him to complain to an interviewer in 1952: "I can do nothing better than grow cabbages and turnips in my little vegetable garden." Relief came, however, from Redstone Arsenal in Huntsville, Alabama. After Eberhard Rees, von Braun's deputy, sounded out Oberth's feelings on the matter during a meeting in Stuttgart, Germany, von Braun wrote a letter confirming his interest: "[We] could make the best use of your abilities by appointing you as scientific advisor to the Arsenal's Technical and Engineering Division." Oberth arrived in Huntsville in July 1955. The employment agreement, arranged by von Braun, was a one-year contract, which was subsequently lengthened to two. In 1957, learning that retirement benefits earned during his brief employment in the United States were much less than the stipend due him in Germany, Oberth returned there when his contract expired.

Three years later, the early guidance Oberth rendered to von Braun was dramatized in *I Aim at the Stars*. Depicted by actor Gerhard Heinze, Oberth's character was filmed in a reconstructed *Raketenflugplatz* playing mentor to a teenage von Braun. Repelled by a distaste for moviemaking acquired through his association with director Fritz Lang thirty years earlier, Oberth scrupulously avoided contact with the production. Nor did he respond to an invitation to attend the premiere. Seated in the orchestra of the Mathaeser Theater, Wernher von Braun envied Oberth's decision to absent himself. The venomous letters of protest to Munich newspapers and chanting pickets outside the theater led him to expect that the scheduled press conference following the film would be more a confrontation than a love fest. He was right.

When von Braun and the film's featured players were escorted later into a nearby hotel banquet room, they faced a huge crowd of reporters representing publications throughout Europe and Great Britain.

Responding to angry questions deploring this cinematic lionizing of the mastermind behind the V-2 assault on London, von Braun resolutely defended himself. The following day an Associated Press dispatch reporting the stormy reception accorded the premiere noted von Braun's contrition and self-justification: "I have very deep and sincere regrets for the victims of V-2 rockets, but there were victims on both sides. A war is a war and when my country is at war, my duty is to help win the war."

Bosley Crowther, film critic for the *New York Times*, summed up the appraisals of many reviewers with the conclusion that "there is little in this made-in-England drama to interest or convince anyone and its synthetic brand of hero worship may be annoying and offensive to some." The furor, however, soon died down and was forgotten as quickly as the film itself. But not before a well-known comedian in America elicited macabre laughter by suggesting that the title *I Aim at the Stars* be lengthened to include *But I Sometimes Hit London*.

49

Finding a "First" for Lyndon

April 29, 1961
Washington, D.C.

THE FOUR-DOOR Chevrolet, by no means luxury transportation, had seen better days. Not yet high enough in the pecking order of the new Kennedy administration to requisition a more prestigious limousine, James E. Webb, head of the National Aeronautics and Space Administration, shrugged resignedly when he saw the government car as he emerged from a side exit of his headquarters near the Mall.

It was Saturday morning. Federal offices were closed and most of Washington's civil servants had fled elsewhere. Webb, however, was still in town to attend a private meeting called by Vice-President Lyndon Baines Johnson. Trailing behind him as he paced briskly toward the car were three subordinates: Drs. Hugh L. Dryden, Abraham Silverstein, and Abraham Hyatt. At the curb, the driver stood by the open rear door as Dryden, Silverstein, and Hyatt clambered inside. Webb took the passenger seat in front. When the car turned east onto Independence Avenue, Webb caught a glimpse of their destination, the United States Capitol, several blocks ahead. He glanced anxiously at his wristwatch. Although not due in Johnson's office for another twenty minutes, Webb, nevertheless, was apprehensive that the vice-president might have wound up his previous business early and therefore might be waiting impatiently for them to arrive.

Surely Webb would have been spared the trauma of this hurriedly scheduled meeting with Johnson had he not overseen a patch of government turf that the vice-president himself personally yearned to cultivate. Johnson, an astute politician, was one of the first Washington insiders to perceive the frustration pervading America in the wake of Russia's initial successes in space. As a result, three years earlier, he had skillfully maneuvered the Space Act through the Senate, creating among other things, the National Aeronautics and Space Administration. That legislation also established an advisory body, the National Space Council, to be chaired by the president of the United States. Its high-ranking membership was to include the secretary of state, the secretary of defense, and the chairman of the Atomic Energy Commission. Although President Dwight D. Eisenhower signed the Space Act into law on July 29, 1958, the nation's chief executive subsequently evinced scant interest in its objectives and did not fulfill his responsibility to assume chairmanship of the Space Council. Lacking committed leadership, the advisory body atrophied and lay dormant for the balance of the Eisenhower presidency. New life was breathed into it, however, when John F. Kennedy succeeded him. Diligently searching for ways to rescue his vice-president from a do-nothing political limbo, Kennedy saw the chairmanship of a rejuvenated Space Council as a vehicle to keep Johnson busy and, he hoped, happy.

Johnson seized his new responsibilities with gusto. Jubilantly announcing to the press that he would work energetically to advance America's interests in space, he added that as chairman he would "advise the president, upon his request, of what the nation's space policy should be." The first space policy guidance Johnson offered to Kennedy was a plea to endorse an effort that the vice-president had initiated when he chaired the Senate Committee on Space. Early in 1958, Johnson had pressed for a national commitment to development of a massively powerful propulsion system, known among rocketmakers as the "big booster." Although legislation was passed by the Senate and House of Representatives, the bill was aborted by an Eisenhower presidential veto. Now, with a more compliant chief executive at the helm, Johnson persuaded Kennedy to look favorably on his pet project. Although Kennedy agreed, he harbored more far-reaching concerns—an appropriate response in space to Russia, for example. America had not yet achieved anything comparably dramatic as the successful Soviet launches of several mammoth satellites, many hundreds of pounds heavier than those orbited in the Vanguard and Explorer series. Determined that the United States score a spectacular "first" in space, Kennedy dispatched a memo to Johnson on April 20, 1961, directing him to select and recommend a suitable goal.

This was the hot potato that Johnson was eyeing warily when, in desperation, he summoned the head of NASA for a consultation. Unlike T. Keith Glennan, the previous NASA administrator, James E. Webb was not an engineer. His forte was business management, law, and government administration. After graduating Phi Beta Kappa from the University of North Carolina in 1928, Webb worked for a year in his alma mater's Bureau of Educational Research. He then became a law clerk in the firm of Parham and Lassiter in Oxford, North Carolina, as well as a U.S. Marine Corps reservist. Winning his wings and a commission in 1931, he served a year as a naval aviator based in Quantico, Virginia. Next was a two-year stint on the staff of Democratic Representative Edward W. Pou of North Carolina, during which he studied law in evening classes at George Washington University. Admitted to the District of Columbia Bar in 1936, Webb then joined the gyroscope division of the Sperry Corporation. Seven years later he had risen to be a vice-president of the subsidiary as well as assistant secretary-treasurer of the parent company. In 1946, President Harry S. Truman named him director of the Bureau of the Budget, where he became a major architect in organizing the newly created Department of Defense and also helped set up the financial structure for the Marshall Plan, the massive aid program for war-ravaged countries in Europe and Asia. In 1949, he became under secretary of state, serving in that post until the Truman administration ended in January 1953. For the next eight years, Webb immersed himself in the private business sector. Before his appointment to NASA in February 1961, he was assistant to the president of Kerr-McGee Oil Industries and concurrently a director on the boards of several companies and banks in the Midwest.

Although these credentials qualified him for virtually any high-level job in government, the multiple skills Webb offered were not those needed by Johnson at the moment. Webb, of course, knew this. In office less than three months, and overseeing an unfamiliar bailiwick, he was still at the base of the learning curve. Webb, nevertheless, was not helpless. Lacking answers is no handicap when there are experts available who can elucidate informed responses for you. Upon learning that the vice-president sought his help in formulating an agenda for America's future in space, Webb organized a brain trust of his own.

The first of a triumverate recruited by Webb for this Saturday-morning meeting was his deputy, Dr. Hugh L. Dryden. Until the formation of NASA in mid-1958, Dryden had been the director of its predecessor, the National Advisory Committee for Aeronautics. Established in 1915, NACA grew to become an internationally respected research organization that, during Dryden's tenure, employed over three thousand engineers and scientists in research centers at Langley Field, Virginia; Moffett Field, California; and the Lewis Flight Propulsion Laboratory near Cleveland. Trained as a physicist, Dryden joined the National Bureau of Standards in 1918 immediately following his twentieth birthday and was awarded a Ph.D. degree from the Johns Hopkins University. Shortly thereafter, as chief of the aerodynamics section, he collaborated on pioneering studies of airflow around aircraft wings at velocities exceeding the speed of sound. During World War II, he headed a project for the National Defense Research Committee that produced the "Bat," the first American guided missile used successfully in combat. In January 1946, he was appointed assistant director of the Bureau of Standards. Fifteen months later, he became head of aeronautical research for NACA, and two years later he advanced to the post of director.

Abe Silverstein, the second member of Webb's backup team, had joined NACA in 1929 after graduation from Rose Polytechnic Institute in Terre Haute, Indiana. A hard-driving personality endowed with an encyclopedic recall in technical matters, Silverstein rose through the ranks of NACA to become associate director of the Lewis Flight Propulsion Laboratory in 1952. Upon formation of NASA in 1958, Dryden tapped him to direct the office of space flight systems. Abe Hyatt, the third of Webb's advisers, had emigrated with his parents from Russia as a small boy. After serving as a lieutenant in the U.S. Marines during World War II, he was assigned to a navy team that interrogated the German rocket scientists at Garmisch-Partenkirchen in the summer of 1945. Following his discharge from the marines, he continued as a civilian employee in the navy's Bureau of Aeronautics, rising to become its chief scientist by the time he went to work for Silverstein as a NASA flight vehicle and propulsion expert in 1958.

Only a few minutes were needed to negotiate the light traffic on Independence Avenue before the chauffeur turned onto the circular drive surrounding the Capitol. Moving slowly along the east front, he drove into an arched vehicle accessway beneath the huge marble staircase entrance to the Senate wing. Webb emerged from the front seat and the others followed him quickly through the doors opening into the ground floor. After identifying themselves to a guard behind a desk, they followed an usher to the Brumidi corridor, where walls and ceiling are adorned with brightly painted birds, flowers, medallion portraits, and renderings of important inventions. Then they entered a secluded private elevator, which whisked them to the first floor near an entrance to the Senate chamber.

Moments later, they were guided into the vice-president's suite and found Johnson waiting at his conference table. Webb hurriedly introduced Dryden, Silverstein, and Hyatt. Johnson, growing impatient, waved them to seats and immediately got down to business. The president, he began, had asked him to define a project that would ensure a dominant lead for the United States in the space race with Russia. Once such a program was selected, he emphasized, the president would wholeheartedly support it, and, Johnson added, so would he. Placing the palms of both hands on the table and leaning forward as he studied the faces turned toward him, Johnson then asked, "Now, what can you do for me?"

Dryden, Silverstein, and Hyatt exchanged quick glances and then looked at Webb. Although he was a newcomer to the space business, Webb was fortunate to have inherited an agency that was well prepared to answer Johnson's question. For more than eighteen months preceding John F. Kennedy's inauguration, NASA had been engaged in studies that were structured to unravel the myriad problems of landing men on the moon and bringing them back. The conclusions drawn were a happy surprise. No insurmountable barriers blocked ultimate achievement of that goal. No escape clauses cited some yet undefined future scientific breakthroughs. Ahead were only gut-wrenching engineering challenges and plenty of hard work if sufficient funding was committed to support the effort.

Webb, who had been thoroughly briefed on these matters during his short tenure as NASA administrator, said he thought that a manned lunar program might fulfill the president's requirements. Johnson promptly replied that he thought so, too. Gesturing to his companions, Webb invited the vice-president's questions. Glancing at his watch, Johnson frowned and announced that he was flying to Texas in the afternoon. There was no time for questions. But would Webb bring over a short statement on a proposed manned lunar program before 2:00 P.M.? Johnson said that he needed it to give to the president. Webb replied that he would. Then suddenly everyone was on their feet and Johnson was gone. It was nearly noon. Walking back along the Mall to NASA headquarters, Webb turned to Silverstein and Hyatt and asked them to compose a statement for Johnson. Within minutes, Silverstein and Hyatt had secluded themselves in an office and set to work. Three quarters of an hour later, with Webb's blessing, their proposal was spirited to the Capitol and inserted in the briefcase that Johnson was taking to Texas.

At 11:25 A.M. on Thursday, May 25, 1961, William "Fishbait" Miller threw open a door on the Democratic side of the House of Representatives and bellowed: "Mistah Speakah, the President of the United States." Then, amid thundering applause, John F. Kennedy made his way down a crowded aisle to the well of the House and mounted the rostrum to address, for the second time in three months, a joint session of Congress. After presenting proposals to increase aid to developing nations, strengthen world alliances, and revitalize the structure and responsiveness of the armed forces, Kennedy urged that America take "a clearly leading role in space achievement." Perhaps to emphasize that he was not asking merely for a show-biz spectacular, he went on to predict that the path ultimately chosen "in many ways, may hold the key to our future on earth." Then, pointing out that America already had the necessary resources, skills, and talent, he acknowledged that the only lacking ingredient had been leadership: "We have never specified long-range goals on an urgent time schedule; or managed our resources and our time so as to insure their fulfillment." But now was the time for change: "I believe that this nation should commit itself to achieving the goal, before this decade is out, of landing a man on the moon and returning him safely to the earth. No single space project in this period will be more impressive to mankind or more important for the long-range exploration of space."

With that declaration, the rocketmakers shouldered an awesome national responsibility. Their dedication and ultimate success were to change America, and the world, for all time.

Epilogue

THE BOLD MOVE to fuel upper stages of Saturn with liquid hydrogen-oxygen proved to be the pivotal technical decision of the manned lunar landing program. Without high-energy propellants, Apollo spacecraft could not have carried three men to moon orbit, landed two of them on the lunar surface, and then returned all three safely to earth. The Silverstein committee was the medium that made that possible.

Credit for designing the first hydrogen-oxygen stage, however, is usually accorded to Krafft Ehricke, the creator of Centaur. The earlier security problem, which prevented Ehricke from originally accepting Karel Bossart's invitation to join Convair, was subsequently resolved and he went to work there in 1954. The Advanced Research Projects Agency approved Ehricke's Centaur proposal in August 1958, and it became a major entry in the space vehicle competition. The U.S. Air Force, which managed the development of Centaur, engineered a long-lasting partnership with the Atlas intercontinental ballistic missile. Atlas-Centaur was initially flight-tested in 1962, and during the ensuing decade, this two-stage combination completed nineteen successful missions.

While Redstone rockets, developed at Huntsville, Alabama, by ABMA, were chosen for preliminary suborbital tests by Project Mercury astronauts Alan Shepard and Virgil Grissom, the booster selected for the historic triple earth orbit by John H. Glenn, Jr., on February 20, 1962, was the air force's Atlas. When Wernher von Braun saw an Atlas for the first time, he was appalled by the "flimsiness" of its thin-wall pressurized tanks. Shaking his head and turning to Convair's Karel Bossart during a good-natured exchange on their divergent rocket-design philosophies, von Braun proclaimed with mock seriousness, "John Glenn is going to ride on that contraption? He should be getting a medal just for sitting on top of it before it takes off!"

Arthur Rudolph, the V-2 assembly expert who had supervised production in the underground factory near Nordhausen, Germany, and later rehabilitated rockets for Operation Backfire, was among the Peenemünde veterans who had followed von Braun to America. At Fort Bliss and subsequently at Redstone Arsenal, Rudolph was known as a skilled troubleshooter and a no-nonsense manager who consistently met deadlines. In 1963, he became program director of Saturn, which, at the time, was undoubtedly the most complex and difficult job in the entire aerospace industry. As a result, around Huntsville, it was he, not von Braun, who was frequently called "Mr. Saturn."

By the time it was terminated in 1973, the Saturn program had transported twenty-one men to the moon and put Skylab in orbit around the earth. Saturn's outstanding record also prompted the award to Arthur Rudolph of the Exceptional Civilian Service Award by the U.S. Army and the Distinguished Service Medal by NASA. But in May 1984, Rudolph's peaceful retirement in San Jose, California, came to an abrupt end. The Office of Special Investigations in the Department of Justice stripped him of his American citizenship and charged that he had been involved in the wartime brutalizing and starvation of slave laborers working on the V-2 assembly line in the underground factory near Nordhausen. Although vociferously proclaiming his innocence, Rudolph and his wife, Martha, were deported to West Germany. Witnesses have been found who accuse Rudolph of war crimes and others who claim that no German civilians mistreated prisoners at Mittelwerk. Several groups in the United States, including the Veterans of Foreign Wars, have rallied to his defense. When the OSI charges became public, retired General John Bruce Medaris, then an Episcopal bishop in Florida, told *San Jose Mercury News* writer John Hubner, "The only thing Arthur Rudolph is guilty of is not committing suicide. If he'd done any more than he did to help the slave laborers, he'd have been shot."

Shortly after his arrival in China in the fall of 1955, Hsue-shen Tsien, like many prominent Chinese scholars, was showered with honorific public offices. Three years later, he won a seat in the National People's Congress, representing the province of Kwantung. Politics, however, may have been mainly a vehicle to allow him free rein in his research. He was also appointed to positions of high authority in several national technical societies. Contact with former friends at Caltech was limited. During the early years in China, his only communications were greeting cards, decorated with red stars, sent around the beginning of the new year. Then nothing other than two messages: one sent on the celebration of Theodore von Karman's seventy-fifth birthday, and the other, a telegram, seven years later after hearing of his elderly mentor's death: "I learn with deep regret the passing of Doctor von Karman, but I believe he, as a brilliant scientist, will live in the hearts of all of us. We can further comfort us by knowing that his scientific contributions will be acknowledged by all countries irrespective of social systems."

By joining the secretariat of the United Nations Educational, Scientific and Cultural Organization in Paris in 1947, Frank J. Malina began the life of an American expatriate. In 1951, he became head of UNESCO's division of scientific research, but two years later, he resigned to devote his full-time energies to an emerging new art form, called kinetic art, which aims to create expressive displays of nontraditional media in order to impart unusual emphasis in terms of color, light, and movement. In the ensuing years, he held several one-man shows and his works are in the permanent collections of the Musée d'Art National in Paris, the National Gallery in Prague, and the Smithsonian Institution in Washington, D.C. He died in Paris on November 9, 1981.

In February 1970, Wernher von Braun left his post as director of the George C. Marshall Space Center in Huntsville, Alabama, to become deputy associate administrator for Planning at NASA headquarters in Washington, D.C. At the time, the Apollo program was entering its final phase, a series of moon landings and explorations extending into 1972. Von Braun envisioned his new assignment as an opportunity to campaign for bases on the moon, a manned space station supported by an earth-to-orbit shuttle, and a manned landing on the planet Mars. He was destined to be thwarted in all those objectives. The mood in Washington was not conducive to any new and costly adventures in space. On June 10, 1972, he announced his departure from NASA and subsequently became vice-president of engineering and development at Fairchild Industries in Germantown, Maryland. Three and half years later, ill health forced his retirement. He died in Alexandria, Virginia, on June 15, 1977.

Notes

THE DREAMERS

3   For background on *Frau im Monde*, see Paul Jensen, *The Cinema of Fritz Lang*.
4-7   Professional and personal relationships of Willy Ley and Hermann Oberth during Ufa Film project: Oberth, 129–142; Ley, 124–132.
8   Adverse critical reviews of *Frau im Monde* in America: "tantalizing incompleteness, and unfortunate genuflection to popular ignorance," Mordaunt Hall, the *New York Times*, February 7, 1931; "unsuccessful, slowly-paced science-fiction effort," Paul Jensen, *The Cinema of Fritz Lang*.
9-11   Rocket test on July 17, 1929: Goddard Papers, 668–674.
11   "Moon Rocket" uproar: Goddard Papers, 337–408; Durant and James, 60–61.
13   "Hey, you two . . .": Ross, 244.
14   "Asked me if there was a possibility . . .": Goddard Papers, 713.
15   "I realized that the object . . .": ibid., 715.
15   "Save us a lot of grief" and "did not have the right attitude": ibid.
18   "To interest as many people": Ley. (1968 edition), 109.
19   "Had performed without mishap": ibid., 124.
20   "To keep further casualties secret": ibid., 125.
21   Nebel's *Mirak* experiments: ibid., 125–6.
24   "A place of honor among my gallery of notables": Letter to Winston Churchill, March 16, 1933. Ivy Lee Papers, Princeton University Library.
24   "He did what most newspapermen don't . . .": Hiebert, 33.
25   "The savings of the poor should be invested . . ." and "these public-spirited men . . .": ibid., 42.
26   "We are preparing for the newspapers a statement . . .": Goddard Papers, 751.
27   "Mr. Daniel Guggenheim has made a grant . . .": ibid., 752.
27   "I take pleasure in offering Twenty-Five Thousand Dollars a year . . .": ibid., 744.
28   "Proved too difficult to be effective . . .": ibid., 755.
28   "Barometers, electrical measuring apparatus, and air traps . . .": ibid., 752–3.
29   "I am quite sure that in [Lasser's] article . . ." and "You have done very well . . .": ibid., 755.

30   "Think I was struck . . .": ibid., 759.
30   "No actual rocket flights were made . . .": ibid., 763.
35   Generales meets von Braun: Durant and James, 75.
36   "All of the organs in the chest . . .": ibid., 76.
37   "Offer real inducements to American scientists . . .": G. Edward
        Pendray Papers, Princeton University Library.
38   "I invite you to visit me . . .": ibid.
38   "Materials, labor and land cost a great deal . . .": ibid.
38   "If you cannot make a beginning immediately . . .": ibid.
41   "I [was] struck by the energy and shrewdness . . .": Dornberger, 27.
43   "Such an ogre as had been represented . . ." and "Broadminded,
        warmhearted, and a scientist . . .": Clarke, 38.
46   "Will have about one minute . . .": G. Edward Pendray Papers,
        Princeton University Library.
47   "In his excitement, or perhaps because of necessity . . .": ibid.
47   "After firing a trifle more than two seconds . . .": ibid.
50   "Greetings from Magdeburg . . .": Clarke, 45.
53   Abbot/Goddard correspondence: Goddard Papers, 845–6.
53   "The investigations under way should be continued . . ." and
        "Impossible!": ibid., 827–30.
57   "Subject to the unqualified approval . . .": ibid., 848.
57   "The Bureau of Ordnance considers . . .": ibid., 864.
58   "If you had lived as you ought to have . . .": ibid., 843.
60   "[Our friend] wishes to see the world a bit . . .": G. Edward
        Pendray Papers, Princeton University Library.
60   Schmiedl's rocket scheme: Ley (1968 edition), 488.
61   Pendray/Ley correspondence: G. Edward Pendray Papers, Prince-
        ton University Library.

THE INNOVATORS

70   "One of our students in aeronautics . . .": Goddard Papers, 1012.
71   "I showed him through the shop . . ." and "the subject of [Malina's]
        work . . .": ibid.
71   "That does not prevent us, however . . .": ibid., 1023.
72   "My work at the present time . . .": ibid., 805.
75   "The large chamber is giving us trouble . . .": ibid., 1028.
77   "Together with a fellow named Apollo Milton Smith . . .": Frank J.
        Malina Papers, Library of Congress.
78   "Here's the first five hundred": ibid.
84   "[Nebel's] name means mist or fog in English . . .": G. Edward
        Pendray Papers, Princeton University Library.
85   "In order to make their knowledge . . .": Ley (1968 edition), 187.
85   "Just tell them we want a gold-plated mirror . . .": Sloop, 208.
86   "I have not in any way changed my feeling . . ." Goddard Papers,
        1133.

90   "We may get through our particular term . . .": Davis, 307.
93   "Since our talk in September . . .": Goddard Papers, 1217.
96   "Hitler has a stranglehold . . .": Deutsch, 189.
97   "I immediately had the impression . . .": Dornberger, 64.
102   "Parsons' method of making the charge . . .": von Karman, 246.
103   "Concerning taking certain things with us . . .": Goddard Papers, 234.
103–08   Goddard/Hickman relationship: ibid., 234–81.
107   "They're now just about where I was . . .": ibid., 1353.
110   "I hope that you may be interested in an invention . . .": ibid., 1325.
110   Goddard/Boushey correspondence: ibid., 1325–37.
114   "No, in *all* capacities . . .": Speer, 234.
119   "We are calling upon the Army . . .": Goddard Papers, 1397.
122   "Provided the work [does] not interfere . . .": ibid., p. 1440
126   "I only hope I have not been mistaken . . .": Dornberger, 70.
128   "It's one thing to help you . . .": ibid., 97.
130   "In view of the difference in the two weapons . . ." and "Put both types into mass production . . .": ibid., 96.
133   "Weren't you mistaken? . . .": Speer, 439.
142   "The war is about to change in a manner that will make our enemies . . .": Reimann, 217.
143   "Left me rather disturbed . . .": Malina (ORDCIT Project), 351.
146   "Upon seeing how much you spent . . .": Goddard Papers, 1533.
146   "There is nothing more conducive to skipping meals . . ." ibid., 1534.
149   "The Ley book tried my patience . . .": G. Edward Pendray Papers, Princeton University Library.
149   "Because Goddard has published little . . .": *Time*, July 31, 1944, 72.
150   "Shall be hospitalized for a week . . .": Goddard Papers, 1608.

THE ADVERSARIES

155–59   Overcast and Backfire references: Project Paperclip records (1945–48), U.S. National Archives.
162   "Goddard had not succeeded . . .": Malina (ORDCIT Project), 358.
166   "Germany lost two wars . . .": Lang, 86.
167   "Royally in a ski hotel . . .": ibid.
168   "Confuses what he hopes to do . . .": U.S. Army, *Peenemünde East*, 284.
171–76   British Army experiments with V-2 rockets at Cuxhaven, Germany: Great Britain, *Report on Operation "Backfire,"* available at U.S. Army Military History Institute, Carlisle Barracks, PA 17013.
177   "An integrated program for missile development": *New York Times*, May 11, 1946, 15.

183   "When we finally got it off . . .": *RMI Rocket* (Reaction Motors, Inc., employee newspaper), December 1951, G. Edward Pendray Papers, Princeton University Library.

183   "I had seen too many motors blow up . . ." and ". . . on Fridays, when I knew . . .": ibid.

189   "Ja, I see the foothills": *Current Biography*, 1953, 677.

190   Malina's burnout: Malina (ORDCIT Project).

191   Malina and UNESCO: ibid.

192   "An excellent chemist . . .": von Karman, 257.

195   Tsien background: Viorst

198   "I am an apparently unwelcome guest . . .": ibid.

The Achievers

209   "Plant is a hobby of the management . . .": Bartlett and Steele, 109.

210–12 Schwidetzky in von Braun/Wooldridge correspondence: Wernher von Braun Papers, Library of Congress.

211   "The water running down the walls . . .": letter from Schlitt to von Braun, ibid.

214   "One day while the inquiry . . .": Lang, 85.

215   "Over there [in wartime Germany] you could get a decision made . . .": Joseph Alsop, *New York Herald-Tribune*, August 18, 1954.

216–17 "I don't know where he is" and "He's here. He's here": Sloop, 192.

219   "They thought Ben was insane": *Time*, April 1, 1957, 16.

220   "Brigadier general . . . technical supervision": Schwiebert, 75.

220   "We created Bennie Schriever in 1953": ibid., 77.

225   Tsien departure for China: *New York Times*, September 13, 1955, 20.

227   Tsien accused by Hynes and Kimple: *New York Times*, November 16, 1950, 18.

230   "Black Saturday" background: Schwiebert, 98–99, and Ramo, 117–18.

233   Atlas tank incident: Sloop, 177.

241   "I kicked four shots . . .": *Current Biography*, 1958, 281.

242   "A stepping stone . . .": ibid.

244   "Ninety days . . .": Medaris, 155.

245   "Congratulations . . .": Ley (1968 edition), 321.

248   "I handled millions . . .": *Washington Post and Times Herald*, June 24, 1955, 40.

248   "While the individual services . . .": *New York Times*, February 8, 1958, 1.

249   "So that significant progress . . .": Sloop, 83.

256   "Nothing yet suggested . . .": ibid., 228.

256   "Whenever given another dollar . . .": ibid.

260   "No, but hell no" and "to shoot Silverstein . . .": Sloop, 238.

260   "Silverstein is right . . .": ibid., 239, and transcript of briefing by Silverstein for Kennedy Space Center Writers Conference, September 1–3, 1977. NASA History Office, Washington, D.C.

262   *I Aim at the Stars* references from promotion and publicity materials in the Theater and Cinema collection of the Free Library of Philadelphia, PA.

262   "Astounded to see that the Nazis . . .": Goddard Papers, 1577.

262   "His equations provided the necessary information . . .": *New York Times*, February 14, 1947, 5.

263   Mintz/von Braun correspondence: Wernher von Braun Papers, Library of Congress.

264   "I would have done it differently": Ley (1968 edition), 203.

264   "I can do nothing better . . .": *Current Biography*, 1957, 417.

264   Oberth offered employment at Huntsville: Wernher von Braun Papers, Library of Congress.

265   "I have very deep and sincere regrets . . .": *New York Times*, August 20, 1960, 15.

265   Bosley Crowther review: *New York Times*, October 20, 1960, 42.

265   "But I sometimes hit London": *New York Times*, June 18, 1977, 24.

270   Meeting with Lyndon B. Johnson, April 29, 1961: Silverstein's 1977 briefing for Kennedy Space Center Writers Conference (see reference p. 260).

EPILOGUE

273   "John Glenn is going to ride on that . . .": Sloop, 177.

273   "The only thing Arthur Rudolph is guilty of . . .": *Philadelphia Inquirer Magazine*, March 9, 1986, 31.

274   "I learn with deep regret . . .": Viorst.

Sources Cited

Bartlett, Donald L., and Steele, James B. *Empire*. New York: W. W. Norton, 1979.

Braun, Wernher von. *Reminiscences of German Rocketry*. London: Journal of the British Interplanetary Society, May 1956.

Clarke, Arthur C. *The Coming of the Space age*. New York: Meredith Press, 1967.

Collier, Basil. *Battle of the V-Weapons, 1944–45*. New York: William Morrow & Company, 1965.

Davis, John S. *The Guggenheims*. New York: William Morrow & Company, 1978.

Deutsch, Harold C. *Hitler and His Generals*. Minneapolis: University of Minnesota Press, 1974.

Dornberger, Walter. *V-2*. New York: Viking Press, 1954.

Durant, Frederick C. III, and James, George S. *First Steps Toward Space*. Proceedings of the First and Second History Symposia of International Academy of Astronautics, Belgrade, Yugoslavia, September 26, 1967, and New York, NY, October 1968. Washington, D.C.: Smithsonian Institution Press, 1974.

Garlinski, Jozef. *Hitler's Last Weapons*. New York: Times Books, 1978.

Goddard, Esther C., and Pendray, G. Edward, eds. *The Papers of Robert H. Goddard*. New York: McGraw-Hill Book Company, 1970.

Great Britain, British Army of the Rhine/Special Projectile Operations Group. *Report on "Operation Backfire."* London: British War Office, 1946.

Hiebert, Ray Eldon. *Courtier to the Crowd*. Ames, IA: Iowa State University Press, 1966.

Huzel, Dieter K. *Peenemünde to Canaveral*. Englewood Cliffs, NJ: Prentice-Hall, Inc., 1962.

Irving, David. *The Rise and Fall of the Luftwaffe*. Boston: Little, Brown & Company, 1973.

Jensen, Paul M. *The Cinema of Fritz Lang*. New York: A. S. Barnes, 1969.

Karman, Theodore von. *The Wind and Beyond*. Boston: Little, Brown & Company, 1967.

Klee, Ernst, and Merke, Otto. *The Birth of the Missile: Secrets of Peenemünde*. New York: E. P. Dutton, 1965.

Lang, Daniel. "A Reporter at Large." *The New Yorker*, April 21, 1951.

Ley, Willy. *Rockets, Missiles and Men in Space* (1968) and *Rockets, Missiles and Space Travel* (1961). New York: Viking Press.

Malina, Frank J. "Excerpts from Letters Written Home, 1936–1941." Frank J. Malina Papers, Library of Congress.

————. "The ORDCIT Project of the Jet Propulsion Laboratory, 1943–1946: A Memoir." Proceedings of the Fifth History of Astronautics Symposium. Brussels, Belgium: International Academy of Astronautics, September 1971.

Medaris, J. B. *Countdown for Decision*. New York: G. P. Putnam, 1960.

Ramo, Simon. *The Business of Science*. New York: Hill and Wang, 1988.

Reimann, Viktor. *Goebbels*. New York: Doubleday, 1976.

Ross, Walter S. *The Last Hero: Charles A. Lindbergh*. New York: Harper & Row, 1964.

Schwiebert, Ernst G. *A History of the U.S. Air Force Ballistic Missiles*. New York: Frederick A. Praeger, 1964.

Sloop, John L. *Liquid Hydrogen As a Propulsion Fuel, 1945–1959*. Washington, D.C.: National Aeronautics and Space Administration, 1978.

Speer, Albert. *Inside the Third Reich*. New York: Macmillan, 1970.

U.S. Army. *Peenemünde East: Through the Eyes of 500 Detained at Garmisch, 1945–46*. Mimeograph copy (753 pages) available at U.S. Army Military History Institute, Carlisle Barracks, PA.

Viorst, Milton. "The Bitter Tea of Dr. Tsien." *Esquire*, December 1967.

Acknowledgments

Invaluable assistance was rendered in the search for sources and background information by: Nancy Bressler, Seeley G. Mudd Manuscript Library, Princeton University; Alice S. Creighton, the Nimitz Library, U.S. Naval Academy; Paula Agranat Hurwitz, Robert A. Millikan Memorial Library, California Institute of Technology; James H. Hutson, Library of Congress; Constance Kaminsky, Chester County (Pennsylvania) Library; John F. Loosbrock, Aerospace Industries Association of America; Martin Manning, U.S. Information Agency; Dorothy E. Mosakowski, Robert Hutchings Goddard Library, Clark University; Victoria S. Mueller, General Dynamics Corporation; Jack Powell, Jr., TRW Space & Defense; Marian Powers, Time, Inc.; Edward J. Reese, National Archives; Cynthia H. Requardt, Milton S. Eisenhower Library, the Johns Hopkins University; Lee D. Saegesser, NASA History Office; Barbara A. Shattuck, National Geographic Society; John J. Slonaker and Randall F. Rakers, U.S. Army Military History Institute; and Delmus E. Williams, the University of Alabama in Huntsville.

Index